ANDY MCINTOSH

Genesis for today

The relevance of the Creation/Evolution debate to today's society

'Genesis **IS** for today'—**JOHN MACARTHUR**

DayOne

© Day One Publications 1997, 2001, 2006

First printed 1997

Second edition 2001, reprinted 2004

Third edition 2006

ISBN 978 1 84625 051 4

ISBN 978-1-84625-051-4

9 781846 250514 >

British Library Cataloguing in Publication Data available

Published by Day One Publications

Ryelands Road, Leominster, HR6 8NZ

☎ 01568 613 740 FAX 01568 611 473

email—sales@dayone.co.uk

web site—www.dayone.co.uk

North American—e-mail—sales@dayonebookstore.com

North American—web site—www.dayonebookstore.com

Designed by Steve Devane and printed by Gutenberg Press, Malta

Dedication

To Philip, David and Grace: that their generation might have a clear witness to the truth of Scripture and the gospel of the Lord Jesus Christ against the flood tide of error all around them.

The truth about the origin of the universe and the creation of life will never be discovered by theorising scientists who start with the presupposition that so much vast and intricate design must be explained apart from any reference to a Designer. Evolutionary theory has been in a state of constant flux since it was first popularized in the 1800s. Today, Darwinism is on shakier ground than ever. Yet the biblical account remains unchanged, unchanging, and unfazed by all the attacks against it. Genesis *is* for today.

I appreciate Andy McIntosh's obvious love for the Bible and his conviction that God's Word will always triumph over every falsehood. He shows in simple language why many of the evolutionists' claims are demonstrably false. In the process, he allows the Word of God to speak plainly for itself. For those who have eyes to see, here is ample proof that God's revealed truth is as trustworthy as ever—and infinitely more certain than every human speculation.

John MacArthur
Pastor of Grace Community Church,
Sun Valley, Los Angeles,
USA

Foreword to the first edition by Verna Wright

D r Andrew McIntosh is a distinguished lecturer in Combustion Theory at our University in Leeds. He is in demand as a speaker on his subject internationally. He is equally well known for his cogent expositions on origins from a scientific viewpoint. Many have appreciated his beautifully illustrated lectures on the mechanisms of flight, and the irresistible conclusion that these diverse methods are highly unlikely to have evolved by chance, but are much more in keeping with a creation model.

In the present volume, however, Dr McIntosh looks carefully at the implications of the creation model in relation not only to the opening chapters of Genesis but also the wider aspects of Christian theology. Many will never have grasped the extensive implications of the creation model and the damage done to basic Christian truths by an unthinking embrace of evolutionary thinking. This book will prove an eye-opener.

V Wright MD, FRCP
Emeritus Professor of Rheumatology,
University of Leeds, UK.

Ken Ham: co-founder of Creation Science Foundation (Australia), founder of *Answers in Genesis* (Kentucky, USA) and well known author and speaker at Creation seminars around the world.

'You can't be a scientist and take the book of Genesis as literal history!' I have heard this statement all too often from non-Christians (and even some Christians) during the 20 years of my involvement in the creation ministry! However, Andy McIntosh, like so many other precious saints of the Lord I have come to know, is a scientist, and is one who also believes that the book of Genesis *is* literal history and is foundational to the rest of Scripture. In *no* way does Genesis conflict with the science he is conducting at Leeds University.

In the academic world where evolutionary thinking is generally accepted as fact, it takes great courage to stand up in this scientific community and insist that the God of the Bible created the entire universe, and everything in it over six literal days and only thousands of years ago. Not only is he subject to great ridicule by his non-Christian peers for holding such beliefs, but sadly many in the church also mock at those like Andy who insist that the book of Genesis *must* be taken literally.

Andy, though, has come to understand an important point that the church in the United Kingdom, by and large, has lost: namely that ultimately *all* Christian doctrine, directly or indirectly, is founded in the literal events of the first eleven chapters of the Bible. Because Andy is a man with a heart for seeing souls saved, he pours out his heart in this book and reveals how his beloved nation has departed so far from the Christian framework that was once so pervasive throughout the culture.

In this book, Andy is going to challenge you in two main areas:

1. That the foundation of Christianity has been undermined and all but destroyed in England because much of the church has accepted the fallible theories of sinful man, and, as a result, has reinterpreted the foundational book of beginnings. Once the church abandoned a literal Genesis, then there was no foundation for a Christian structure. *All* Christian doctrines are dependent on the literal events of Genesis.

For instance, what is sin? If there was no literal garden, literal Adam, literal serpent, literal fruit and literal Fall, then who defines what sin is? How could it be rebellion if there was no literal rebellion? Why did Jesus die physically on a cross for our sins if literal physical death was not the penalty for a literal rebellion?

If you are prepared to put aside all 'outside ideas', and carefully read Andy's expounding of Scripture, you will be challenged to make a decision concerning the clear teaching of the Word of God in Genesis. Frankly, it may even make you feel uncomfortable! However, as you read Andy's challenge *please* be like the Bereans who 'searched the Scriptures daily, whether these things were so' (Acts 17:11).

2. Andy deals with another area that has been sadly neglected in our modern culture: how we treat the Lord's Day. Now, even though you may be like me and not go as far as Andy in this area, nonetheless it is true that to many in the church today, the Lord's Day is little different from any other day of the week.

At the very least, I believe you will be additionally challenged—as I was—to reconsider our priorities and actions as a family, as we consider this day set aside as a special time of rest and contemplation.

I believe that Andy's book will play an active role in a growing world-wide movement to bring reformation again to a church which has sadly compromised the clear teaching of Scripture, particularly regarding the foundational book of Genesis.

Ken Ham
Florence, Kentucky,
USA

When I first put pen to paper it was not with the intention of writing a book. I had already given some thought to chapters 1–3 through being asked to speak occasionally on the subject of creation or evolution from a scientific point of view and also as to why biblically the subject is important. I have always been impressed by the work of the Lord's Day Observance Society and in recent years by the determined leadership of its General Secretary, John Roberts. When an early form of chapter 6 on the Sabbath was submitted for possible publication as a leaflet, John made the suggestion of a book. So with some fear and trepidation I began to draw my thoughts together, not just on the obvious scientific implications of the creation/evolution debate, but on the wider concerns of the relevance of this whole issue to the Church, Family, Society and the Nation.

I freely wish to acknowledge the influence upon my thinking of a number of people who share my concern for a firm stand on Genesis. I have counted it a privilege to have stimulating conversations with some key people involved in creation-based outreach. It is difficult to name them all, but I would particularly like to thank Professor Verna Wright, Mr Ken Ham, Dr David Rosevear and Mr Geoff Chapman for their encouragement over the years.

In no way do I claim that this is the final word on such a vital issue. I have written because of a burden for an up-and-coming generation of Christian believers in the UK who are in the midst of strong attacks on Christian belief from all angles. Even today, with the wealth of materials available, there are immense dangers that we approach this important matter of origins without a sense of the paramount authority of Scripture. If these thoughts are a help to some readers, then I shall be grateful that a useful contribution has been made to this vital debate.

I owe a debt to friends who read and checked my manuscript and examined my arguments. In particular, Messrs Roger Carswell, David Harding, Trevor Knight, Professor Verna Wright and Dr Stephen Taylor have spent many hours on my behalf.

Lastly, this book could not have been completed without the kind and loving support of my family, in particular my long-suffering and patient wife, Juliet, who translated my scrawl into a legible manuscript.

A comment regarding the notes at the end of each chapter. These are not merely references though they contain such. There have been times when I have wished to develop a supporting argument without disturbing the flow of the main text and I have put such arguments in the notes. Some are quite detailed and it is hoped they will make interesting reading.

Scripture quotations are generally from the New King James Version. However in the interests of accuracy, there are occasional places where the Authorized Version is used instead.

Andy McIntosh
October 1997

Preface to the second edition

Since writing the first edition three years ago, the response of readers has been very encouraging, both from at home and abroad. It has been humbling to have people thank me for the clearer understanding they have come to, concerning the Biblical issues surrounding the Creation/Evolution issue, and to realize that under God's good hand, there are those who have had their faith strengthened as a result.

In this second edition I have carefully gone through all the (known) typos that occurred in the first edition. My thanks to all those who faithfully pointed out these mistakes. I have been through minor inaccuracies that have been pointed out to me, and I have also added quite a number of additional notes at the end of each chapter. The section on marriage in chapter 4 (section 4.3) has been partly rewritten, and the section on death in chapter 7 (section 7.3) has been strengthened. More detail has been put in on astronomy (Appendix B), and perhaps to the delight of many, the recent discoveries about the precision aiming of the Bombardier Beetle have been added (also in Appendix B). Further notes have been added at the end of this same appendix, particularly concerning the Flood.

My concern is primarily to have the evangelical church see the seriousness of the Creation/Evolution issue, and to see the very important connection with (a) Biblical Authority, and (b) The gospel itself—through the erroneous teaching of evolution concerning death. My aim is therefore, that as a result, Christians should have their swords sharp, that is deep convictions based on the Word of God. It is only from such a firm base that we will make a deep foundational impression on the very decadent society that we live in. God honours his Word. Christians convinced on the first eleven chapters of Genesis, will have a greater impact in their evangelism. Since the first edition was produced (1997), the question of Origins has received greater prominence in the world's media. This was illustrated by the vast sums of money which were used in the production of the BBC's programme, *Walking with Dinosaurs* in 1999—made with expensive models, brought to life by clever photography and graphics, and yet mixing fact and fiction before millions of viewers. Nevertheless the Creation viewpoint is clearly having some impact, since earlier this year (2000) the journal *New Scientist* was concerned enough to have almost a complete issue devoted to Creationism. This indicates that it only requires a small percentage of Christians to become vocal, before the world takes notice. It is my prayer that in his mercy, God will continue to use this and other literature to awaken the church to the crucial importance of standing firm on a straightforward belief in Genesis. Far from being irrelevant as some maintain, it is one of the major issues of this generation. Let us be faithful to Christ, his Word and his gospel.

Andy McIntosh
January 2001

The year 2001, when the second edition of *Genesis for Today* came out, proved to be momentous: after September 11th the world changed and was catapulted overnight into great political instability. The 21st century, which began with such bright hopes, was now plunged into uncertainty. So the message of Biblical Christianity, with its firm roots in a world made and owned by God, has become more than ever relevant to Western society—a society which has lost its moorings as it has increasingly embraced a philosophy that has no absolutes and thus no means to measure right and wrong. It is with this in mind that the major addition of chapter 10 to this third edition has been written. This chapter is concerned with the shift in thinking in the last decade towards postmodernism, and how we may address it. More than ever we need a vibrant and compassionate outgoing Christianity which is firmly rooted in a thorough understanding of origins. If we do not clearly state the basis of our absolutes from Genesis and Creation, then Islam will gladly fill the vacuum left by a church that no longer believes its own book and does not hold to the reality of these truths.

The only power which can resist the claims of such false religion is a Christianity which places God firmly on the throne of all the physical Universe, not in some box marked vaguely 'spiritual truth—open only on Sundays'. Sadly the evangelical church has, in a large measure, sold its right to be a tangible and relevant force in modern society. In its drive to become contemporary and accepted by secular society, it has taken on the weak view of a God sidelined by his own Creation! If it continues to disown the claims of Christ as Creator, it will in fact become more and more sidelined and be regarded as irrelevant.

There is little lasting strength in a Christianity that skirts this issue of Origins and the true ownership of the world which, ruled by man, is in rebellion against God. To connect with relevance to a dying world fast moving to the climax of all things—Christ's return in judgement—we need again powerfully to assert God's ownership over all the created order. Nothing less than revival of full-blooded belief in the infallibility of Scripture, its plenary inspiration, its relevance to all branches of Science, Arts, Law and Commerce, will address the national wounds left in our benighted land by 150 years of liberalism.

Minor errors have been found and corrected from the last edition. In particular, Figure 2 showing the genealogies to Abraham needed correction concerning the birth of Abraham.

As John MacArthur states in his recommendation, Genesis *is* for today.

Andy McIntosh
June 2006

Contents

Contents

List of figures

Genesis and fundamentals

'Why is the issue important?', many people say today. 'Can't we just ignore the subject of origins and get on with experiencing our lives now?' Many believers in the Bible still say, 'Why be so concerned?' when the subject of origins comes up.

To answer this, in this introductory chapter, let me illustrate. If you meet a stranger, your first query, if not immediately expressed, is 'Where do you come from?' To understand who that person is and how they relate to you, it is important to know about their origin. Suppose now we develop this idea and someone comes saying they represent a landowner from afar who lays claim to all our house and possessions, our indignant response might well be 'Who do you think you are?' followed by a demand for proof of identity. The legal wrangling which follows would be very much to do with original documents and proof of ownership. Eventually a vital document is found showing beyond doubt that the absent landowner not only owns the land, house and possessions, but built the house to begin with. The plans and title deeds are all in his name.

So the analogy follows through. Today in our society, there is no concept of Divine ownership of this world. Atheistic humanism has so dominated western civilization, that there is no sense of responsibility to a Master who owns us, let alone a master builder, planner and Redeemer. How do we counter this man-centred philosophy? Do we join the majority and say 'I don't know clearly where you and I are from, but I've come to say you are nevertheless accountable to the real owner of this world.' This call will only be understood by those who have some sense of God already in their knowledge. But we must realize today that we are up against the powerful forces of atheism (denial that God exists), pantheism (there is a power/life force in the world—some leading thinkers believe that somehow the world and its ecosystem are alive—the Gaia[1] type philosophy), or deism (that God wound up the Universe at the beginning and then left it). There is very little awareness of the true God/Creator. We have to go back to grass roots. We have to start by clearly showing the credentials of the Divine Authorship and Ownership of this world.

It is certainly true that this issue of origins is not of itself vital for salvation, just as a first time parachutist may not know all the details of the parachute which breaks his headlong fall to earth. But if you are responsible for equipping a regiment of paratroopers, you will make it your business to know all there is to know about parachute design!

I anticipate there will be two main types of readers of this book: those who are curious, but who do not claim to be believers in the Bible, and those who are Christians but as yet are uncertain on the question of origins. Let me say first to those of you who are seeking, that the question of origins is important, for you need to know at the very least, that the Bible *does* speak on these matters and has answers regarding such questions—however unpopular those answers are. What is more, you need to be aware that there is a growing body of professional, educated opinion which does not accept atheistic humanism and its portrayal of evolution as a fact. Often it is a startling revelation to many sincere thinking people that there is any other way of thinking! We have got so used to the 'box in the corner' giving us pre-digested ideas that we are surprised to see that there is an alternative. What is more, the media is *heavily biased* against a Christian stance. It is significant that Professor Richard Dawkins in March/April 1996 was given three multicolumn opportunities in *The Times*[2] to publicize his overtly atheistic views with excerpts from his latest book *Climbing Mount Improbable*[3] and it is also significant that the BBC promotes one-sided presentations on origins (e.g. David Attenborough's *Life on Earth* series), and anything which attempts to undermine orthodox Christianity. For example, in the autumn of 1996 the BBC screened a major series on the old Gnostic claims to finding the body of Christ. The truth will wear such attacks, but the real danger is that many serious-minded people are led to thinking only from one side, without a clear recognition that there is a wealth of biblical, archaeological, historical and scientific evidence, which is entirely consistent with a belief in Christ as the Son of God, the Creator and Redeemer.

There will be other readers who are already believers in Christ, but who have not yet faced the issue of origins. For you, it is important to realize that the whole basis of our salvation hinges upon Genesis. Without

Genesis and a real Garden of Eden, a literal serpent, a genuine historical Fall, the whole account of redemption itself falls like a stack of dominoes. Sadly, even evangelical writers have brought the historical basis of Genesis into question.4 This then weakens considerably the high view of Scripture which is necessary in order to preach against sin and unfold God's plan of redemption. Though you may believe in Christ, to avoid putting stumbling blocks in the way of others it is essential you have clear-cut views on the authority of Genesis, scientifically, historically and socially.

As Ken Ham ably brings out in his uncompromising book *The Lie— Evolution*,5 Genesis is not only the basis of the gospel, but gives the basis for the fabric of our entire society—clothing; marriage for life of man and woman (not man-man, or woman-woman); the value of human life from the womb (no abortion); good government and care for the land and animals; scientific enquiry and many other issues. All these find their roots in Genesis. The aim of this book is to show how in the West, we need to take stock as to where we are and how far we have moved from the clear-cut well-tried principles of Scripture. In this nation of Britain today, we think we have become 'free', 'emancipated from the shackles which held down our fore-fathers'. How wrong we are. Far from being free, whole sections of our communities are increasingly slaves to gambling (the National Lottery), vice, pornography and crimes of the worst sort. Is it freedom if caring parents cannot walk with their children from a swimming trip without fear of being assaulted? This happened in the spring of 1996 in Kent when a mother and her two children with their dog were viciously attacked leaving all but one child dead. If only men and women would realize that, as the Bible says, our hearts will never naturally go the way that even our consciences say is right. Rather than shackling us, the opposite is true when we turn to the Bible. Belief in the Scripture and the Christ of the Scripture, enables us to *turn* from our sin and failure and gives us a fresh start; a transformed life in which we are no longer a slave to doing wrong. Calling on the name of Christ as the one who came to take the punishment for our sin liberates and frees individuals from the grip of sin and death. When whole groups of people turn, it transforms communities and the nation is affected. My purpose in writing this book is that from whatever angle, we shall see the fundamental relevance of Genesis for Today.

Chapter 1 notes

1 **JE Lovelock,** *Gaia—a new look at life on Earth* (Oxford: Oxford University Press, 1987).

2 *The Times,* London, 29/3/96, 1/4/96 and 2/4/96.

3 **R Dawkins,** *Climbing Mount Improbable* (London: Viking, 1996).

4 **R Clements,** *Masterplan* (Leicester: InterVarsity Press, 1994), pp. 12–14; **MA Noll,** *The Scandal of the Evangelical Mind* (Leicester: InterVarsity Press, 1994).

5 **K Ham,** *The Lie—Evolution* (Colorado Springs: Master Books, 1988).

Genesis and science

2.1 Order in the natural world

'In the beginning God created the heavens and the earth'; So read the American astronauts—Anders, Lovell and Borman—as they gazed in awe at the earth from their orbit round the moon on Christmas Eve, 1968. For them, there was a deep conviction that what they saw then could only be explained by creation. Many would not only agree but also argue further, that the careful balancing of all the ingredients necessary for life could not have arrived here by chance. It was none other than Albert Einstein who wrote that 'the harmony of natural law reveals an intelligence of such superiority that all the systematic thinking of human beings is utterly insignificant'. Yet we are living today in an age when a large majority of people doubt that intricate design means there is a great designer.

2.2 Scientists are affected by their world-views

In the last analysis, no scientist is entirely objective. We are always governed by our assumptions. If a scientist does not believe in God, then his starting point of atheism will be bound to affect his judgement as he looks at the world around him. If his mind is closed to the possibility of a designer, his own assumption will *force* him to adopt what to many will seem an 'unlikely' explanation for what he observes. We should not be surprized to find arguments being used which stretch the imagination and are based on little concrete evidence, since the last thing that the *natural* man will wish to admit is design. Often assumptions are cleverly hidden behind so-called evidence. It is not necessarily the case that these scientific writers are insincere. Their conclusions are the product of a mind-set which is so deeply affected by atheistic humanism that they are barely aware that their assumption of there being no external influence in the Universe has been the major factor affecting such conclusions.

A good example of this type of thinking is that concerning our own planet. Even the inanimate world that we live on is remarkable for the delicate balance of the atmosphere, oceans, tides and energy from the sun. The fact that the moon is at just the right distance from the earth so as not to leave stagnant oceans on the one hand or to give daily tidal waves on the other, is a witness to design, yet some respected scientists turn to the notion that Earth itself has mysteriously controlled its own environment and atmosphere to sustain life (e.g. Lovelock and the Gaia hypothesis[1]). Such thinking is not new but is a modern form of pantheism which has been believed in Eastern religions for centuries. This illustrates the fact that it is one's *assumptions* (emanating from the *world-view* of a writer) which have a large bearing on the conclusions reached. The letter to the Romans (Romans 1:28) speaks very clearly of the wilful nature of natural man— that 'they did not like to retain God in their knowledge'.

When we move from the inanimate world to examining the animal and plant kingdom, there are countless examples of intricate mechanisms which have to be given some kind of natural explanation.[2] One example is flight, which is used by four types of creatures: mammals (for instance bats), birds, insects and the now extinct pterodactyls. Even if one accepts the dating system of the rocks, the lack of any unquestionable transitional forms in the fossil record has led many scientists seriously to question the whole basis of evolutionary thinking. At least some are prepared to reconsider the assumptions they have made. In spite of this, some still prefer to find ways of escaping the alternative conclusion of design. A notable example is the molecular biologist and writer Richard Dawkins (author of *The Blind Watchmaker* and *The Selfish Gene*). He is very open about his atheistic starting point. In an interview he said:[3]

Most people grow up and go through their lives without ever really understanding Darwinism. They spend enormous amounts of time learning church teachings. This annoys me, out of a love for truth. To me, religion is very largely an enemy of truth.

Nevertheless, despite his attempts to justify his objectivity, the religious fervour of his atheism is quite evident in his own writings. To most of us, looking at the intricacies of a mechanically driven watch, we would immediately recognize design as we see the cogs and wheels all working in perfect harmony and rhythm. But Dawkins, when looking at intricate mechanisms in the plant and animal world right down to the cellular scale and smaller still, is prepared to argue that 'the watch made itself'. This, against all the laws of probability of making even *one living cell* from inanimate chemistry![4] These views of Dawkins are held with fervour, not so much because there is any hard evidence to support them but because, as Thomas Huxley the ardent evolutionist of the 19th century said, 'the alternative of Special Creation is unthinkable'. That which seems a straightforward deduction to a scientist who believes in creation (and is not prepared to close his mind to the possibility of the Divine) has to be avoided *at all costs* by the scientist who 'will not have this man [Christ] to reign over [him]' (Luke 19:14). His assumptions have driven him to his 'amoeba making men' conclusion. Whether it be David Attenborough with his famous *Life on Earth* series on television[5] or Stephen Hawking and *A brief history of Time,* all such authors and commentators are effectively propagating *religious* assumptions. They are doing this just as much as a creationist, since the assumption of whether or not One outside was involved at the beginning (and still is involved) reflects one's world-view, and profoundly affects one's thinking and subsequent conclusions.

The religious nature of the debate on origins is recognized by the leading proponents of belief in evolution. According to Sir Julian Huxley, quoted in a leading humanist publication, a humanist is,

someone who believes that man is just as much a natural phenomenon as an animal or plant; that his body, mind and soul were not supernaturally created but are products of evolution.[6]

Pierre Teilhard de Chardin, quoted by Ayala, went further,

[Evolution] is a general postulate to which all theories, all hypotheses, all systems must henceforward bow and which they must satisfy in order to be thinkable and true. Evolution is a light which illuminates all facts, a trajectory which all lines of thought must follow—this is what evolution is.[7]

In a frank admission of the religious nature of evolution, two well respected scientists, Birch and Ehrlich, stated in the journal *Nature:*

Our theory of evolution has become ... one which cannot be refuted by any possible observation. Every conceivable observation can be fitted into it. It is thus 'outside of empirical science' but not necessarily false. No one can think of ways in which to test it. Ideas, either without basis or based on a few laboratory experiments carried out in extremely simplified systems have attained currency far beyond their validity. They have become part of an evolutionary dogma accepted by most of us as part of our training.[8]

The above authors have rightly acknowledged the religious nature of the debate on origins. No scientist is without bias. He will always be coloured by his or her world-view. It is no wonder that Lewontin said,

… whatever the desire to reconcile science and religion may be, there is no escape from the fundamental contradiction between evolution and creationism. They are irreconcilable world views.[9]

2.3 Assumptions or prejudice?

We must recognize that both the thinking and conclusions of the scientist who believes in creation and one who starts out with atheistic humanism, are entirely consistent with their starting assumptions. To avoid prejudice, which is the refusal to alter one's opinion in the light of careful scrutiny, requires an openness to have one's presuppositions and subsequent thinking examined. The scientist who believes in creation looks at the world around him, and he observes that many facts are consistent with the presupposition of a designer and even demand this to be so. He considers the inanimate world and notices the intricate balance of the water cycle, tidal forces on the oceans and the dynamic equilibrium of oxygen and carbon dioxide in the atmosphere. In the living world he observes the intricacies of DNA, the mechanisms of breathing, seeing, hearing, flight and countless other devices and concludes that this is the mark of a Divine designer. As long as his position is open to being tested by alternative theories, this is not prejudice. Equally well he (the creationist) must be allowed to examine the evolutionist position by showing that many mechanisms cannot be produced by chance processes, not even if an infinite amount of time is allowed. Good science from the creationist quarter needs to be encouraged and recognized. Even if the evolution position were true, it could only gain from such a healthy exchange of opposing opinions in an open forum. This is the ideal, but in fact the scientific world is far from allowing such an open exchange. Because in our society the prevailing opinion is undoubtedly on the side of atheistic humanism, sadly many scientists will not allow the starting assumptions to be questioned, so it would not be an exaggeration to say that scientific progress in some areas is in danger of being stifled.[10]

A refreshing addition to the debate is the book *Darwin's Black Box* by Michael Behe.[11] Although he is not a creationist, he shows that design in biochemistry cannot be ignored or explained away. He rightly argues that science has limits when he says,[12]

… the fundamental philosophical principles that underlie reality and the theological principle, or lack of principles, that can be garnered from philosophy and historical experience are at root chosen by the individual.

Here, Behe acknowledges the vital point concerning the presuppositions governing a scientist's interpretation of data. In reply to the arrogance of Dawkins, who said[13] that anyone who denies evolution is either 'ignorant, stupid or insane (or wicked—but I'd rather not consider that)', Behe argues for a far greater openness and freedom to disagree:[14]

It isn't a big step from calling someone wicked to taking forceful measures to put an end to their wickedness. John Maddox, the editor of *Nature,* has written in his journal that 'it may not be long before the practice of religion must be regarded as anti-science'.[15] In his recent book *Darwin's Dangerous Idea,* philosopher Daniel Dennett compares religious believers—90 percent of the population—to wild animals who may have to be caged, and he says that parents should be prevented (presumably by coercion) from misinforming their children about the truth of evolution, which is so evident to him.[16] This is not a recipe for domestic tranquility. It is one thing to try to persuade someone by polemics; it is entirely different to propose to coerce those who disagree with you. As the weight of scientific evidence shifts dramatically, this point should be kept prominently in mind. Richard Dawkins has said that Darwin made it possible to be an 'intellectually fulfilled atheist'.[17] The failure of Darwin's theory on the molecular scale may cause him to feel less fulfilled, but no-one should try to stop him from continuing his search.

Van Inwagen,[18] reviewing Behe's powerful answer to the far-fetched arguments of Dawkins against design, has to admit:

If Darwinians respond to this important book [*Darwin's Black Box*] by ignoring it, misrepresenting it, or ridiculing it, that will be evidence in favour of the widespread suspicion that Darwinianism functions more as an ideology than as a scientific theory. If they can successfully answer Behe's arguments, that will be important evidence in favour of Darwinianism.

No amount of evidence will necessarily change a person's mind if he is determined to exclude the possibility of God's existence. The Bible (Psalm 14:1; Psalm 53:1) refers to the fool who 'has said in his heart, "There is no God"' and to those who 'did not like to retain God in their knowledge' (Romans 1:28) or even the possibility of him. Few people standing at the end of Runway 28 Left at Heathrow and watching a large Boeing airliner make the final adjustments before landing, could seriously question the planned thousands of man-hours of purposeful design that went into making such a craft. Yet equally impressive is the dive (often with far greater precision) of any of the birds we see around us. Mechanically, the flexibility of the latter is much greater, yet if you say birds are designed, you are regarded as unscientific!

Of course if someone seriously did doubt the design of a modern airliner, that person could be convinced by taking him into Boeing's factory in Seattle, Washington State, USA, and introducing him to the teams of design engineers. In the same way man's prejudice against design in creation can only really be answered by a radical change of heart and by meeting the Author of all personally. In the end the difference between these two world views is due to *religious* differences. It is because men *do not want to be accountable* to a Creator God, that they persist with a theory which has little evidence to support it.

Every scientist, if he is honest, has assumptions, even a religious (and sometimes an overtly anti-Christian) starting point. Scientists can often be terribly prejudiced, as Lord Lister found to his amazement last century. He had proved time and again that by washing carefully before an operation, the death of patients could often be avoided. Few of his colleagues believed him at first and he was much ridiculed and criticized until it became evident that Lister's patients lived and those of other surgeons died! Science is a process of careful, logical deduction based on assumptions. In the purest of sciences, mathematics, one must always recognize the starting assumptions in a logical deduction and, if the answer contradicts other evidence, be prepared to abandon one's starting point. The evolutionist assumes either God 'is not there' (Dawkins) or that God 'set evolution going' (the view of many sincere but misguided Christians). Either way, it is claimed that there are natural forces which made molecules into men.

It is not the primary purpose of this book to be another apologetics title on the subject of creation/evolution. There are plenty of very good texts on this subject. However, for the interested reader, further reasons concerning the scientific arguments are listed briefly in the appendices at the end.

2.4 Scientific endeavour

The world-view of a true Bible-believing Christian is not just a small matter. It has a big effect on how he thinks and how he relates to those around him. The Christian world view is fundamentally and radically different to that from an evolutionary perspective. No area is so much affected as the whole purpose behind scientific endeavour.

Scientific endeavour for the Bible-believing scientist must be subject to scriptural principles, as must every area of his or her life. In Genesis 1:28 before the Fall, God said to Adam and Eve, 'Be fruitful, and multiply; fill the earth, and subdue it; have dominion over the fish of the sea, over the birds of the air, and over every living thing that moves upon the earth.' Again, after the Flood, Noah was given a similar command (Genesis 9:1), 'Be fruitful, and multiply, and fill the earth', repeated again in Genesis 9:7. In the beginning man was to be vegetarian (Genesis 1:29–30) and his task was to dress and keep the garden of Eden (Genesis 2:15). Only after the Fall did this task of tilling the ground become hard work—Genesis 3:19, 'In the sweat of your face you shall eat bread …' He ceased to be vegetarian in his diet when Noah was instructed to eat meat (see Genesis 9:3, 'Every moving thing that lives shall be food for you'). Indeed, God speaks of the animals as now having fear (Genesis 9:2) and that 'They are given into your [Noah's] hand'. There is little doubt that the Bible teaches man's pre-eminence over the rest of the natural world but this does not justify cruelty. To demonstrate this there are a number of Scriptures which teach against cruelty:

Deuteronomy 22:6–7: not taking the mother bird with the eggs or young hatchlings;

Deuteronomy 25:4: not muzzling the ox which treads out the corn;

Proverbs 12:10: 'A righteous man regards the life of his animal, but the tender mercies of the wicked are cruel.'

In the original instruction of Genesis 1:28, God goes on to say that man is to have dominion over (literally: rule, tread down) every living thing and subdue (literally: keep under, bring into subjection) the earth. It is evident from the naming of the animals in Genesis 2 (verses 19 and 20) and the instruction to tend the garden (verse 15), that this dominion was not harsh. Fear and bloodshed were not known until after the Fall. Consequently, scientific endeavour involving humane control of the animal world and controlled farming is to be encouraged. Many great scientists of the past have been Bible-believing men. One of the most notable English scientists last century was Faraday, who demonstrated the principle of electromagnetism, and who humbly stated that the greatest discovery he had made was of the Lord Jesus Christ as his own Saviour.

Faraday's humility is borne out by the following excerpt from the book *Researches in Chemistry and Physics* and originally from a lecture on 'Mental Education' delivered before the Royal Institution on 6 May 1854:[19]

I believe that as a man is placed above the creatures round him, there is a higher and far more exalted position within his view; and the ways are infinite in which he occupies his thoughts about the fears, or hope, or expectations, of a future life. I believe that the truth of that future cannot be brought to his knowledge by any exertion of his mental powers, however exalted they may be; that it is made known to him by other teaching than his own; it is received through simple belief of the testimony given. Let no one suppose, for an instant, that the self-education I am about to commend, in respect of the things of this life, extends to any considerations of the hope set before us, as if man by reasoning could find out God. It would be improper here to enter upon this subject further than to claim an absolute distinction between religious and ordinary belief. I shall be reproached with the weakness of refusing to apply these mental operations which I think good in respect of high things to the very highest. I am content to bear the reproach … I have never seen anything incompatible between those things of man which can be known by the spirit of man that is within him and those higher things concerning his future, which he cannot know by that spirit.

Thus Faraday found no difficulty in accepting that 'there is a higher and far more exalted position within his view' and that the knowledge of the Divine is received 'through simple belief of the testimonies given'. God has spoken perfectly in Scripture. We would do well to follow Faraday's example and realize the limitations of man (and those who say 'man by reasoning can find out God')[20] and accept that God has directly spoken to us in Christ and the Scriptures.

In their science, such men as Faraday saw no conflict between their Christian faith and their scientific careers. It was Newton who spoke of 'thinking God's thoughts after him'. Believing in an ordered, well-planned Universe, a number of God-fearing scientists have made immense contributions to scientific discovery for instance Kepler, who showed that the planets for instance have elliptic orbits round the sun, and thus greatly furthered progress in astronomy, and Pasteur, who was doubted for many years because he insisted that life could not come from non-life and consequently non-living decaying matter could not give birth to microbes and bacteria, and thereby to disease. Nevertheless, due to his careful scientific work, agricultural and farming methods improved in France and much of Europe. His name has become synonymous with the treatments of milk and other produce. The belief in design and purpose in the Universe prompted men and women of such convictions to understand better the order *already placed in the Universe*. The verses of Scripture, Hebrews 1:3, 'upholding all things by the word of his power' and Colossians 1:17, 'in Him all things consist' (literally: hang together) have very deep philosophical implications for the Bible-believing scientist. He *expects* to see well-ordered principles governing life on Earth, albeit he knows that, 'the whole creation groans and labours with birth pangs …' (Romans 8:22) as a result of the principle of sin and death now in this world. All the Universe is declared by the Bible not only to be made *by* the Lord, but *for* him. Thus Proverbs 16:4 states, 'The Lord has made all things for himself' and Romans 11:36 at the end of a glorious doxology, states, 'For *of* Him and *through* Him and *to* Him are all things, to whom be glory for ever. Amen.' The final Lordship of Christ is a constant recurring theme. Philippians 2:10 states, 'that at the name of Jesus every knee should bow, of those in heaven, and of those on earth, and of those under the earth'. The glory of an existing ordered Universe is only surpassed by the glory of that to come. The primary purpose of Christ's death is to redeem lost sinners to himself. But Ephesians 1:10 goes further, 'that … He might gather together in one all things in Christ, both which are in heaven and which are on earth—in Him.' Colossians 1:20 is similar, '… by Him to reconcile all things to Himself—by Him, whether things on earth or things in heaven, having made peace through the blood of His cross.'

The contrast with scientists of evolutionary thinking is great. All those of evolutionary persuasion end up either with a Darwinian principle (accidental 'good' mutations survived as environments changed—survival of the fittest) or Lamarckianism (there was a need for a species to alter, so the genes of parents produced altered characteristics in the offspring—e.g. a small necked ancestor of the giraffe gave birth to longer necked offspring in order to reach a better food supply). For an evolutionist there is always a search for *why* order has come about since he has no framework of order in his starting assumptions. Yet the question 'Why?' is really outside the realm of science and to force an answer to this question from scientific enquiry is to push the scientific method beyond its remit. Indeed this is the fatal flaw in Huxley's argument in his famous essay *The lights of the Church and the light of Science,* when he claimed that science *alone* could answer the question of origins[21]—a claim which is so obviously false since (a) no man was there to observe and (b) there is no warrant to discount the alternative of special revelation.

Basic to a scientist with evolutionary assumptions is that, in all his investigations, the simple *somehow* became complicated. For Lovelock and his Gaia hypothesis,[22] the *how* is explained by the earth itself and its biosphere, atmosphere, oceans, and soil; the totality constituting a feedback or cybernetic system which seeks an optimal physical and chemical environment for life on this planet.

Thus he comes to a virtually pantheistic conclusion that the planet is itself in some way 'alive' and able not only to sustain life now, but also that in the past conditions were exactly 'right' for life to evolve from an ammonia-like reducing atmosphere. Alternatively, others would prefer to say that life from outer space sparked off the first organic process and that from these beginnings came the long billions-of-years climb to the complexity of man himself. All evolutionists are driven to arguments such as the following:

If we can imagine a planet made of nothing but the component parts of watches, we may reasonably assume that in the fullness of time—perhaps 1,000 million years— gravitational forces and the restless motion of the wind would assemble at least one working watch. Life on Earth probably started in a similar manner.[23]

Such speculative reasoning is clearly not science, but wishful thinking on the part of the writer, despite his being a Fellow of the Royal Society. One has to appreciate that however unbelievable to many of us, these views are seriously held to by people just as eminent as Lovelock.

There was an interesting exchange in the newspapers in September 1996 which reported the forthright statements by Peter Atkins, Professor of Chemistry at Oxford University. He argued in a debate at the British Association for the Advancement of Science (BAAS) at Birmingham University that science had ruled out belief in God. A few days later a brief letter appeared which I quote in full:

Sir—Professor Peter Atkins' diatribe (report, Sept. 11), which included the claim that it is impossible to believe in God and be a 'true scientist', contrasts interestingly with the following quotation: 'The religious feeling of the scientist takes the form of rapturous amazement at the harmony of natural law—which reveals an intelligence of such superiority that, compared with it, all the systematic thinking and acting of human beings is an utterly insignificant reflection'. The source of these words? Some scientist by the name of Albert Einstein. Prof. Atkins may have heard of him.[24]

Einstein's greatnes[25] was in some measure not only due to his mental brilliance, but also to something sadly lacking in many scientists today—a sense of humility and an awareness of the boundaries and limitations of the scientific method. True genius does not need to resort to arrogance.

What drives ardent evolutionists such as Lovelock, Attenborough, Dawkins or Atkins is an atheism which itself is as religious an assumption as special creation. Thus, for an evolutionist, the teleological (design implies a designer) argument *has* to be dismissed and it is now important to see that his or her subsequent scientific investigation is motivated no longer by a wonder at the order already *there*, but by a desire to *find* a 'life-force' principle within the world around him. This is exactly as Romans 1 states. Those who refuse God as Creator (verse 20) are then described (verse 25) as those, 'who exchanged the truth of God for the lie, and worshipped and served the creature rather than the Creator'. The survival of higher and better life forms is now his determining philosophy. Not only science but sociology and anthropology have been much influenced by Darwinian thinking. Such scientists argue that there are no absolute laws and man is essentially no different from the animals. We have no right to 'alter' the earth or its creatures. Man is but one of them and the natural life on earth must not be disturbed. Friends of the Earth, Animal Rights, and many similar organisations today largely flow from such thinking. A sense that the Earth itself is shaping its own future and that man is but part of this global machine is very prevalent in the media. For Christian Bible-believing people it is important that we understand where such thinking is coming from. Though we believe we should not misuse the world's resources, we must resist the unbiblical idea that man is but a 'naked ape'. Evolutionary science reduces man to a beast, with no purpose and little future. Biblically based scientific inquiry regards man as fallen yet noble, still entrusted with the delegated and princely authority to rule the Earth.

Indeed, we should not be brow-beaten by the evolutionary outlook of the majority around us. Too often Bible-believing thinkers are defensive. In every walk of life—scientific, cultural, medical, humanitarian—there should be a bold offensive on the ungodly pragmatism which on the one hand holds man to be only an animal, yet on the other hand desperately searches for a reason to treat his neighbour with altruism. Even Huxley who, more than any, was the antagonist of Christian belief in the 19th century, makes a plaintive call for morality and endeavour when he knows that evolution, if it is true, implies an opposite course. In his essay, *Evolution and Ethics*,[26] he has to appeal to the individual to counter evolution:

Let us understand, once for all, that the ethical progress of society depends, not on imitating the cosmic process, [i.e. evolution], still less in running away from it, *but in combating it*. It may seem an audacious proposal thus to pit the microcosm against the macrocosm and to set man to subdue nature to his higher ends; but I venture to think that the great intellectual difference between the ancient times with which we have been occupied and our day, lies in the solid foundation we have acquired for the hope that such an enterprise may meet with a certain measure of success.

Though two world wars have passed since Huxley's day and the so-called 'higher ends' of man have been painfully absent, present thinking is still dominated by the evolutionary world-view. *The Ascent of Man*[27] thinking of Huxley's time has gone,[28] but now we are faced with New Age philosophies based on evolutionary, pantheistic ideas. Schaeffer, one of the best Christian thinkers of the last century, saw clearly the impossibility of morality flowing from evolution when he said:[29]

If man is not made in the image of God, nothing then stands in the way of inhumanity. There is no good reason why mankind should be perceived as special. Human life is cheapened.

Schaeffer, in the same book, also comments on the abuse of genetic engineering:

Once the uniqueness of people as created by God is removed and mankind is viewed as only one of the gene patterns which came to earth by chance, there is no reason not to treat people as things to be experimented on and to make over the whole of humanity according to the decisions of a relatively few individuals. If people are not unique—as made in the image of God—the barrier is gone.[30]

So the ethical basis of scientific enquiry is vital and is most properly rooted in the firm foundation that all life has been created by God. Without this, nothing is sacrosanct. There are no absolute rules.

December 1996 saw the death of Carl Sagan, one of the most prolific of writers on astronomy and with a determination to oppose any creationist viewpoint. How significant that his last major statement left the following empty and forlorn hope:

We live on a hunk of rock and metal that circles a humdrum star that is one of 400 billion other stars that make up the Milky Way Galaxy which is one of billions of other galaxies which make up a universe which may be one of a very large number, perhaps an infinite number of other universes. That is a perspective on human life and our culture that is well worth pondering.[31]

The evolutionist can, in the end, only be definite about one fact—that he has no idea where we are from, no idea where we are going or why we are here! What a contrast to the Bible-centred view which teaches *why* there is sin and death and gives a lasting and secure hope to a fallen race through Christ alone.

A Bible-first, creationist world-view is essential if we are to make an impact on the decadent western society as we begin the millennium. Contrary to popular thinking, a literal belief in Genesis is entirely consistent with true scientific enquiry, and only a thorough-going biblical outlook will provide the radical foundational change that is so evidently needed today.

Chapter 2 notes

1 JE Lovelock, Gaia—a new look at life on Earth (Oxford: Oxford University Press, 1991).

2 R Milton, The Facts of Life—shattering the myth of Darwinism (London: 4th Estate, 1992).

3 R Dawkins, 'Interview' Omni 12 (4), 60–61, January 1990.

4 See M Poole, 'A critique of aspects of the philosophy and theology of Richard Dawkins' in Science and Christian Belief 6 (1994) 1–49 for a detailed critique of Dawkins' ideas.

5 See also the book David Attenborough, Life on Earth (London: Collins & British Broadcasting Corporation, 1979).

6 *What is Humanism?,* San Jose, CA 95106: Humanist Community of San Jose quoted in **DT Gish,** ICR Impact Article 262, 'The Nature of Science and of Theories on Origins', April 1995.

7 FJ Ayala, 'Nothing in biology makes sense except in the light of evolution', review of the work of T Dobzhansky, *The Journal of Heredity,* 68, 1977, 3–10.

8 LC Birch, and **PR Ehrlich,** *Nature,* 214; 1967, 369.

9 R Lewontin, Introduction to **LR Godfrey** (ed.) *Scientists confront Creationism* (New York: WW Norton, 1983), p. xxvi.

10 It is noteworthy that Sir Fred Hoyle, no friend to the Christian viewpoint, agrees. Quoted by **J Horgan** in 'The return of the maverick', *Scientific American,* 272(3), March 1995, p. 25, Hoyle states, 'Science today is locked into paradigms ... every avenue is blocked by beliefs that are wrong, and if you try to get anything published by a journal today, you will run up against a paradigm, and the editors will turn it down.'

11 M Behe, *Darwin's Black Box—The Biochemical Challenge to Evolution* (New York: Free Press, 1996). See particularly chapter 11 'Science, Philosophy, Religion'.

12 M Behe, op. cit., p. 250.

13 R Dawkins, *New York Times,* 9 April 1989, sec. 7, p. 34.

14 M Behe, op. cit., p. 250.

15 J Maddox, 'Defending Science against anti-Science', *Nature,* 368, 185, 1994.

16 DC Dennett, *Darwin's Dangerous Idea* (New York: Simon and Schuster, 1995), pp. 515–516.

17 R Dawkins, *The Blind Watchmaker* (Harmondsworth: Penguin, 1991), p. 6.

18 P van Inwagen, Professor of Philosophy, Notre Dame University, on the flyleaf of **M Behe,** *Darwin's Black Box,* op. cit.

19 Wilfred L Randell, *Michael Faraday (1791–1867)* (London: Leonard Parsons; Boston: Small, Maynard & Co., 1924), pp. 149–150. This book is an archive of valuable biographical detail of the man behind the science. The biographer (Randell) now deceased, was the grandfather of ACM. See also **JG Crowther,** *British Scientists of the 19th Century,* Vol. 1 (Pelican, 1940). He discusses the lives of Davy, Faraday and Joule. Joule who brilliantly demonstrated the principle of the conservation of energy, stated (p. 159) 'After the knowledge of, and obedience to, the will of God, the next aim must be to know something of His Attributes of wisdom, power and goodness as evidenced by His handiwork. The study of nature and her laws ... [is] ... essentially a holy undertaking ... [and is of] ... great importance and absolute necessity in the education of youth.' This quote shows a similar humble attitude to that of Faraday.

20 Job 11:7–9 teaches that finite man cannot search out the deep things of the Infinite—Almighty God.

21 TH Huxley, chapter 6, 'The lights of the Church and the light of Science' in *Science and Hebrew Tradition—Essays by Thomas H Huxley* (London: Macmillan, 1903), pp. 201–238. See particularly p. 212, 'The origin of the present state of the heavens and the earth is a problem which lies strictly within the province of physical science ...'. See also p. 234 where he boldly asserts 'it can be demonstrated that the earth took longer than six days in the making, and that the Deluge, as described, is a physical impossibility.' Such dogmatism indicates the religious nature of his assumptions (rather than scientific).

22 JE Lovelock, op. cit., p.11.

23 JE Lovelock, op. cit, p.14.

24 See *Daily Telegraph,* 11 September 1996.

25 Sadly Einstein's greatness scientifically was not matched by faithfulness before and within marriage. The book *Einstein: a life* by Denis Brian (New York: Wiley, 1996), shows both sides of the man.

26 TH Huxley, *Evolution and Ethics and other essays* (London: Macmillan, 1903), p. 83 (italics and part in square brackets, mine). The essay is *The Romanes Lecture* given in 1893.

27 The book *The Ascent of Man* by **Henry Drummond** (London: Hodder and Stoughton, 1894) represented the sincere (but misguided) attempt by Christian scholars in the 19th century to show that evolution could be regarded as part of biblical thinking. In fact Huxley was far more consistent and much clearer in his thinking, since he realized the two approaches could never be joined. Neverthless both sides had a view of a positive, expanding society where peace would reign. Drummond and others like him were ardent supporters of world evangelical missionary outreach. In other respects, Henry Drummond, Professor of Natural Science in the Free Church College, Glasgow, was exemplary. His classic little book *The Greatest thing in the World* (London: Hodder and Stoughton, 1890, 1980) is a masterly exposition of 1 Corinthians 13 and is regarded by many as unsurpassed. In the recent 1980 edition of *The Greatest thing in the World,* **Denis Duncan** has a postscript on Drummond's life where, on p. 60, he refers to the criticism that 'The Ascent of Man' rightly evoked. It seems even the great DL Moody did not appreciate the seriousness of the error of evolution it contained.

28 J Bronowski bravely produced a book again of this title in 1990 (**J Bronowski,** *The Ascent of Man* (London: BBC, 1990)) but the violence of the 20th century has caused many humanists to despair of any ascent.

29 FA Schaeffer & CE Koop, *Whatever happened to the human race?* (Westchester, Illinois: Crossway Books, 1983), p. 10.

30 FA Schaeffer & CE Koop, op. cit., p. 8.

31 C Sagan, Interview with Ted Koppel on the US TV programme *Dateline*. This interview took place a few days before Carl Sagan's death. Ted Koppel asked Carl Sagan whether he had any closing remarks or words of wisdom he would like to share with the Earth's people.

Genesis and history

3.1 Recognising the issues

As a scientist, I believe that it is entirely reasonable to hold that the world was made of the order of 6,000 years ago in six 24–hour days. But the basis for my belief is unashamedly Scripture first. As I have sought to explain in the previous chapter, this is not undermining science. It is simply recognising that true science has limitations. Genesis records in a matter-of-fact way that the world was created by a definite act of special creation by God. Consequently the truth of the whole Bible itself is at stake if we are not to believe it on its first few pages. As the little child said 'If God didn't mean what he said, why didn't he say what he meant?' We are not dealing with poetry, but the blow by blow account of a series of major events. Most of the leading University theologians today (including liberal thinkers) would agree that the writer of Genesis clearly *intended* to convey that this is what actually happened. Thus it is foolish even to try to attempt to marry evolutionary views with Genesis either by Theistic Evolution (that is, God *used* evolution to make the world) or Progressive Creation (God *interrupted* the evolutionary process with a few jumps, notably to give an early hominid a soul). This latter view is the one primarily put forward by Hugh Ross,[1] and both this view and Theistic Evolution are clearly answered by recent creationist writings.[2] The aim of this chapter is to show that if we take the Bible as our starting point as the inerrant Word of God, we must accept that the Genesis creation account is to be taken at face value and cannot be reconciled with creation over long periods of time.

3.2 The whole Bible stands or falls with the historicity of Genesis

It is crucially important to have a straightforward view of Genesis. The secular world recognizes this more than the church. Thomas Huxley (1825–1895), the ardent defender of Darwin's ideas and the one who (more than Darwin himself) propagated evolutionary thinking, wrote:

I am fairly at a loss to comprehend how anyone for a moment can doubt that Christian theology must stand or fall with the historical trustworthiness of the Jewish Scriptures.

The very conception of the Messiah, or Christ, is inextricably interwoven with Jewish history; the identification of Jesus of Nazareth with that Messiah rests upon the interpretation of the passages of the Hebrew Scriptures which have no evidential value unless they possess the historical character assigned to them.[3]

In recent years a somewhat strange trend has developed in Christian circles. While some secular authors have begun to doubt the traditional evolutionary thinking of Darwin, Huxley and others who first made popular such views, some sincere evangelical Christians have been developing the concept that 'God used evolution to make the world'—the view which here is termed 'Theistic Evolution'. Such an idea is, of course, by no means new, but it is now becoming more fashionable among evangelicals (who supposedly hold to the infallibility of the Scripture) as well as liberals (who do not). Some books by evangelical writers doubting the straightforward creationist position on Genesis are *Beyond Belief: Science, faith and ethical challenges* by Alexander and White,[4] *Rebuilding the Matrix* by Alexander and *The Scandal of the Evangelical Mind* by Noll (published by InterVarsity Press, who have a strong evangelical tradition).[5] These books give the impression that one can be 'evangelical' and believe in evolution. They are really advocating liberalism and reflect an equivocal stand on a most vital issue. The Christian evangelical is increasingly being led to believe that the literal interpretation of Genesis is simply a matter of opinion. This is particularly brought out by the book *Creation and Evolution*[6] in the series *When Christians disagree*. The implication is that the issue of creation is as secondary as other titles in the same series (e.g. 'Pacifism and War' or 'Politics'). Is this really the case? Is the Bible really so unclear as to the method of creation? Many would have us believe so, and the irony is that secular authors, whilst in no way adopting a special creation approach, are beginning to question the fundamentals of progressive evolutionary thinking (e.g. the 'Punctuated Equilibrium' view of Stephen J Gould and others which, in brief, states that there was sudden change within species so that there was no time for any transitional fossils to form in the rocks).

It is foolish not to recognize the relevance of the question of the historicity of Genesis to other very important areas of belief and practice.

Huxley, though a convinced atheist, was clear-cut in his thinking, at least on this issue. He knew that the influence of Christianity would wane if one could cast doubt on the truthfulness of the first book of the Bible. He knew the Bible better than many Christians who falsely tried to marry the tenets of evolution and Christianity, by first of all abandoning a belief in a global world-wide flood. Huxley knew that in time, all the major doctrines held by the established church would be abandoned once they had compromised on Genesis.[7]

Once Creation, the Fall and the Flood are brought into question as history, then this brings immediately into disrepute, not just the statements of the Apostles (who, one recognizes, were fallible men), but of the Lord Jesus Christ himself who appealed to Genesis as history. The whole meaning of sin and redemption is blurred and lost if we lose the anchor of Genesis. The Puritan poet Milton saw the grandeur of redemption based on a firm belief in the Bible. The greatness of seventeenth century commitment to a biblical worldview is reflected in his epic poems 'Paradise Lost' and 'Paradise Regained'.

Are we right to dismiss the outlook of Bunyan (author of 'Pilgrim's Progress') and Milton of the 17th century with their straightforward belief in Scripture? Are we right to turn from the fervent preaching of Wesley and Whitefield of the 18th century who, with their appeal to Scripture, by God's grace turned England from moral and political disaster? Should we let loose from the anchor that held England steady in the 19th century? Were Spurgeon, Ryle and Müller all mistaken in their firm adherence to the Book of books, such that the Prime Minister (Gladstone) spoke of the 'impregnable rock of Holy Scripture'?[8] Nobody denies that 19th century England had its faults, such as the inhumane social conditions endured by many workers in coal mines, factories and mills. Dickens so eloquently pointed out all these in *Oliver Twist* and other classic books, but Britain's faults were *not* in its belief in the Bible as history.[9] The faults of a bigoted and narrow spirit are not the fault of the Scripture but of a pharisaical self-righteousness which completely denies the Bible. Christ condemned hypocrisy wherever he saw it. It was a full-blooded, total belief in Scripture in the 19th century that, in fact, produced world-class men and women of catholicity and generosity: people such as Hudson Taylor, the great missionary of China; David Livingstone and Mary

Slessor, who gave up all to win the heart of Africa for the gospel, and Lord Shaftesbury, who gave a fortune in time, money and energy to abolish the cruel misuse of children and see them won to the Saviour. These all believed that there was coming a day when Christ would return to usher in the great judgement and that only those trusting in Christ's redemptive work at Calvary could be forgiven. They knew the Scriptures taught that just as there was a literal fall, there would be a literal return of Christ and the resurrection of believers to an eternity with him.

If we are to believe we originally came from monkeys and apes with generations of violence and bloodshed, and that there was no literal Eden, what are we to make of the Bible's promises concerning the new heavens and new earth 'in which righteousness dwells' (2 Peter 3:13)?

Below I consider why, if we believe the Bible, we should believe in the historicity of Genesis 1–11, creation in six 24–hour days and no gaps in the creation week.

3.3 The historicity of Genesis 1–11

THOSE ACCEPTING THE BIBLE'S AUTHORITY

First of paramount importance is whether Genesis 1 to 11 is to be regarded as historical. The answer to this is in the affirmative for the following reasons:

i. Christ regarded the major characters and events as historical. Adam and Eve are referred to indirectly (Matthew 19:4), Abel directly (Matthew 23:35; Luke 11:51), Noah directly (Matthew 24:37; Luke 17:26) and the Flood directly (Matthew 24:38–39; Luke 17:27).

ii. The genealogy of Christ in Luke 3 backs up the genealogies of Genesis 5 and 11 (and also that of 1 Chronicles 1). This repetition of the genealogies strengthens the view that they should be regarded as an accurate history of the ancestry of man. (This point is expanded on in section 3.6.)

iii. The Apostles regarded the major characters and events as historical. Paul refers to Adam and Eve directly (Romans 5:14; 1 Corinthians 15:22,45; 2 Corinthians 11:3; 1 Timothy 2:13–14). The latter reference is in the context of an argument which specifically depends on the order of the creation of the first pair of human beings. The possibility of Genesis not being literal with no real Adam and Eve makes the argument of 1 Timothy 2 nonsense. Even if one assumes a real Adam and Eve, but with many hominid ancestors to this pair, one still removes the meaning of this chapter which is that Eve came from *Adam*, *not* a hominid pair before both of them. (The view that Adam and Eve had hominid ancestors is put forward by Stott.[10]) In fact the literary analysis of Genesis 1–11 conducted by a number of experts has revealed that

these chapters cannot be identified as non-historical on the basis of any generally applicable literary criteria. Neither are they distinguishable from Genesis 12–50 by significant differences in their literary character. There is no great divide between Genesis 11 and Genesis 12. In fact, Genesis 11 interlocks with the preceding and following narratives.[11]

Hebrews 11:4 and 12:24 refer to Cain and Abel as historical. John and Jude also confirm this in 1 John 3:12 and Jude 11. A further reference in Jude (verse 14) speaks forcibly of the genealogy from Adam to Enoch as history when it refers to Enoch being the seventh from Adam. Peter, in both his epistles, refers to Noah historically (1 Peter 3:20; 2 Peter 2:5). In the context of the second reference it is clear that Peter regards the Flood as a major catastrophe in history, not so far removed from his own time. 2 Peter 2 describes the Flood of the 'old world' and the 'world of the ungodly' (verse 5). The following chapter leaves no room scripturally for any argument concerning 'local flood' theories (2 Peter 3:4–7). The same word from God which brought the Flood on the world, is the same word which reserves the world to final judgement. If the latter is worldwide (and of this there is no doubt), then so is the former. The conclusion must follow that the New Testament leaves *no* doubt that Adam and Eve were historical, with their ensuing Fall, that the genealogy to Noah is historical and that the Flood was a *worldwide* historical event.

THE SCEPTIC

Of course the sceptic will not accept the testimony of either the Old or the New Testament, and thus the appeal to the Lord's own words and that of the Apostles will not be heard. So the sceptic relies heavily on evidence which claims to prove that the world must be extremely old. In Appendix C *Fossils and the Rocks* some of these so-called proofs of great age are countered, and the reader is referred to the Bibliography for some notable creationist apologetic books on this subject. Huxley was premature a hundred years ago when he stated:

Notwithstanding diligent search, I have been unable to discover that the universality of the Deluge has any defender left, at least among those who have so far mastered the rudiments of natural knowledge as to be able to appreciate the weight of evidence against it.[12]

The 'weight of evidence' that Huxley sincerely thought was there, far from undermining Scripture, has in fact confirmed it. This is particularly true of archaeological finds in Palestine and the Middle East. The investigations at Ur are consistent with the Patriarchal journey of Terah and Abraham, the digging near Jericho shows remarkable evidence of catastrophic demolition of the walls in the time of Joshua.[13] Since Huxley's time, both the lack of *any* clear-cut 'transitional' fossils and the embarrassing discovery of mass graves of fish and animals all over the world substantiates greatly the world-wide flood and leads not a few professors in world-class universities to deny his arrogant claims. For the sceptic reader, let me ask him or her just for a moment to leave aside the matter of rock dating often raised by evolutionists (and dealt with in the section *The dating of the rocks* in Appendix C); consider for a moment the unthinkable! Suppose that the Bible were true in its account of a world-wide flood. In my travels, each time I go across the Pacific, I am always amazed as to its size and depth. Scientists refer to the 'ring of fire' of volcanoes and earthquake zones running down the west coast of the USA, the Andes of South America, the islands of Indonesia and up through south east Asia, Japan and north east Russia. This has led some Creation/Flood scientists to propose that the Flood was due to an impact with a large asteroid which catastrophically broke the Earth's mantle (possibly in the Pacific which would explain its great depth), tilted the Earth off a 'vertical' spin axis and caused earthquakes and volcanoes of cataclysmic proportions.[14] Not only did water fall from above, but water originally beneath the earth was released with tidal waves of immense depths sweeping across the globe. Let the reader consider. *If* such an event took place, what would one expect to see? Surely massive mud layers, rocks, debris scattered across the globe and millions of dead creatures buried in the sedimentary rock layer which would form as the waters receded. That is exactly what is found. There is nothing found in the rock layers which is inconsistent with such supposed events. In fact much that is found is *only* traceable to a catastrophic cause (see for example the discussion in Appendix C about polystrate tree trunks running through a number of rock layers which evolutionists would have us believe were deposited over millions of years). Thus coming with an open mind, the historicity of Genesis 1–11, and in particular the Flood, is not as far-fetched as the media would have us believe. It is very damaging when professing Bible-believers dismiss the straightforward view of a young earth on the basis of the so-called certainties of scientific dating methods.[15] Firstly, Scripture should always come first (not man-made scientific theories) and secondly, the dating schemes are based on unproved assumptions. Because we are heavily indoctrinated by questionable deductions from rocks made out to be extremely old, there is little awareness of (a) the experimental evidence that hardened stratified rock layers can be formed quickly (such as the Toatle Canyon below Mount St Helens after the volcanic explosion of 1980—see Appendix C) (b) experimental evidence that coal can be formed quickly if there is rapid heating (again see Appendix C) and (c) the documentary written evidence of ancient flood accounts all over the world from Russia to Mexico, Greece to Hawaii.[16] These matters are quietly put to one side before the juggernaut of evolutionary prejudice. But the sacred records live on, and humble minds should never put the Scriptures aside lightly when they have been tried and tested for centuries. The old records are corroborated by other ancient evidence and it is foolish and arrogant thinking which assumes that truth was never known in the past.

3.4 Creation in six literal 24–hour days

The scientific evidence for creation is dealt with in Appendices A, B and C. Some Christians, whilst believing Genesis to be authoritative, seek to hold to evolution as well. The aim of this section is to show that this view leads to impossible inconsistencies in biblical interpretation.

The Scriptures teach that creation was in six literal 24–hour days. Many Christians would be with us up to the previous point, but would sadly diverge at this juncture. Whilst accepting that Genesis is historical, some sincere believers take on the view that in order to harmonize Genesis with scientific theories, each day of creation must represent long periods of thousands or millions of years. Superficially this sounds plausible until one realizes that the order of creation, though similar to evolutionary 'family trees', is not exactly the same. One must beware of giving heed to the temptation of putting science first *before* Scripture. Science, like any other interest of man, is not neutral. It must be subject to Scripture. Great scientists are those who know the limitations of the scientific method. When science is forced beyond the remit of understanding the 'how' of the world around us and into the realm of pronouncing on the 'why' as well, it fails. We need to return to the humble spirit of Faraday and others (see chapter 2). While it can be seen, by looking at history, that great scientists are not necessarily believers in Scripture, it will always be true that a proper reverence for Scripture will spawn clear thinking, not just in science, but in all matters, sociological, economical, political and in every area of life. Put another way, a love for the Bible will encourage good science, but good science on its own with fallible men, can easily go awry. If we consider the six day creation, we must conclude that the days were literal 24-hour periods for the following reasons:

i. Genesis 1 reads as historical Hebrew literature (not poetry). The characteristics of Hebrew poetry are parallelism and repetition. In his book *The Great Brain Robbery*,[17] David CC Watson points this out by comparing Psalm 33 and Genesis 1. Psalm 33:6 reads, 'By the word of the Lord the heavens were made, and all the host of them by the breath of his mouth.' This is an example of parallelism and repetition which is quite absent from Genesis 1. That account is no poem. Rather, in a very matter-of-fact way, it is simply recording, stage by stage, what God *did*. This point is important as we now go on to consider the meaning of the word 'day'.

ii. The context of Genesis 1 demands that the word 'day' be a literal 24–hour period. The original word 'yom' in the Hebrew can mean a period of time but it is always obvious from the context. In Genesis 1:5 the word 'day' initially signifies the daylight hours and then, in the same verse, goes on to refer to the completion of the first day of creation, thus implying literal 24–hour periods. At this point many argue that 2 Peter 3:8 ('… with the Lord one day is as a thousand years, and a thousand years as one day …') is justification for regarding the days as non-literal. But one must be very careful not to jump to a conclusion here. 2 Peter 3:8 does *not* say one day *equals* 1,000 years, but rather that with God, time is of no consequence. The verses are in the context of teaching on the second coming of Christ. He is coming, but it may be in some thousands of years and not in days. The word 'day' here is still meaning a 24–hour period. As David CC Watson[18] has aptly commented, 'To toss 2 Peter 3:8 into the middle of Genesis 1 is about as sensible as to affirm that Matthew 27:63 means "After three thousand years I shall rise again"!'

iii. The most conclusive of all arguments concerning the days of Genesis 1 being literal 24–hour periods is to be found in Exodus 20:8–11. 'Remember the Sabbath day, to keep it holy … For in six days the Lord made the heavens and the earth, the sea and all that is in them, and rested the seventh day …'. Although opponents of a six-literal-day creation assail many of the other arguments listed here, it is very rare that Exodus 20 is brought into their reasoning. Of course this is hardly surprising since it is impossible to force the word 'day' to mean a 'period of time' in the context of the fourth commandment. The creation ordinance, repeated by Moses in this passage, is that man is to keep every seventh 24-hour period—not every seventh week or century! It clearly states the reason—'For in six days the Lord made the heavens and the earth' (where the word 'made' is 'asah' and is the same as that used in Genesis 1:31—'God saw everything that He had made'—and is widely used in the Genesis accounts for God's creative acts. The other word 'bara' is reserved for God's creation out of nothing as in Genesis 1:1.). It is most significant that this major argument from Scripture put forward by one of the creationist writers in the IVP book 'Creation and Evolution' (ref. 6 above) was left unanswered by those denying a six literal 24–hour day creation.

A final word on this matter is that only when the theory of evolution came on the scene did Bible commentators ever begin to consider day-age theories. Though this is no proof, the fact makes one question as to whether the theory arose from a priority of good exegesis and exposition, or whether it was simply expediency at the time. A person placed in a room with a Bible and no knowledge of current scientific opinion, would never consider for one moment that Genesis 1–11 was other than a straightforward historical account.[19] Neither would that person do anything but reject evolutionary ideas (theistic or atheistic) had they been presented as originating in the Bible itself. Rather, if theistic evolution had not originated as a response to, and in the context of, atheistic evolution, it would have been denounced immediately as a fantastic theological and exegetical contortion. Evolution as a concept must start *outside* the Bible, for it has no friend within it.

3.5 No gap before the creation week

The Scriptures do not allow for a gap before the creation week. There are a number of Christians who propose that there can be a gap between Genesis 1:1 and 1:2. Such writers translate (incorrectly) Genesis 1:2 '... and the earth *became* waste and void ...'. This is called the 'Gap Theory' and they take the view that God judged the earth in some way before Adam and Eve were made. Since the word used in Exodus 20:11 is 'made' (asah) and not 'created' (bara), Genesis 1:2 onwards is regarded as a restoration of the earth and not an original creation. However Watson[20] lists a number of verses where 'created' and 'made' are quite indistinguishable. For example, Genesis 1:31 'God saw everything that He had *made*' is referring to the acts of *creation* in Genesis 1:1, 21 and 27. Thus the distinction between the two words in the context of Genesis is not due to a different *mechanism* on the part of God Almighty in bringing the world into being. So there is no biblical warrant for a time gap between Genesis 1:1 and Genesis 1:2. If it were not for evolutionary ideas it is unlikely any exegetical argument would have been put forward for a gap between Genesis 1:1 and Genesis 1:2. Once again it seems that some are trying to find a way of marrying two diametrically opposed world views. The idea that somehow things went wrong between Genesis 1:1 and Genesis 1:2 is not consistent with Isaiah 45:18 which states that the Lord 'created the heavens ... formed the earth and made it ... who did not create it in vain, who formed it to be inhabited.' This shows that the express aim of God was for a world inhabited by man in his image. The Gap Theory appeared as a footnote in the Scofield

Reference Bible when evolutionary thinking was first being widely felt. As will be seen later in this book, theologically it presents a major problem since death and violent survival are supposed to have been going on for millions of years before the appearance of Adam and Eve. The reader is referred to an excellent critique of the Gap Theory by Fields.[21]

3.6 How long ago was creation?

The Scriptures read straightforwardly, do not allow for any gaps in the Genesis genealogies, except in one minor instance where, at the most, a few hundred years may be inserted. This point needs careful thought by all Christians. Our approach to this particular matter often reveals our true attitude to Scripture as a whole. Do we really believe the Scriptures as they stand or not? An article by David T Rosevear[22] entitled 'The genealogies in Scripture' is one of the clearest treatments of the subject of genealogies in Scripture. There are places in the Bible where some names are missed out of genealogies since the word 'begot' can signify heritage and not sonship. One example is Matthew's genealogy from Abraham to Joseph. Comparison with 1 Chronicles indicates that from David to Christ, Matthew removes some names in order to achieve patterns of fourteen steps (e.g. Matthew 1:11 'Josias begot Jechonias' compared to 1 Chronicles 3:15–16 where Josiah is the grandfather (through Jehoiakim) of Jeconiah.[23] These clear examples of omissions in genealogies are sometimes used to justify the omissions of many generations in earlier lists. Sadly in Appendix II of their book *The Genesis Flood*,[24] Whitcomb and Morris use the scarcity of names in Exodus 6:16–20 from Levi to Moses (compared to 1 Chronicles 7:20–28 between Joseph and Joshua) to argue for many gaps both there and, significantly, in the earlier genealogies of Genesis 5 and 11.).

However, as an example of the care one must take with biblical genealogies, let us consider the supposed discrepancy between four generations, Levi—Moses (Exodus 6) and 10 generations, Joseph—Nun (Joshua's father) (1 Chronicles 7) with Joseph being contemporary with Levi, and Nun roughly contemporary with Moses. As is apparent on close examination of these texts, we are considering two different sets of generations in the same time span. One salient Scripture can easily be overlooked. Leviticus 10:4 states that Uzziel, brother to Amram (Exodus 6:18), is the uncle of Aaron which precludes any possibility for a gap between Amram and Aaron/Moses. Then, examination of the context of Exodus 6:16–19 where the descendants of each of Levi's children are listed in turn, would strongly suggest there is no gap from Kohath to Amram. So why are there more names on Joseph's side (through Ephraim) than on Levi's? We can turn to other Scriptures to find the answer to this. Two facts emerge. (a) The Lord prophesied to Abraham (Genesis 15:16) that after his death, '… in the fourth generation they shall return here …' Jacob, later on, does indeed leave to dwell in Egypt *with the fourth generation* from him (Levi-Kohath-Amram-Moses). By now a nation, they make the journey back to Canaan. So Genesis 15:16 holds true, and gaps in Levi's line cannot be allowed. The other fact is (b) Joseph's children (particularly Ephraim who means 'fruitful') were prophesied to 'grow into a multitude in the midst of the earth' (literally: 'as fishes do increase', Genesis 48:15–19). Again in Genesis 48:22 the principle is repeated. These two facts give us the answer to the apparent discrepancy in the chronology of the two tribes. It would seem that either a tribe became great in number through many children per generation, or by earlier marriage of each descendant (as in Ephraim's case).

This point is relevant to the *earlier* genealogies of Genesis 5 and 11. Morris and Whitcomb[25] argue that there is a possible gap between Eber and the generation of Joktan and Peleg (Genesis 10:25) by making the comparison with Exodus 6:20 concerning Moses and Aaron descending from Amram.[26] But we have seen that Leviticus 10:4 shows this must be regarded as a tight genealogy and by the same token, so are Genesis 5, Genesis 10 and 11. We cannot insert names just where we please. Indeed, the situation is far tighter in Genesis 5 and 11 than in any of the other genealogies. The reader is referred to Rosevear's article[27] on this point. He poses the question 'Can the term "begot" imply only "descent" as with Matthew's line?' The answer is a clear 'No' since in these genealogies we are given *extra* details which exclude the possibility of missing generations. Only by making the term 'begot' mean 'fathered the line leading to', could substantial gaps be argued for. But such thinking is tortuous, when the straightforward reading is plain and understandable and secondly, the overall thrust is so the reader may know who were the ancesters of Abraham/Noah and how long ago they lived. It is highly unlikely gap theories would ever be considered were it not for external evolutionary thinking. Internal Scripture evidence would never support such interpretation of Genesis 5 and 11 on their own. We read that when Adam was 130 years old, he fathered Seth, that Adam lived a further 800 years after this (having other sons and daughters), and that he died at the age of 930 years. There is thus no room here for ambiguity. We have already referred to Jude 14 which teaches that Genesis 5 *cannot* have gaps since Enoch is referred to as the seventh from Adam. Indeed it is very significant that from Jude 14 we can infer that the New Testament (which is always the key to understanding the Old) shows that *we are meant to take the genealogies* literally. The only difficulty in the early genealogies is in Luke's account (Luke 3:36). Cainan is added between Arphaxad and Salah. Rosevear suggests here that Luke seems to be drawing from the Septuagint manuscripts (the Greek translation of the Old Testament). However the Septuagint manuscript here is an unreliable source, particularly in its chronology.[28] This suggestion would cast a shadow of doubt over the accuracy of New Testament revelation and in particular the accuracy of Luke's account. An alternative is in fact that Luke is giving *extra* information; A possibility[29] which does no violence to the years of Arphaxad and Salah in Genesis 11 is that Arphaxad's daughter was married at an early age to Cainan (son of Ham), thereby giving a right (by marriage[30]) for his name to be included in the princely line, and further giving rise, by the skilful plan of Satan, to the occupation of the Promised Land by an evil nation. Whatever the answer to this question, it is a difficulty which in no way alters the overall thrust of Genesis 5 and 11, as a straight history with no gaps (notice that Genesis 4 has a similar number of generations for Cain's line). Every biblical historian accepts that the major point of these genealogies is that the Israelites might know both *who* were their ancestors and *when* they lived.

Further it must be emphasized that, though the ages of the patriarchs seem unbelievable, they are not at random. They decay roughly in an exponential way after the Flood, strongly indicating that an acceleration of the ageing process accompanied this cataclysmic event. The reader is referred to the charts (Figures 1 and 2) which illustrate graphically the declining age spans of the Patriarchs.[31] One possible explanation is that a water vapour canopy was acting as a shield from harmful radiation before the Flood. The large wingspan of pre-Flood pterodactyls suggests a greater air pressure before the Flood to support such creatures. It is known that increased air pressure can aid health and furthermore, it is quite possible there was also greater oxygen content in the atmosphere than the 1 in 5 ratio today. Consequently these *may* also be explanations for the longevity of the patriarchs before the Flood. The great ages also explain how such detail of early events (e.g. right down to days, months and years in the record of the Flood: Genesis 7 and 8) could easily be handed down to succeeding generations. The remarkable implication of these genealogies (see Figs 1 and 2) is that Adam overlapped Methuselah for over 200 years, that Methuselah overlapped Noah for 600 years, Noah overlapped his own son Shem for over 400 years and that Abraham was outlived by Eber six generations before him! These direct implications from the biblical record show (a) how easily information can be transmitted from early times across thousands of years (e.g. only four people are needed to span creation to Abraham: Adam—Methuselah—Shem—Abraham). Consequently for Abraham, the account of creation was like referring to his great-grandfather's records. This enables us to understand how well the truth of early history was handed down. These records also show (b) how recently, in terms of modern thinking, the world was made. In fact this is not out of keeping with many non-biblical records which speak of long-lived ancestors and a flood. A simple extrapolation back in time of population figures indicates that the human race is only thousands of years old and not tens of thousands of years (let alone millions!). Even the severe infant mortality rate before c.1850, and shorter life spans, would only alter such calculations by centuries, not millennia. The straight addition of the chronologies gives a figure of approximately 2,000 years from Adam to Abraham. The latter is accepted by historians to have lived at roughly 2,000 BC. Thus Scripture teaches a creation date around 4,000 BC. Even accounting for the difficulties with Cainan, and the later dating of the Exodus, the uncertainty is only of the order of 200 years at the most.

Let us take note that the early genealogies have been recorded by God four times (Genesis 5, 1 Chronicles 1, Matthew 1 and Luke 3) with the names the same except for Cainan in Luke. When God repeats something we notice it. Three times and we know it is important. Four times and we know there is no doubt that these genealogies are to be treated with the utmost reverence.

This principle of repetition in Scripture is explained by Joseph in Genesis 41:32 when interpreting Pharoah's dream 'And the dream was repeated to Pharoah twice *because the thing is established by God.*' The same principles occurred when Peter was spoken to by God in a dream that he might understand that Gentiles were no longer to be regarded as unclean (Acts 10:9–16). The dream was repeated three times to emphasize the importance to Peter of its meaning.

The author is well aware that many from the evangelical faith would argue for a lengthening of the pre-Abraham period.[32] One such giant was BB Warfield, who in all other respects was very conservative in his view of Scripture. But he conceded a vital point when he stated:[33]

The question of the antiquity of man has of itself no theological significance … the Bible does not assign a brief span to human history.

Firstly, were it not for the desire of some to disprove Genesis, nobody would normally read Genesis without the obvious implication that here indeed was a tight history. Secondly, I would enquire of all those with a belief in Scripture being the inspired Word of God, would one not expect that the Divinely perfect and accurate scriptural records would correct other ancient writings, and *not the other way round*? Lastly, contrary to Warfield, the significance of an old earth view is two-fold: (i) the lengthening of man's history is used to justify evolutionary ideas and (ii) the authority of Scripture is brought into question since the reading of the text in a straightforward way is denied. Jude 14 makes it perfectly plain that Enoch was the seventh from Adam (and thus that the genealogies are a tight record of history). Consequently such views of the antiquity of man undermine the authority of the *New* Testament as well as the Old.

YEARS AFTER CREATION ▶

	0	100	200	300	400	500	600	700	800	

Adam

Seth

Enos

Cainan

Mahalaleel

Jared

Enoch **622**

Methuselah

Lamech

Noah

Notice:

1: The death of Methuselah (by his name) heralded the flood.

2: Lamech the son of Methuselah, and father of Noah, died 5 years before the flood, aged 777 years.

3: Lamech knew Adam for 56 years, but Noah missed him by 126 years.

4: The first recorded 'natural' death was of Adam. But the 2nd departure was **not** Seth, but Enoch who was translated. (NB: excluding the **murder** of Abel and possibly others).

5: No gaps can be found: (i) The early genealogies occur 3 times in Scripture: Genesis 5&11; 1 Chronicles 1; & Luke 3.

(ii) Jude 14 refers to Enoch, the **seventh** from Adam. This is strong New Testament evidence for the fact that these genealogies contain no break.

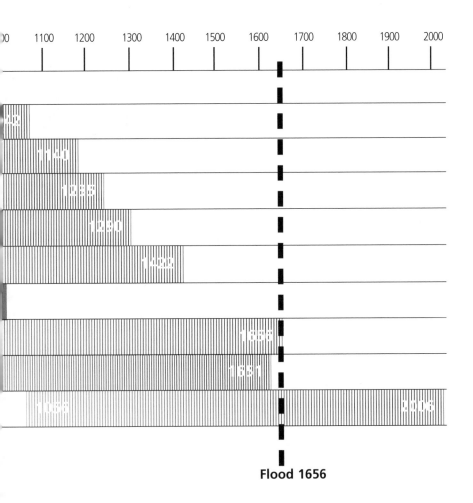

Flood 1656

Figure 1

YEARS AFTER CREATION ▶

	600	700	800	900	1000	11000	1200	1300	1400

Methuselah

Lamech

Noah

Shem

Arphaxad

Salah

Eber

Peleg

Reu

Serug

Nahor

Terah

Abraham

Notice:

1: Careful comparison of Genesis 11:26, Genesis 12:4 and Acts 7:4 shows that Abraham is 75 years old when he leaves Haran and that this is not long after the year of Terah's death (2083 after Creation).

2: Abraham overlapped Shem by about 150 years.

3: Eber *outlived* Abraham by about 4 years.

Genesis and history

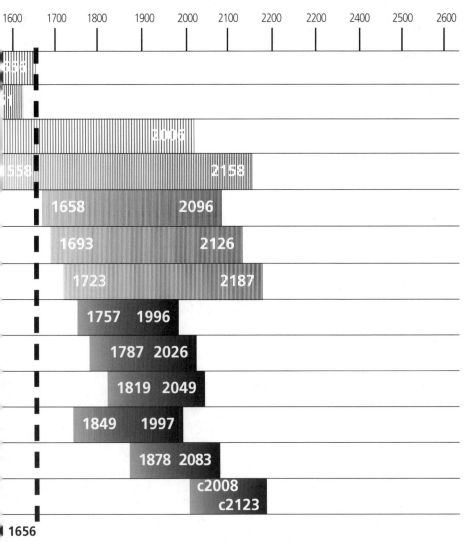

1656

4: Of this series of 10 generations, Noah—Abraham, the early generations (Shem—Eber) are living as Terah initially departs from Ur of the Chaldeans (Genesis 11:31–32).

5: The gradual reduction in lifespan after the flood.

6: Comparing Genesis 5:32, 9:22,24, 10:21 and 11:10, the order of Noah's children was probably Japheth, Shem, then Ham.

Figure 2

Genesis for today **55**

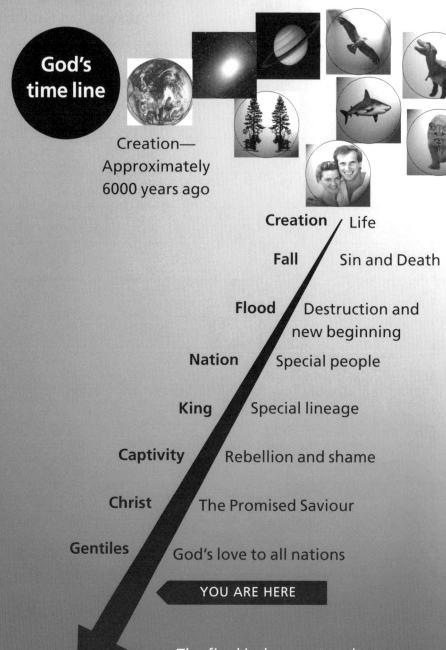

God's time line

Creation—
Approximately
6000 years ago

Creation / Life

Fall Sin and Death

Flood Destruction and
new beginning

Nation Special people

King Special lineage

Captivity Rebellion and shame

Christ The Promised Saviour

Gentiles God's love to all nations

YOU ARE HERE

The final judgement and
the glorious hope of the Church

**Christ's
return**

Figure 3

3.7 The Great Catastrophe 4,400 years ago

For the Bible-believing Christian, history dates back to the Flood which took place in about 2400 BC. To the average person this seems incredible, but as Cooper points out in his recent fascinating book *After the Flood*,[34] there are *many* records in Europe alone of claimed descendency of kings and rulers back to Japheth (son of Noah). Some have argued that because these references are to Scripture they are not an independent record and thus are not further confirmation. However, the fact that these refer to biblical names at all is testimony that the Bible was much honoured then as an historical document. These records coupled with accounts from the Eskimo to the Aborigine of a flood long ago, bear great testimony to (1) a common ancestor, Noah and (2) a world-wide flood. These matters are covered briefly in Appendix B *Summary of Scientific Evidence for Creation and the Flood* (see the section entitled 'Population Growth and ancient genealogical records'). The reader is also referred to the article by Peet.[35] It is to our discredit in the West, that we accept too readily 'pre-packed' history over the media. Few really examine *all* the evidence and thus are entirely objective in considering the fascinating origin of the races of the world. Thus anthropologists too easily dismiss the above records as legend and fable without recognising a common (albeit corrupted) thread of truth. There are too many of these early accounts (20+) of Noah and the Flood for them to be discounted.[36] What is more, is it mere coincidence that all written records go back to the Sumerians and the region of the Middle East to about 4–5,000 years ago? The records are consistent with the Bible's portrayal of history and the dispersion after Babel.[37,38] The evidence points to mankind after Noah coming from the Middle East with Japheth forming the European nations, Shem forming those nations of the East (including the oldest known unconquered civilization—China) and Ham forming the nations of Africa. It may well also be true that ancient legends are correct that the American Indians came over the Bering Strait from Siberia as they pushed further eastward.

Only in latter centuries with the drive for exploration, have the tribes of Noah met again. Thus western explorers (sons of Japheth) met what they thought were primitive tribes people in North and South America, in the Pacific islands along with Aborigines in Australia and Maoris in New

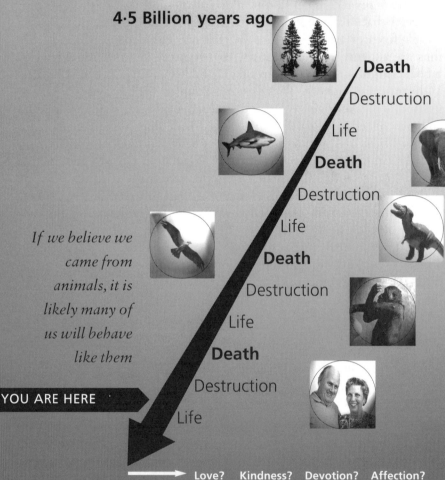

Figure 4

Zealand. But they were really meeting, generations later, the descendants of Ham and Shem. It is fascinating to reconsider world history from a biblical perspective. Rather than tenuous connections between nations millions of years in the past, the biblical position is that our international connections are very great, and relatively recent. This gives a very different perspective on the attitude we should adopt to other nations. If we are connected by blood only a few thousand years ago (as against the old earth view of Warfield and others), then oppression is all the more unjustified and racism and apartheid finds no warrant in Scripture. Hitler's Third Reich was built on a racist foundation with the Aryan race regarded as supreme. It is important to see that to view the human race as having a record beyond the few thousand years of Scripture is to leave the way open to those who would justify even today the evolution of a master race.

3.8 A sense of responsibility

In this chapter it has been the author's intention to encourage a far greater reverence for the written Word of God as history whenever its mode of writing obviously demands such. Scripture is neither primarily a history text nor a scientific handbook, but where the Lord touches on such matters, he is true and never contradicts himself. Both history and science must follow the perfect Revelation and not come before it; else we shall be led astray. In order for the reader to appreciate the very different (and irreconcilable) world views of evolution and creation, four charts (Figs 3–6) are included to illustrate God's time line and that from an evolutionary perspective. The Scriptures teach a six literal day creation of the order of six thousand years ago with a flood covering the whole world only about 1,650 years later. The Lord taught very clearly using the major catastrophe of the Flood and the disaster of Sodom, that these were real events and a forewarning of the final judgement yet to come (Luke 17:26–30). Belief in a real historical world-wide flood is connected to belief in the second coming of Christ. The biblical teaching of a flood around 4,400 years ago concertinas the huge ages we are brainwashed with by the media. Suddenly when we look at matters from a proper biblical perspective, we realize that Eden and the Fall of Man were not so far in the distant past as many would have us believe. Our responsibility before God

Two diametrically opposed world views

Evolution

Somehow it all began four and a half thousand million years ago...

The Bible

In the beginning God created the heavens and the earth.

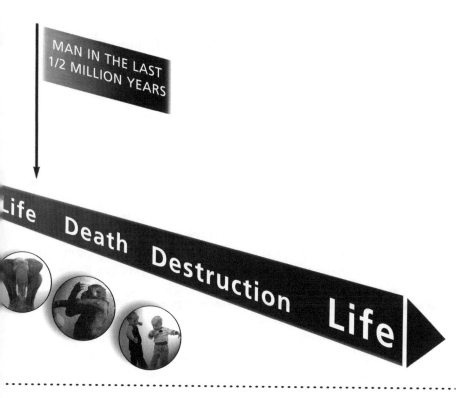

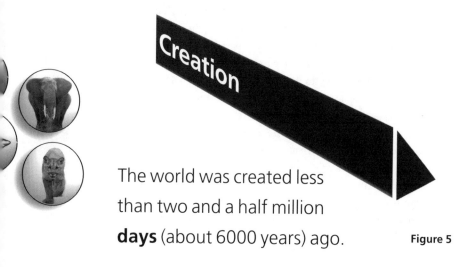

The world was created less than two and a half million **days** (about 6000 years) ago.

Figure 5

is accentuated as it is not more than 100 generations since the Flood and 110 generations to Adam and the Fall. *We* fell in Adam, *we* rebelled, *we* died.[39] In the light of this, the brevity of life here becomes much more apparent and our responsibility before God is all the greater as we see the day of his appearing close at hand.

Chapter 3 notes

1 **H Ross,** *Creation and Time: A Biblical and Scientific perspective on the Creation-Date controversy* (Colorado Springs: NavPress, 1994).

2 **M Van Bebber,** and **P Taylor,** *Creation and Time—A Report on the Progressive Creationist Book by Hugh Ross* (Mesa, AZ: Eden Communications, 1995).

3 **TH Huxley,** *Science and the Hebrew Tradition—essays by Thomas H Huxley,* chapter 6, 'The lights of the Church and the light of Science' (London: Macmillan, 1903), pp. 201–238. The quote in the text is from p. 207.

4 **DR Alexander,** and **RS White,** *Beyond Belief: Science, faith and ethical challenges* (Oxford: Lion, 2004). These two authors are closely associated with 'Christians in Science' and the journal *Science and Christian Belief* (of which Alexander is editor). These outlets propagate the view that Theistic Evolution is the only way to approach the apparent conflict. Professor White (a Geophysicist) has written a web article 'Science: Friend or Foe?' (see web site http://www.cis.org.uk/resources/articles/article_archive/white_friendfoe.htm). This typifies the 'science-first' thinking which is the error of this group of writers. He states in the above article, 'So if our understanding of the universe and the world around us from our reading of scripture does not agree with our experience of nature, and of the world in which we live, then we have to allow for the possibility that maybe we have misinterpreted scripture on this point.' The answer to the dilemma he posed should in fact be the reverse. Where the Scripture is repeatedly emphatic (and we have argued in this book that this is the case), and there appears to be a conflict, then we must consider that we have not understood the science correctly. See also chapters 7–9 of the book also by Alexander: **DR Alexander,** *Rebuilding the Matrix: Science and Faith in the 21st Century* (Oxford: Lion, 2002).

5 **MA Noll,** *The Scandal of the Evangelical Mind* (Leicester: InterVarsity Press, 1994). Noll is disparaging of the creationist position, but is answered very ably in the review by **Carl Wieland**—see *Creation Technical Journal,* 10(1), 1996, pp. 18–19.

6 **DF Burke** (ed.), *Creation and Evolution (When Christians disagree;* Leicester: Inter Varsity Press 1986).

When he is come

Christ's first coming Christ's second coming

Bethlehem Micah 5:2; Matthew 2:1	**Olivet near Jerusalem** Zechariah 14:4; Acts 2:11–12
Quietly to the world Luke 2:7	**With the trumpet** 1 Thessalonians 4:16
At a time of relative peace Luke 2:1	**At a time of immense falling away** 2 Thessalonians 2:3
Came to save his people from their sins Matthew 1:21; Luke 2:11–14	**Will come to bring judgement** 2 Thessalonians 1:8
Not expected—yet announced Luke1 John the Baptist; Matthew 2 Star; Luke 2 Shepherds	**Not announced— yet expected** 1 Thessalonians 4:13–18

7 K Ham, *A child may see the folly of it,* Creation 17(2), 20–22, March-May 1995, published by Creation Science Foundation.

8 Quoted by **Winston Churchill** in *Thoughts and Adventures* (London: Odhams Press, 1949), p. 225.

9 C Hill, *The English Bible and the seventeenth century revolution* (London: Penguin, 1994). See chapter 1, 'A Biblical Culture' and chapter 8, 'The Bible and Practical Politics'. Hill's thesis is that belief in the Bible as the supreme authority causes wars and evil in society. Like so many before him, he refuses to see that the worst and most subtle of human evils is to corrupt even the best of godliness and then, rather than blame the counterfeit, to blame the original.

10 John Stott, *Understanding the Bible* (London: Scripture Union, 1984).

11 MD Kline, 'Genesis: Historicity and literary parallels' in **D Guthrie, JA Motyer, AM Stibbs, DJ Wiseman** (eds), *New Bible Commentary, Revised* (London: Inter-Varsity Press, 1967), p. 80.

12 TH Huxley, *Science and Hebrew Tradition—Essays by Thomas H Huxley* (London: Macmillan, 1903), chapter 6, *The lights of the Church and the light of Science,* pp. 201–238. See particularly p. 217.

13 For a very useful summary of excavations in Palestine, the reader is referred to **JD Douglas, FF Bruce, JI Packer, RVG Tasker and DJ Wiseman (eds)** *The New Bible Dictionary* (London: IVP, 1962), pp. 60–76. In particular the tables of excavated sites on pp. 72–76 are a mine of further information for the serious student. What has been borne out by these studies is that there is no part of Scripture which is in fact brought into question by the spotlight of archaeology. Rather, the detail bears testimony to the sacred record. Concerning Jericho, see the references in the New Bible Dictionary and in particular those referring to **Professor E Sellin.** In 1908 he excavated Jericho and J Politeyan (*Biblical Discoveries in Egypt, Palestine and Mesopotamia* (Elliot Stock, 1922), p. 120) records 'Dr Sellin showed a well-preserved city wall built upon a foundation of loam and gravel 3 or 4 feet thick. Upon this a wall of stones and rubble, 6½ to 8 feet thick, and 16 feet high; upon this again a brick wall, 8 feet high, and 6½ feet in thickness was reared, making a total of 24 feet. This wall bulged outward, thus making the scaling of it impossible.' There was also evidence of the walls collapsing. Some scholars date these walls as prior to Joshua's time. With severe difficulties in dating methods, one wonders whether these liberal scholars are coming to such a conclusion from an objective standpoint or from prejudice, when so much of the excavations clearly substantiates the Jericho campaign described in the book of Joshua.

14 The asteroid impact theory is not held to by all creation/flood scientists. This possible explanation is but one of many alternatives.

15 See article 'Can Science and Christianity both be true?' (Ch. 9, pp. 121–123) by **C Humphries** in the book, *Real Science, Real Faith*, edited by **RJ Berry** (Eastbourne: Monarch, 1995). See also chapter 2 'Down to Earth' by **Martini Bott** who on pp. 26–27 makes the same mistake of putting science first.

16 Byron C Nelson, *The Deluge Story in Stone* (Minneapolis: Bethany Fellowship, 1968), see also **Henry Morris,** *Science and the Bible* (Amersham: Scripture Press, 1986), p. 134.

17 David CC Watson, *The Great Brain Robbery* (Worthing: Walter, 1975), p. 12.

18 David CC Watson, op. cit., pp. 25,26.

19 I am indebted here to the very valuable contribution of **David Harding,** Pastor of Milnrow Evangelical Church, near Rochdale, Lancashire. A growing number of Bible-believing pastors seeking to evangelize this generation, regard this issue as crucial in presenting the reliability of Scripture to the outsider.

20 David CC Watson, op. cit., pp. 14,15.

21 WW Fields, *Unformed and Unfilled—A critique of the Gap theory* (Collinsville, Illinois: Burgener Enterprises, 1994).

22 David T Rosevear, 'The genealogies in Scripture' in **EH Andrews, W Gitt,** and **WJ Ouweneel** (eds), *Concepts in Creationism* (Welwyn: Evangelical Press, 1986), pp. 68–77.

23 It should be noted that Matthew's genealogy is the line of Joseph, the legal guardian of the young Christ. This is consistent with Jeremiah 22:30 which clearly stated no descendent of Jechoniah would prosper and sit on the throne of David. Mary's line is given in Luke 3 where the blood line of Christ is traced through David's son Nathan, not through Solomon. The literal translation of Luke 3:23 is 'Jesus … being (as was supposed) the son of Joseph, which was of Heli.' The 'which was' relates to Christ. His mother Mary was the daughter of Heli.

24 HM Morris and **JC Whitcomb,** *The Genesis Flood* (Presbyterian and Reformed Publishing Company/Evangelical Press), p. 481, Appendix II, 1969.

25 HM Morris and **JC Whitcomb,** op. cit., p.483.

26 Morris and **Whitcomb** argue on the basis that 8,600 Kohathites in Num. 3:28 could not have been generated in so short a time. However we read Kohath had four sons, Amram, Izehar, Hebron and Uzziel (Exodus 6:18 and Num. 3:19). This means on average 2,150 descendants per son. From Exodus 6:16–20, Amram is recorded as having two sons (Moses and Aaron—see Exodus 6:20) and Miriam (Num. 26:59); Izehar had three sons; Uzziel had three sons; Hebron's sons are not recorded, but we know he had sons since Num. 3:27 refers to the Hebronites. Let us take an average of three per son (but there may have been more sons than those recorded for each of Kohath's four sons). Three sons each implies in that generation about 716 descendants from the sons of Moses' generation in the subtribe of Kohath. If the number of sons from this point on increased greatly per generation and they married earlier, then it is conceivable three more generations could be added from Moses by the time the count was made in Numbers 3. It is possible some had more than one wife and thus again the number of sons could increase markedly. It is also possible that Amram in particular had other wives and descendants. Nine sons per generation would then give 729 for three generations. If in fact Hebron had as many as twelve sons (like Jacob), then any difficulty in reaching 8,600 for the whole of the Kohathites is removed at a stroke. The context of Exodus 6 and Numbers 3 strongly suggests these are straightforward records.

27 DT Rosevear, op. cit., p.73.

28 David CC Watson, *The Great Brain Robbery* (Worthing: Henry E Walker, 1975), Appendix D, p. 100. Watson discusses the other manuscripts and highlights the systematic alterations to the chronology in the Septuagint group of texts and the Samaritan manuscripts.

29 I am indebted to some most illuminating discussions with Mr Roy Pibworth of Wilstead, Bedforshire, whose knowledge of Hebrew language and thinking have deepened my respect for the accuracy of Old Testament records.

30 Compare Matthew 1:16 where Joseph only by marriage (but not by blood) has his ancestors included in the princely line [Note again that Matthew has the genealogy of Christ through Joseph and Luke the genealogy of Christ through Mary]—see note 22.

31 Using the year markers referring to the years since Creation, Genesis 11:26 indicates that Terah's sons Abram, Nahor and Haran were born after the year 1948. Since Genesis 12:4 tells us that Abram was 75 when he left Haran, and Acts 7:4 indicates that Abraham left Haran only when Terah was dead, Abraham must have been 75 years old around the year 2083 (Terah's death). Abraham's birth must have been in the year 2008—this is 60 years after the mention of Terah's children being born in Genesis 11:26. But Abram is mentioned first in Genesis 11:26 only because of his prominence later. Though unusual, it is likely (i) that there was a sizeable gap between the sons born to Terah, and (ii) that with the place name Haran being prominent in the Genesis account, Haran was the eldest son born in 1948, and (iii) that he settled such that the area where he lived was named after him. From Genesis 25:7 we know that Abram lived to be 175 years old so that Abram (by that time renamed Abraham) died in the year 2183. The reader is referred to Appendix II, 'Genesis 11 and the Date of the Flood' in **HM Morris** and **JC Whitcomb's** *The Genesis Flood*. On pp. 479, 480 footnote 1 discusses the view that Stephen was mistaken in his statement in Acts 7:4, even though Acts faithfully records his statement as given. Such a view is mischievous and means that Scripture is no longer its own interpreter. They rightly come to the conclusion that such a view arises from a motive of men seeking to undermine Scripture inerrancy, not promote it.

32 **WH Green,** 'Primeval Chronology', *Biliotheca Sacra* 1890, reprinted in *Classical evangelical essays on Old Testament Interpretation*, ed. **WC Kaiser** (Grand Rapids: Baker, 1972). See also, **TC Mitchell** and **AR Millard,** 'Genealogy in the Old Testament' in *Illustrated Bible Dictionary* (Leicester: IVP, 1989), where there is a useful discussion of the various views.

33 **BB Warfield,** 'On the antiquity and the unity of the human race', *Princeton Theological Review,* Vol. 9 (1911), pp. 1–25—see also the *Works of Benjamin Warfield,* Vol. 9, 'Studies in Theology' (New York: Oxford University Press, 1932), pp. 235–236.

34 **W Cooper,** *After the Flood: The early post-flood history of Europe traced back to Noah* (Chichester: New Wine Press, 1995).

35 **JHJ Peet,** 'The Bible and Chronology—A Geochronological View', *Origins—Journal of the Biblical Creation Society,* Vol. 22, pp. 2–26, March 1997.

36 **Byron C Nelson,** *The Deluge Story in Stone* (Minneapolis: Bethany Fellowship, 1968).

37 **WF Albright,** one of the greatest Old Testament historians and author of many articles and books (see for instance *Archaeology of the Old Testament* (1956)) has stated of Genesis 10 and the early record of the nations that it is 'an astonishingly accurate document'.

38 It is intriguing evidence that still today in Iraq, there is a mound 6 miles southwest of Hillah called 'Birs nimroud'. **Henry Morris,** in his book *Science and the Bible* (Amersham: Scripture Press, 1988) describes (p. 93) the excavation of this ancient Babylonian Ziggurat which today has a base 49,000 square feet and 300 feet high. This is large enough for it to be the possible remains of an eight section ziggurat described as 650 ft. high and 1/4 mile square at the base, by the Greek historian Herodotus (440 BC) and reckoned in that day to be very old. This may be the remains of the Tower of Babel built by Nimrod at around BC 2200. The reader is referred to the book by **John Urquhart** *Modern Discoveries and the Bible* (Marshall, 1898), p. 285–310 and in particular pp. 298–300. See also A Parrot *The Tower of Babel,* 1955. It should also be noted that just as with the Flood accounts, there are accounts of Babel in other parts of the world. Most striking is the account from ancient Mexico which speaks of the Flood and later the tower of Babel being left unfinished and language being suddenly confused. Such accounts are very strong indications that the Flood and Babel were real events and not to be discounted by serious historians (see Urquhart, op. cit., p. 170, and pp. 295–6).

39 Contrast this with the book *Masterplan* by **Roy Clements** (Leicester: InterVarsity Press, 1994). That book suggests a literal view of Genesis 3 is not essential and that we need simply to concentrate on what the text means to us. Such teaching allows the Fall to be regarded as far

in the past. Not only does it encourage a weak view of Scripture, but it weakens the teaching of our responsibility in Adam, in the Fall. Human nature will always belittle sin. It will always be the tendency to think, if not express, that my connection and hence responsibility in Adam is diminished, since Adam was allegedly hundreds of thousands of years ago. Sadly Clements, some years after writing this book, fell into a moral crisis involving homosexuality. A right view of sex (see chapter 4) finds its roots in a literal view of Genesis 1–3.

Genesis and marriage

If there is one area where the subject of origins has a major effect, it is concerning marriage. Many Christians are not aware of this today and do not realize that by imbibing a mind-set from the humanist philosophy which surrounds us in the western world, they are sowing seeds of contention in marriage.

4.1 Marriage is man to woman

Over the past decade there has been a vast erosion of accepted scriptural values in our society in Great Britain, notably in the established church. In recent years there have been religious leaders *openly* condoning homosexuality.[1] What is the answer to this? Do we simply wring our hands and lamely say that it is 'not good', 'not acceptable', 'unpleasant'? Many will say 'Of course not!' They will say this because Scripture condemns it in the Old Testament (Genesis 18:20; 19:5, Leviticus 18:22) and in the New Testament (Romans 1:27). In Matthew 19:5, [AV] Christ speaks of '... a man leaving his father and mother and cleaving [being joined—not just physically but emotionally] to his wife.' However, unless we are clear on origins, those who accept evolution and yet argue from the Bible are in trouble, for the Lord gives reasons (Matthew 19:4), 'Have you not read, that he who made them *at the beginning*, made them *male and female'*. The New Testament elsewhere teaches the basis of marriage between a man and woman is that God made Eve from Adam (1 Timothy 2:13), so that Genesis is the foundation for all the Bible's reasoning concerning the whole area of sex and relationships. Genesis 2:18–25 teaches that Eve was specifically made for Adam's physical, mental and emotional needs. She was made from Adam's rib and designed to be Adam's helpmeet. As Matthew Henry[2] in his famous commentary aptly remarks, she was 'not made out of his head to rule over him, nor out of his feet to be trampled upon by him, but out of his side to be equal with him, under his arm to be protected, and near his heart to be loved'. It may be a shock to realize this, but if Genesis 2 is not to be seen as historical and to be taken literally, then there is no waterproof argument against the liberal thinkers of the day who would even have us

Chapter 4

believe that there is such a thing as 'Christian' homosexuality. We are living in very evil days. Christian students in our Universities must stand up and be counted on this crucial issue. Is it preposterous to wonder how long any Christian Union which firmly holds views on morals (particularly in this area) will be allowed to meet on campuses where the tide is moving firmly in the opposite direction? The Lord judged Sodom and Gomorrah for this sin (Genesis 19) and he will certainly bring severe judgement on those who justify and perpetrate such practices (1 Corinthians 6:9).

4.2 Marriage is the only basis for sexual fulfilment

The Bible clearly teaches that 'marriage is honourable among all and the bed undefiled' (Hebrews 13:4). But where are the roots of this teaching? Again the basis of sexual morality begins in Genesis. For in the beginning God said 'it is not good that man should be alone; I will make him an help meet for him' (Genesis 2:18 [AV]). The Lord made Eve from Adam's rib and Adam said, 'This is now bone of my bones and flesh of my flesh' (Genesis 2:23). Thus it is important to realize God made sexuality. Despite all attempts by evolutionists, no-one has ever been able to remove the obvious explanation of design in the function of man to woman. The Lord teaches in Genesis 2:24 [AV], 'Therefore shall a man leave his father and his mother, and shall cleave unto his wife: and they shall become one flesh.' Notice here it does not say that a man shall cleave to *a* woman—that would justify licentious and permissive behaviour. Rather, a man is to cleave to his wife (lit.: 'his woman'). There is a sense of *belonging*. There is a recognized public and legal agreement, so that all know that two people have agreed before God to commit their lives together. Though weddings as such are not directly spoken of in the Old Testament, there is ample evidence of a covenant commitment in marriage. Such public commitment is taught in Genesis 24 when Abraham's servant finds a wife for Isaac from Abraham's family left behind in Mesopotamia. The seriousness of this commitment is implied in Exodus 20:17, 'you shall not covet your neighbour's wife ...' (the seventh commandment) and is illustrated beautifully in the book of Ruth when in the climax of that book, not only the land but Ruth (and thus Naomi's heritage) are redeemed. Boaz and Ruth are thus committed publicly to each other at the meeting of the elders in the gate at Bethlehem.

70 Genesis for today

What a far cry from the casual relationships entered into today. Marriage is a covenant within society in which one man and one woman enter a public covenantal contract before God to belong to each other. The Lord recognized this by himself being present at a wedding (John 2). Later, in John 4, the Lord commanded the Samaritan woman to 'Go, call your husband, and come here' (John 4:16). After her sad admission that she had no husband, he said, 'for you have had five husbands and *the one whom you now have is not your husband*' (John 4:18). This clearly teaches that in the Lord's eyes (i) to be joined physically without commitment as husband-wife is wrong and (ii) physical union does not *define* marriage—a husband/wife relationship is far more than only sexual fulfilment. Turning to 1 Corinthians 6:18 we read, 'Flee sexual immorality. Every sin that a man does is outside the body; but he who commits sexual immorality sins against his own body...'. Paul again warns Timothy, 'Flee also youthful lusts' (2 Timothy 2:22). The Lord set man as different to the animals, along with the lifelong man-woman partnership as his plan for the basis of human love and the stable home. The irony is that in our permissive society and the emphasis on so called 'free love', real care, compassion and security have been lost and many people have become enslaved to selfishness. In particular, many young people have increasingly felt a sense of despair, with an alarming growth in the suicide rate.[3]

4.3 Marriage is a deep friendship for life

It is significant that there are very few verses in the Bible which speak of divorce. The main passage is Deuteronomy 24 where laws guarding against a wife returning to her first husband are written down. The Lord made it abundantly clear in Matthew 5:32 that divorce and remarriage (except in the case of adultery/fornication) were not the way for God's people. Some would argue the exceptive clause does not cover remarriage. Certainly, if it does, there can be no basis for separation besides infidelity. The strong words of Christ in Matthew 5:32 are a condemnation of the immorality so rife even in our churches. God never intended us to have broken relationships, because he *made* (lit.: 'built') Eve in the beginning. The saddest statistic in Britain today is the increasing break up of marriages, including even Christian marriages. Much difficulty could be avoided if we had a correct view as to the *origin* of marriage in Genesis. In Genesis 2:18ff. the whole purpose of the making of Eve was for *relationship*. Even before the Fall, it is evident that Eve's function is to be a 'help meet' for Adam. As quoted earlier (Section 4.1—Matthew Henry's commentary on the passage) this is in no way to justify male dominance and abuse of women. There is no superiority or inferiority implied, simply a difference of function. Nevertheless headship is implied as we shall come to in a later section. What I seek to stress here is the permanence of what God did. Eve was not brought to be 'named' as another animal and then left to make her own way in life. Her role was to relate to Adam. Notice it was only later that Adam knew his wife. Sexual fulfilment is part of marriage and certainly should generally play a significant role, but it does not *define* it. Many marriages go wrong because they begin and end with the physical. There should be a firm relationship and friendship of which the physical part is a final confirmation. If a couple are not clear that God made Eve differently to Adam in the beginning, a whole host of hang-ups will continue as the woman tries to act like a man and the husband expects his wife to think like him. It is vital to realize that it was always thus! God made us differently. The important things to note from Genesis 2:18–25 are that:

i. Adam was created from dust but Eve was *made* from Adam. The verb used in verse 22 is 'banah' which over 300 times is translated 'built'. Thus God shows us in his Word that woman is not constructed in the same way. Man is designed to be more rugged and geared to the outward—the mastery of the world around him. Woman is made fundamentally differently. Not only are there obvious physical differences, but she is crafted and constructed in such a way that in general she has a greater ability to show empathy and concern to those around her (though now marred by the cruelty and abuse of others). Although obviously there is great variety in any group, women are in the main more self-contained than men. It can be argued that it is easier for a woman to live singly than a man. No doubt some women long to be married and have sublimated that desire for marriage to devoted service to Christ in missionary endeavour; however the Scripture in Genesis 2 makes it very clear that Eve was made for Adam, not Adam for Eve. Genesis 39 (Potiphar's wife) and Proverbs 5 (the strange woman) show the grave danger of overturning God's decree. The woman's role is primarily to be responsive rather than to initiate. Clearly there is a variety of temperament such that in particular, single women missionaries have shamed men with their courageous initiative (e.g. Mary Slessor, Amy Carmichael). Nevertheless in these days of feminism, Christian marriages need particularly to guard against an incorrect view of each other's role. Thus Paul appeals in 1 Timothy 2 to Genesis 2 to show that the woman should not lead in church or in marriage: 1 Timothy 2:13 '... for Adam was formed first then Eve ...'. The Biblical teaching is of different roles played by men and women. There is no implication of superiority or inferiority.

ii. Man is to cleave to his wife. Genesis 2:24 instructs all husbands in an important principle. A man is to 'leave his father and mother'. This tacitly underlies the point already made that a man needs a home and a home-maker. When he marries, he cannot keep the close ties with his parents. He must make new roots with his wife. This is also taught concerning the wife (see Genesis 24 and the need for Rebekah to leave her parents to become the bride of Isaac). Few marriages will work with in-laws close at hand! (Even the secular world knows this with all the 'in-law' humour!) The Lord allows a man exemption from responsibility in the army or burden in business matters, for the first year of marriage (Deuteronomy 24:5) in order that a firm foundation of relationship can be established. We do well to take heed to this today. We cannot expect a marriage to be established overnight. Roots take time to grow. Foundations take time to build. Thought, energy, time and patience are needed. In this push-button age we are too hasty in giving up because something does not work immediately. It is significant that when Rebekah came to Isaac's home in Genesis 24, he had been praying in the fields. How many more couples from God's people would stay together if they had learnt to pray, both individually (as here, Genesis 24:63) and together (1 Peter 3:7)?

iii. Man and wife are to be one flesh. Genesis 2:24 says man and wife became one flesh in marriage. As mentioned earlier, the physical union of man and wife does not define marriage. It is the covenant agreement before God that defines it. The physical union is the natural expression of close relationship and intimacy that should exist in a true friendship based on love and respect. Genesis 2:25 specifically states they were naked and not ashamed. This is often a stumbling block for Christian couples. One or both considers the physical side to be dirty because of the filthy behaviour of the world. Not so, says the Scripture. Both here (Genesis 2:25) and in the New Testament (Hebrews 13:4), God specifically states the cleanness and purity of sexual relationships *within* marriage. No doubt behaviour before conversion can be washed by the blood of Christ; undoubtedly 1 John 1:7 teaches that *all* sin can be cleansed and forgiven. However, there needs to be careful preparation of engaged couples coming to marriage from the unclean environments surrounding us. The 'one flesh' will also be expressed in a number of other ways—the shared house, money, goods and life-style. It is rarely a wise course of action for husband and wife to have separate bank accounts. There must be total and unreserved commitment for marriages to work. One wise-crack said, 'man is incomplete until he is married, and then he is finished!' The jest actually contains an important truth: A man must not carry on thinking he will not alter after marriage. Some hobbies and pleasures need to be given up for the needs of his wife. In closing the chapter of bachelorhood, he finds a new fulfilment. A godly Christian marriage should produce a unity far more effective than the two individuals on their own.

4.4 Marriage and the Fall

All that we have said so far concerns Genesis 2—God's ideal before sin came into the world. Our discussions would not be complete if we were to leave it there. Adam and Eve fell and their relationship altered significantly as a consequence. This is an important matter. If we do not have a firm view on Genesis and our beginnings, we will not understand some of the greatest dangers to stable marriages. According to Scripture, death came *after* the Fall, not before it, as evolution teaches. Sorrow and death are due to sin, not a means of generating beauty, structure and diversity as the philosophy of evolution maintains! The Bible and evolution are diametrically opposed when it comes to sorrow and death. Evolution teaches the endless discarding of the individual to make way for the species of the future. The Bible teaches sin leads to death and decay. Rather than a new and 'better' race forming out of the old, the opposite is true as, ultimately, the same but fallen human race faces judgement and punishment before God. I have stated this here because it was *within marriage that the first temptation came*. If one does not accept Genesis 3 or regards it as something not to be taken literally, then there will be little understanding of God's plan for Christian marriage. The following are important truths we should recognize.

4.4.1 EVE WAS DECEIVED, ADAM WAS NOT

This point is brought out by Paul in 1 Timothy 2:14. Eve herself knew she had been cleverly tricked when she said to the Lord in Genesis 3:13 'The serpent deceived me, and I ate'. She listened to the serpent who lied with the words 'You will not surely die' (Genesis 3:4), forgot God's command, saw the fruit of the tree of knowledge of good and evil, desired it and took it. Adam's sin was different. 1 Timothy 2:14 tells us that he was not deceived. Genesis 3:6 says Eve '… also gave to her husband with her; and he ate …'. For Adam, it was downright rebellion, not deception. His was the defiance, where Eve's was neglect. Adam's sin was full in the face of conscience and clear instruction; Eve's sin was in careless disregard for what had been said and a hasty yielding to covetous desire.

Herein lies the way husbands and wives are often tempted today. The man will easily rebel against what God has clearly said. The woman is more readily deceived because she can generally be more quickly moved by the heart. Though such tendencies may at times be reversed, they give an insight into how the enemy generally attacks us. We should be 'wise as serpents and harmless as doves' (Matthew 10:16), aware of the entrance of sin, aware of the need for personal repentance, and prepared to forgive others when wronged. This is clearly taught in the parable of the unforgiving servant in Matthew 18:21–35. If we have been forgiven much then love must characterize our walk and a preparedness to forgive. Hardness of heart to the Lord and to others who have failed, is the way the enemy enters. As 2 Corinthians 2:11 states 'we are not ignorant of his [the devil's] devices'.

4.4.2 THE CONSEQUENCE OF THE FALL IN MAN AND WOMAN

We know God did *not* curse Adam and Eve for their sin. He *did* curse the serpent (Genesis 3:14) who now would have to slither along the ground (the implication being that it previously would have had legs like other reptiles)

Adam
and **Eve**

Man—glory of God
1 Corinthians 11:7

Woman—glory of Man
1 Corinthians 11:7

Adam—made first
1 Timothy 2:13

Eve—made second
1 Timothy 2:14

Adam—made from dust
Genesis 2:7

Eve—'built' from man
Genesis 2:21–22;
1 Corinthians 11:8

Adam—not deceived
1 Timothy 2:14

Eve—deceived
1 Timothy 2:14

Figure 7

and would be despised above all other creatures. The serpent personified the devil. In Genesis 3:15, God decrees he will be dealt the fatal blow on the head by the woman's Seed (the first reference to the promised Saviour and the virgin birth) but that he (the Serpent—The Devil) would bruise the Saviour's heel (Christ's suffering on the cross). As the Lord deals with Adam and Eve, he causes them to receive three major consequences:

i. Eve will now know pain in childbirth and she will now be ruled by her husband. Whereas before, there was always the mutual respect which meant that Eve naturally could follow Adam's lead, her desire is now 'subject to thy husband' [AV]. Collision of will will take place and Adam is to 'rule over' her (see Genesis 3:16 [AV]).4

ii. For Adam (Genesis 3:17–19), he was to know difficulty in providing for his wife and family. The ground which previously grew produce with little difficulty was now cursed, and thorns and thistles would throttle plants grown for food. 'In the sweat of your face you shall eat bread' (Genesis 3:19). Sweat speaks of the toil due to the curse, supremely seen on the Saviour's brow in the Garden of Gethsemane as he grappled with the awesome task before him of carrying our sin (Luke 22:39–44). Man cannot take it easy. It will be hard and difficult to provide for his own.

iii. Man and woman both needed a covering (Genesis 3:21). God made coats of skins. As we shall see in a later chapter, this shows God's care and provision spiritually in providing the atonement for our sin. In the context of sexuality and man-woman relationships, we also see here the important origin of clothing. Whereas in Genesis 2:25, they were naked and not ashamed, Adam and Eve now knew that they were naked and were ashamed before God (Genesis 3:7). Clothing was essential, for lust and greed must be restrained. The reason for clothing is difficult to justify if we accept the tenets of evolution and deny the historicity of Genesis. The animals are essentially unclothed. Why shouldn't we be? The ultimate appeal can only be to Genesis 3. It is noteworthy that it is always of the enemy (the devil) to bring confusion and moral degradation by unclothing men and women. (See for example the disaster of the worship at the golden calf in Exodus 32 where (verse 6), 'the people sat down to eat and to drink and rose up to play' and in verse 25 it says, 'Aaron had not restrained them to their shame among their enemies.') It is vitally important that Christian

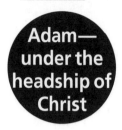

Adam— under the headship of Christ

Made in the image of God   Genesis 1:26

Under the headship of Christ   1 Corinthians 11:3

Made first—did not come from a female hominid   Genesis 2:7; 1 Timothy 2:13

Leader of all Creation— Named the animals   Genesis 2:19–20

Not deceived—rebelled   Genesis 3:17; 1 Timothy 2:14

Sorrow and hard labour— sweat, to gain daily bread   Genesis 3:19

Dying spiritually, he (and Eve) would now die physically   Genesis 2:17

Called on the name of the Lord   Genesis 4:26   **Figure 8**

young people are not led by modern-day fashion which to a large extent is governed by the prince of this world (that is the devil). When it comes to courting with a view to marriage, immodesty in clothing can be a big cause of stumbling. The choosing of a partner should not be by the way a person dresses, but by character and personality.

4.5 Leadership in marriage

Though we have touched on headship (Section 4.3) it is most important that we understand that in the light of the literal fall of man and woman before God, we will no longer *naturally* function correctly as couples in marriage. Who could not agree that there is something very beautiful when two young people, engaged to be married, are obviously happy in their love and romance together? But it would be foolishness indeed to think that this alone could carry a marriage through to maturity. The rose-bed will easily grow weeds as well; the calm sunny days give way to ferocious storms. It is because of the Fall that God has laid down clear rules for his people within marriage. One of these cuts right across modern-day views. This concerns the headship within marriage. Genesis 3, 1 Timothy 2 and 1 Corinthians 11 all teach that the man is to lead. Ephesians 5:22 says 'wives, submit to your own husbands, as to the Lord.' The wife is to submit not because the husband is better than his wife, who may well be his intellectual superior. No, the reason simply is for the *Lord's* sake. Ephesians 5:22 says 'as to the Lord'. She may be far better at making quick and accurate decisions, but for the Lord's sake and his blessing on a marriage, she is to sublimate her will to God's word and her husband (Genesis 3:16). Ephesians 5:23 says 'the husband is head of the wife, even as Christ is head of the church'. This is explained further in 1 Corinthians 11 where Paul teaches that there is a line of authority, God—Christ—Man—Woman. Thus 1 Corinthians 11:3 states, 'the head of every man is Christ, the head of woman is man …'. The woman (1 Corinthians 11:10) is 'to have a symbol of authority on her head because of the angels'.[5] The outward expression of this is that the woman, who is 'the glory of man' (1 Corinthians 11:7) should have a head-covering in public worship to recognize God's order of authority. 1 Timothy 2:9–15 explains further that headship in marriage lies with the man because of the danger of deception. This means that though there will certainly be

Eve– built for relationship

Made in the image of God Genesis 1:26

Under the headship of man 1 Corinthians 11:3

Helpmeet Genesis 2:18

Deceived 1 Timothy 2:14

Sorrow and conception multiplied Genesis 3:16

Mother of all living Genesis 3:20

Looked for the Lord Genesis 4:1

Picture of the Church Genesis 2:23; Ephesians 5:30

'The woman was ...

not made out of his head to rule over him,

nor out of his feet to be trampled upon by him,

but out of his side to be equal with him, under his arm to be protected,

and near his heart to be beloved'.

Figure 9

Matthew Henry

discussion, the responsibility and decision-making will lie with the man. This has been accepted for centuries by the Christian Church and to a great extent by the secular world. It is significant that only in the last century, since the rise of liberal attacks on Genesis and biblical authority has there been a serious questioning of male and female roles. Not only has the role of women within marriage been questioned, but also the belief that women should lead and direct in the church has been put forward. Rather than emancipate women, this in fact forces a lady to be put in a vulnerable position. The enemy, the devil, is a real and dangerous force to contend with. We cannot expect blessing if we flout God's authority and wilfully reject his Word. For those who seek by God's grace to lead married lives consistent with his Word, readers are encouraged to study the helpful book by Brian Edwards[6] and the collection of writings also edited by Edwards[7] on the whole question of authority in the church.

In order to summarize the main points taught in this very important area of relationships, three charts with the major teachings are included (Figures 7–9).

4.6 The picture of marriage

To conclude this chapter, I would like to draw the reader's attention to the clear injunction for the husband in Ephesians 5:25, 'Husbands, love your wives, just as Christ also loved the church and gave himself for it'. This completes the matter. Just as wives are to submit to their husbands 'as to the Lord' (verse 22), so husbands are to love their wives 'as the Lord does the church' (verse 29). Then Paul states, 'we are members of his body, of his flesh, and of his bones' (verse 30) and quotes Genesis 2:24 concerning a man leaving his father and his mother. He exclaims (verse 32), 'This is a great mystery, but I speak concerning Christ and the church'. The Lord requires the love, compassion and tenderness of a Christian husband to his wife to emulate Christ himself! A high calling indeed! But attainable through obedience to the Lord and submission to him. The 'one-flesh' is a picture of Christ's unity with his Bride, the Church. Remove Genesis, and one of the most beautiful pictures of salvation is lost. Christian marriages are meant to be a firm and lasting testimony to a rebellious world that Christ's love is deep, sacrificial and eternal to his people.

Chapter 4

Chapter 4 notes

1 See for instance *Evangelical Times*, Nov. 1996, p. 2 concerning homosexuality practised by church leaders. See also *Evangelical Times*, Jan. 1997, p. 5 where it is recorded that **Bishop John Gladwin** (of Guildford) preached at Southwark Cathedral to the 20th anniversary Festival of the 'Lesbian and Gay Christian' Movement! In his address (see *Guildford Diocesan Herald* Issue 106, Dec. 1996, p. 6) he spoke of his hearers as being both 'gay and Christian' of being 'members of God's Holy Church'. The Biblical teaching is that same sex and opposite sex immorality are **both** wrong, and to be renounced at conversion.

2 *Matthew Henry's Commentary on the Whole Bible*, edited by **LF Church** (London: Marshall, Morgan & Scott, 1970), p. 7.

3 **C Wieland,** *Teen Tragedy—What's behind the explosion in youth suicide?*, Creation *Magazine*, 18(4), Sept.–Nov. 1996, pp. 42–43.

4 Many see Genesis 3:17 as God explaining the tension that would now exist in marriage. Whereas before the Fall, Eve had the overwhelming assurance that she was made for Adam, now there is a corruption of nature in Adam and Eve. She will now have a nature that desires to rise up and dominate. As the Puritan **John Gill** comments, he will now rule over her in a sinful and selfish way 'with less kindness and gentleness, with more rigour and strictness'. Marriage becomes corrupted by the stresses created by two fallen natures conflicting in a desire for leadership. Another Puritan commentator, **Matthew Henry,** in his commentary on the whole Bible (London: Marshall, Morgan & Scott, 1970, p.11), aptly comments: 'Those wives who do not only despise and disobey their husbands, but domineer over them, do not consider that they not only violate a divine law, but thwart a divine sentence'. Nevertheless her sentence 'in sorrow thou shalt bring forth children; and thy desire shall be to thy husband, and he shall rule over thee' [AV] was (to quote Matthew Henry again) 'not a curse, to bring her to ruin, but a chastisement, to bring her to repentance.'

5 It is the conviction of the author that this refers to the angels that sinned and rebelled in earlier ages (2 Peter 2:4; Jude 6). In other words, man is to lead and to be the head of the woman lest the devil rise up and accuse the Lord's people of rebellion when his angels were condemned for such behaviour. Her head-covering in worship, though a symbol, is still to be observed as a sign of godly submission. (See also Numbers 5:11–31, particularly v. 18).

6 **B Edwards,** *No Longer Two* (Epsom: Day One Publications, 1999).

7 **B Edwards** (ed.), *Men, Women and Authority* (Epsom: Day One Publications, 1996).

Genesis and family life

The backbone of a strong nation is the family unit. If this is torn apart, the government of such a nation becomes impossible, both legally and economically. Britain has for many years been advocating permissive lifestyles which even secular politicians of today are concerned about. To a great extent, because family values had been put to one side by its own members, the Conservative government's *Back to Basics* campaign of 1995 failed to take off. Nevertheless, many politicians and leaders in our country are genuinely concerned, since the high divorce rate leads to much hurt and sorrow for the children of each succeeding generation. Christians need to wake up to the vice which is gripping our inner cities in particular. The church where I worked for a number of years lies in such an area in Leeds and as we reached out into the immediate neighbourhood, it was easy to see that the norm now is one-parent families. DL Moody rightly said 'If we don't crack the cities, we lose the nation'. Many believed that what saved Britain from a bloody revolution similar to that in France 200 years ago was the powerful preaching of Whitefield, Wesley and other men of the revival that swept through the country. They reached the common people in their thousands. The revivals in New England, Connecticut and much of the Eastern Seaboard of the United States similarly grounded the USA again in the Word of God. What followed was an immense return to family stability and authority which in turn led to a firm base from which industry brought prosperity. Though much vice from slavery, the opium trade, abuse of children and women remained, even this (see chapter 9) was to a great extent driven out by Bible-believing men and women.

5.1 Authority

It is important to realize how much the Bible played a part in the everyday life of the family in the eighteenth and through into the nineteenth century. The break-up of the family marked the end of the twentieth century and continues into the twenty-first. Where does this stem from? It goes hand in hand with a disbelief in Genesis and the power of the Scriptures. How many Christians (let alone nominal believers and those overtly against Christian belief) read the Scriptures to their families each day? How many believers talk over the Word of God at meal times rather than the anti-social mentality of TV with every meal? It is surely no wonder that when Dad seeks to curb Peter over the rock music he's playing, that a discussion ensues leading to an argument which goes nowhere. Dad has no absolute measure to prove his point beyond saying 'It's always been this way.' Such reasoning carries no weight. There has to be a final authority. When courtship begins, how do parents convince their children that sex should only be within marriage? As in the last chapter, one must appeal to the Bible. However, if you as a parent do not believe in a literal Genesis, most children pick this up pretty quickly and there is usually little patience with grey reasoning. That is, if one book (Genesis) is doubted, a child's mind will often speedily see the implications and ask an awkward question, 'why did Jesus refer to Adam and Eve in the beginning when it wasn't the beginning?' We sow the seeds of trouble in the family when we deny the historical accuracy of Genesis. We should not be surprized when outlandish clothes, behaviour and music are all justified as teenage years test all the barriers. Firm and yet kind discipline flows only from a strong belief in Scripture.

5.2 The first family

The first family saw division and bloodshed. The grief to Adam and Eve must have been immense as they witnessed the tragedy of Cain and were bereaved of Abel. Genesis 4 teaches a number of truths:

i. The same parents can bring totally different children into the world. This is obvious physically but for Christian parents who long to see spiritual understanding in their children, they must recognize that all are born in sin (Psalm 51:5) and not all will humble themselves before God.

ii. A truth which is easily missed from Genesis 4 is that God had *direct* dealings with both Abel *and* Cain. Both brought an offering to God, though only one offering was accepted. We must encourage each child to have direct dealings with their Creator.

iii. A blood sacrifice alone can please God. Just as God covered Adam and Eve with skins (Genesis 3:21) and made the first animal sacrifice on the part of Adam and Eve, so he only accepts an offering of the flock from Abel and refuses the offering of the fruit of the ground. Hebrews 9:22 is an abiding principle, 'Without shedding of blood is no remission'. One can only approach the Lord with a blood sacrifice. This also shows clearly that man and animals are distinct. Adam was given control of the animal and plant world in Genesis 1 with Adam clearly regarded as greater than the animals when he named them in Genesis 2. Skins of animals were used in Genesis 3; the firstling of the flock was offered in Genesis 4. We see that any idea of animal liberation finds no basis in Scripture, whilst in no way justifying the abuse of creatures (e.g. 'You shall not muzzle an ox while it treads out the grain' Deuteronomy 25:4— as discussed in section 2.4).

iv. The origin of murder. So Genesis 4 leads into the first murder due to jealousy. Cain killed Abel. The first son (carnal/natural) rose up against the second son (spiritual). The flesh hates the spirit.[1] It will always be so. The important matter in family life is that relationships are learned and made with others in a loving, caring environment. The Lord taught that hatred is tantamount to murder (Matthew 5:21–22). Thus in every temper, harsh word and confrontation, the battle of evil versus good is being conducted. The quiet and firm authority of Christian parents at some time will be fought against, since in each child there is the principle of original sin. Only a belief in Genesis gives the right attitude to discipline which the Lord himself instituted in bringing a curse upon Cain and banishing him from his presence.

The second account of murder is later in Genesis 4 by Lamech, whose name means 'overthrower, wild man, despairing'. His name and life typify the natural man who is proud and rebels against God. Matthew Henry comments that, by his proud boast in Genesis 4:23–24, Lamech 'owns himself a man of a fierce and cruel disposition, that would lay about him without mercy, and kill all that stood in his way'.[2] Lamech brings great doom upon any who dare to try to avenge the blood of the one he has killed. We see here the natural development of sin. First Cain's murder, now Lamech's with no shame but blatant arrogance. Unrestrained sin always leads to this, which is why God has ruled that Governments do not bear the sword in vain (Romans 13:4).

Chapter 5

5.3 God's dealings with families

As Genesis unfolds, from Genesis 5 onwards we see clearly that God's order is for man to have the headship and to govern his family. Adam—Seth—Enos through to Noah. All the genealogies imply a strong family unit. This is particularly borne out as the account of Abraham (Abram) unfolds in Genesis 12 and subsequent chapters. The respect and honour of parents by children is written across these early accounts.

By the time Noah comes on the scene, violence and bloodshed were common (Genesis 6:5). These events brought God's severe judgement on the whole human race with a world-wide flood. However, his care for the one family left (i.e. Noah and his wife) is indicative of his desire for all families to be secure, trusting him.

Abraham's wife, Sarah, is taken as a model wife (1 Peter 3:6) and Isaac the model son (Genesis 22), willing to go with his father Abraham to the place of sacrifice. Though the main lesson of Genesis 22 is undoubtedly Abraham's willingness to sacrifice his own son, the strong bond of father-to-son and son-to-father is an example in itself of the love there should be in the homes of God's people.

The next generation of Isaac's children, followed by Jacob's difficulties with his family shows the principle of sin entering a family just as with Adam and Eve. The Lord said of Esau and Jacob (Malachi 1:2–3; Romans 9:13), 'Jacob I have loved, but Esau I have hated'. Esau, the man of the field—picturing the world, never found repentance (Hebrews 12:16–17). Yet Jacob, though crafty and cunning, was brought to see his own desperate need and finally sought the Lord as God's man. However, it was not until after much sadness had occurred in Jacob's family, that the wiser, God-fearing Jacob emerged. He started with a reliance on his own cunning; he ended his days lame, but worshipping, leaning on his staff (Hebrews 11:21). Genesis teaches God's dealings with families as entities and gives hope for the wanderer and the prodigal.

Before we move on from this heading, note that Cain and Abel, Jacob and Esau both had the same privileges of care and instruction (note with Cain, God even spoke directly to him), yet one walked with God and the other did not. Parents should pray for, teach and lead their children, but in the end conversion is of the Lord, not man.

5.4 Abortion

One further matter is very relevant here. In the account of the birth of the twins Jacob and Esau (Genesis 25), there are, in verses 22 and 23, the clear statements that 'the children struggled together within her' and when Rebekah asks, 'Why am I this way?' there is the remarkable statement by the Lord: 'Two nations are in your womb'. Already Jacob and Esau are called children and God knew their characters just as he knew David in the womb (Psalm 139:13) and Jeremiah (Jeremiah 1:5). Thus Genesis 25:22–23 is the first of many very clear texts which show that the baby in the womb is fully a human being and is to be treated thus. Genesis has no room for abortion—even the murderer Cain was not aborted at birth, neither Esau who brought much trouble to the Lord's people later. God's way is not to allow the slaughter of children to justify promiscuous behaviour.

How far removed then we are in our modern western society from biblical family values, when we justify the murder of children on a colossal scale in most western nations. In the UK alone it is at least 3,000 a week. This is the major expression of a total disregard for the value of other people in our society. With the child helpless to defend itself, we literally dismember it before we can hear the cry of anguish. No wonder that we are fast seeing the break up of family values of care and support in our nation, when many are simply treating partners as toys and human lives due to come in to the world from such behaviour are put on the scrap heap like used cars.

Where does this stem from? Undoubtedly there is a strong connection with the prevalent world-view in our society—atheistic humanism. It is important to think carefully here. It is by no means the case that all those that are of this persuasion justify the break up of the traditional family unit and many would be very troubled by abortion and the corollary at the other end of the scale, euthanasia. But the dilemma they face still flows from their world view. Their consciences shout 'Society is corrupt; evil people must be curbed'. But their philosophy beats to a different drum, for where are the rules which say that men should live any differently to the animals? Atheistic humanism can have noble ideals but it has no constructive answers to man's inhumanity to man. During the writing of this book, one of the worst child mass murders took place in Dunblane, Scotland (March

1996). Families were destroyed by the mindless behaviour of an embittered individual who entered a primary school and gunned down 16 children and a teacher before killing himself. As with the Hungerford massacre in 1987, the whole nation reels in shock at such evil. But the fault lies with ourselves. As a nation we are breeding wickedness on an ever increasing scale. During the news coverage on the BBC during the aftermath of Dunblane, it was reported that in America there are an average of 30 mass murder incidents each year. Fundamental questions concerning the rearing of the next generation have to be asked. Can strict laws ever stop atrocities like the murder of toddler James Bulger in 1993? How does one produce stable, balanced children who can be an asset to others and to the nation? Undoubtedly it is through bringing back family values; and where is the power to achieve this? Externally imposed laws do not change hearts. Only in one place—the Scriptures, the Book of books with each family unit reading and trusting the principles taught therein—only by this means has it been proved by our ancestors that there is real power to change the human heart. But no teaching of itself will have lasting effect if the foundations of Genesis are doubted. The fundamental malaise is the sin of disbelief in God's Word. Strong Bible-believing families will only be produced where a clear unequivocal stand is taken on Genesis.

5.5 Practical implications

In closing this chapter, the following are practical helps which some may find useful in this important matter of rearing a family.

5.5.1 ROLES

As brought out in chapter 4, the roles of man and woman are different. Neither husband nor wife is greater or lesser than the other, but their roles are different. The man's domain is to lie further than the home. He is to till the ground (Genesis 2) and after the Fall, he is to find work hard and difficult. The wife's responsibilities will lie primarily within the home and she will find difficulty in bearing children (Genesis 3).[3] It is important that *attitudes* are right. Though there may sometimes be no alternative for the wife having to work (because of the difficulty of the husband finding a job), the norm for the Christian family should be the man working, with his wife's activities focused on the home and children. 1 Timothy 5:14 speaks of married women bearing children and managing the house. Titus 2:5 refers to 'homemakers'. Are we as an evangelical church teaching this? This is particularly important with young children who need the security of the mother's presence in the home. However, even in later years, the accessibility of both parents is vital to achieve balanced maturity.

5.5.2 PRIORITIES

One of the greatest dangers in modern family life is that the home itself becomes more important than the family. Often the reason why the wife works full-time as well as the husband is not of necessity, but to have the extra luxuries in the home. It may even be that having children is delayed for this selfish reason. The tenth commandment against covetousness is vital here. A Christian couple have to realize the importance of God and relationships coming first, as against material goods. As children enter the world, a warm loving environment is far more important than having the latest in hi-fi equipment or computers.

5.5.3 TIME

Both in early years and later, it is vital that the husband makes time both for his wife and his family. Teaching in the morning together gathered round the Scriptures is invaluable, and eating together at breakfast and in the evening should be the norm. If there is a television in the home, it should be strictly controlled as, apart from the obvious evil content in many of the programmes, it can dominate and intrude, so that meal-times and family life are impaired. The husband also has to be careful that both his work and recreations do not cut him off, or make him inaccessible to his family. No plant grows without watering. Time simply talking and sharing is vital in any relationship. We all have experienced times of failure in this area, and invariably it can be traced back to lack of personal prayer *for* the other person combined with time *with* them. Most helpful can be the Lord's Day in this regard. Sunday can be a day when more time can usefully be spent in speaking to others in the family (see following chapter). The hardest area of all to get right is the balance of time spent on the Lord's work outside the home (in church or other Christian activity) and that spent with the family directly. The call to serve the Lord and put him first must never be side-stepped (Matthew 19:29), but caring for one's family is also a God given responsibility (1 Timothy 5:8; Ephesians 6:4). This underlines the importance of prayerful unity between husband and wife in the vital area of child rearing. One of the most moving testimonies to the power of the Christian family from recent history is from Russia before the fall of Communism in 1991. The unregistered churches often experienced bitter persecution when the buildings were ransacked and the leaders had to flee from home and family and some spent years in terrible prison conditions. But their faithfulness was honoured, as wives formed the Council of Prisoners' relatives. The majority of the children, some of whom had never seen their fathers, followed their parents' footsteps and trusted the Saviour. They *knew* it was for the Lord's sake that their fathers were absent. Crucial in this matter is motives. If our Christian work is self-centred, this will affect the blessing we wish upon our own families. But selfless service for the Master, which is an outflowing of selfless service to wife and family, will be owned of him. Matthew 6:33 'Seek first the kingdom of God, and his righteousness; and all these things shall be added to you.'

Chapter 5 notes

1   1 Corinthians 15:47 states a fundamental principle 'The first man was of the earth, made of dust; the second man is the Lord from heaven' which teaches that natural man cannot save himself. Christ (the second man) alone can save. This principle is represented by many examples in the Old Testament. Cain and Abel, Ishmael and Isaac, Esau and Jacob, Saul and David. The first is natural, the second is spiritual.

2   **Matthew Henry's** *Commentary on the Whole Bible,* edited by **LF Church** (London: Marshall, Morgan & Scott, 1970), p. 15.

3   Nevertheless, 1 Timothy 2:15 teaches that the mother will be saved in child-rearing. The word 'childbearing' is 'teknognonia' in the Greek, denoting not only birth but the duties of motherhood (see *Vine's Expository Dictionary*). The same word is also used in 1 Timothy 5:14 mentioned further on in section 5.5.1.

Genesis and the Sabbath

The change in the British law is already putting pressure on Christians to work on this day as on any other. Why is this day important? How is it connected to the creation/evolution debate?

6.1 The body clock

In each one of us is a seven day clock which medical experts acknowledge is deeply ingrained in our make-up.[1] There are other clocks, such as the need for rest every 24 hours and other daily rhythms concerning the natural functions of the human body, but one which is just as vital is the weekly cycle. Atheistic-led societies have tried to extend the working week and failed. Notably the French Revolutionaries tried to make a ten-day week. This could not work because the body just cannot cope without a rest every seven days. This is a testimony to the truth of Genesis that our human bodies, as at creation, need to have the weekly rest. This is why the Lord said 'The Sabbath was made for man and not man for the Sabbath' (Mark 2:27) not to in any way remove the Sabbath rest, but to remove ungodly additions.

6.2 The day of rest at creation

God's original plans for the whole of the human race are all in Genesis. Many Christians do not realize that the law concerning the Sabbath day (which simply means 'cessation') did not begin with the Ten Commandments in Exodus 20, but was in fact the very first command ever given to *all* of mankind (not just the Israelites). In Genesis 2:3 '... God blessed the seventh day, and sanctified it ...'. This means the day was 'set apart' as a special day by God right at the beginning for all the human race. In Exodus 20 it is explained further. Exodus 20:10 states '... the seventh day is the Sabbath of the Lord your God. In it you shall do no work: you, nor your son, nor your daughter, nor your manservant, nor your maidservant ...' The *principle* of the Sabbath is laid down in the Ten Commandments. It is important to recognize that the actual day of the week is not explicitly referred to at Sinai. Rather it is simply laid down that every seventh day there is to be a day of rest. Thus the Christian Sabbath and change of day is allowed for in the fourth commandment. What is more is that the reason for the Sabbath law is that 'in six days the Lord made the heavens and the earth, the sea, and all that is in them, and rested the seventh day …'. This verse is rightly used in our debates with theistic evolutionists (those who believe in long ages for the six days of creation) to show that the Bible clearly teaches that the days of creation are six 24-hour days. The Sabbath command would have no sense if we were being required to keep every seventh millennium! The 'day' in the fourth commandment is the word 'yom' in Hebrew and clearly has to mean a 24-hour period for the Sabbath law to make sense. Since the reason given for the Sabbath in Exodus 20 is that God made the world in six days with one day of rest, there is no way round the clear implication that the six days of creation have to be six 24-hour periods for the argument to have meaning. But if it is right to use this verse to show that the creation 'days' were 24-hour periods, it behoves us also to acknowledge the authority that the Sabbath holds over us as a *creation* ordinance—not Jewish.

6.3 The Sabbath today—moral or ceremonial?

However, some say, it is surely just part of the Jewish ceremonial law which passed away, for did not the Apostle Paul say in Colossians 2:16–17 'Therefore let no one judge you in food … or of a new moon, or sabbaths, which are a shadow of things to come'? If this was the only reference in the New Testament, it would be a very doubtful argument on which to base the destruction of the whole Sabbath law, since there are many other passages (notably the words of the Lord in Mark 2:27) which indicate it stands today. In the Authorized Version the word 'days' in Colossians 2:16, is added in italics (meaning the word is not in the original) and gives the impression that only the word sabbath (singular) is there in the Greek. The New International Version translates the Greek as '… a Sabbath day …' which is again misleading. A straightforward literal translation of the original text (very similar to the NKJV quoted above) is 'or the new moon, or of sabbaths, which are a shadow of coming things …' The word is 'sabbaton' and has a plural ending (a long 'o'), but is writtem 'sabbata' in some manuscripts. Vine[2] has argued that 'sabbata' is transliterated from the Aramaic, and thus does not prove conclusively the plural is correct. However a firm view of the plenary inspiration of Scripture does not exclude usage of words which are of non-Greek origin, and the existence of texts with 'sabbaton'—a definately plural ending—strongly argues against this referring to the weekly Sabbath day. For a correct interpretation we must turn to the verses surrounding Colossians 2:16–17. The context is clearly what is called the ceremonial or Levitical law. So it is evident that Paul is referring to the ceremonial sabbaths, else he would be directly undermining the teaching of Christ's Lordship of the Sabbath in Mark 2:27–28. What has passed away is the sabbaths of the period leading up to the Passover (days of unleavened bread), the Day of Atonement (six months later) and the Feast of Tabernacles. There were three main periods in the Jewish year which were to be strictly kept. These were the Passover, Pentecost and the Day of Atonement. Leviticus 23, Numbers 29 and Deuteronomy 16 detail these special days which have all now passed away.

In order for the reader to understand the difference between the ceremonial law (which has passed away) and the moral law (which still stands today) the chart below shows the major differences between them:

Moral Law (10 Commandments)	Ceremonial Law (Sacrifices)
Written by God	**Written by Moses**
Deuteronomy 5:22, Exodus 31:18	Deuteronomy 31:9, 24–26
Spoken by God	**Spoken by Moses**
Deuteronomy 4:12–13	Leviticus 1:1, 2; 7:37–38
Put *in* the Ark of the Covenant	**Kept at the *side* of the Ark**
Deuteronomy 10:5	Deuteronomy 31:26
Defines sin	**A shadow of things to come**
1 John 3:4; Romans 3:20; James 2:10–11	Hebrews 10:1–4, Colossians 2:17
Everlasting	**Abolished**
Matthew 5:18–19; Luke 16:17; Psalm 111:7–8	Ephesians 2:15, Colossians 2:14–17;

God's law (The moral law, Ten Commandments) was *enlarged* on in the New Testament, not taken away from. This is shown in the following verses: Isaiah 42:21 (prophetic), Matthew 5:17–19, Romans 3:31, 1 Corinthians 7:19, Ephesians 6:2, James 2:10–11, Jeremiah 31:33 (prophetic), Hebrews 8:10 (fulfilled).

Table 6.1: The Difference between the Moral Law (Ten Commandments) and the Ceremonial Law.

A number of New Testament Scriptures make it clear that the Sabbath is a law to be observed today : James 2:10 says '… whosoever shall keep the whole law, and yet stumble in one point, he is guilty of all …'. James goes on to quote the sixth and seventh commandments, making it crystal clear that he is meaning the Ten Commandments, when he is referring to the law and by immediate implication, all of them are binding for the Christian. This is consistent with the prophecy of the gospel age in the Old Testament since in Jeremiah 31:33 God says 'I will put my law in their minds, and write it on their hearts; and I will be their God, and they shall be my people.' A mark of God's people is that they keep his commandments (John 14:15), not seeking to earn favour with God, but out of deep love for the one who gave his life for the church.

It is kept not for salvation, for no-one was ever saved by the law, not even Abraham (this is the message of Galatians), but as a mark of being God's people with his law written on their hearts (Jeremiah 31:33). A notable passage concerning the perpetuity of the sabbath in the gospel age is in Hebrews 4. The Lord's Day is a witness that Christ has finished his work of redemption just as the seventh day was a witness that the work of creation was finished. Hebrews 4:1–10 is a careful argument based on this comparison. Just as God rested when he had ceased his work of creation (verse 3), so Christ (verse 10) rested when he had completed the work of redemption. Thus verse 9 states 'There remains therefore a rest [literally: 'keeping of a sabbath'—the Greek is 'sabbatismos'] for the people of God'. The argument is that Christians should keep a sabbath still as a testimony both of the redemption completed by Christ (verse 10) and of the rest in heaven yet to come (verse 11). This day (now Sunday) is a pledge of the heaven which is ours. Verse 3 reads 'We who have believed, do enter that rest' (the Christian Sabbath and rest, as a pledge and preparation of the heavenly), and verse 11 states that we should 'be diligent … to enter that rest' (the rest of heaven to come).[3]

Many Christian families can testify to what an oasis the Christian Sunday can be made. This is because we are able to shut off the pressures due to work and other responsibilities for one complete day and remind ourselves as to our destiny with Christ. Hebrews 4 speaks of the heavenly rest to come, of which we receive a foretaste every time we keep the Lord's Day here.

6.4 The authority of the Sabbath—for all time

Genesis 2:3 teaches that God rested on the seventh day so that God himself set his seal upon the Sabbath. As with God's killing an animal to provide covering for Adam and Eve (and thus teaching the importance of blood-sacrifice), so God setting the standard of rest on the Sabbath, shows that he has set his authority on it. Furthermore Christ said '… the Son of Man is also Lord of the Sabbath' (Luke 6:5). Christ gave authority to all the Ten Commandments (implied in Mark 10:19) but admonished, not those who kept the Sabbath, but rather those who had missed the whole point of the day (Mark 2:27–28) and who hypocritically criticized the doing of good on it (Luke 13:15; John 5:18). The keeping of the Sabbath as a day set apart from work and one's own pleasure was never in question. The Lord sets his seal on the Sabbath. The seventh day rest is a *creation* ordinance, not a Jewish one. What God did in the first week was set as a principle for all nations to follow in every age.

It is important to note that the Ten Commandments were given by God directly, which is why Deuteronomy 5:22 is important, 'These words the Lord spoke … and he added no more'. Then Moses records 'And he wrote them on two tables of stone, and gave them to me.' God *spoke* the decalogue directly and *wrote* it directly. This law is not to be regarded in any way as transient. Those who still think that the Sabbath is only part of a Jewish Ceremonial Law which was to fade away should recall that *before* the giving of the decalogue (the 'ten words' of Sinai) the Sabbath rest instituted at creation in Genesis 2 was being practised. In Exodus 16 (before the events at Sinai), the Israelites are told to gather twice the amount of manna on the sixth day. The reason is clearly stated in Exodus 16:23 'Tomorrow is a Sabbath rest, a holy Sabbath to the Lord'.

Furthermore the fourth commandment is the most detailed, with four verses given to it in Exodus 20 and Deuteronomy 5. The commandments naturally split into two. The first group (which may well have been the first table), sets out laws concerning the relationship of man to God, with the fourth coming at the end of this group detailing the time we should specifically dedicate to him. This is the key to keeping the first three. The second group in a similar way covers six laws concerning the relationship of men with one another, with the last commandment again being the key to laws five to nine. The last command restrains greed and selfishness which 1 Timothy 6:10 affirms is the root of all evil.4 We remove the fourth commandment and his day at our peril. For then we will find it difficult to keep the first three concerning idolatry and blasphemy. If Christ is Lord of the Sabbath (Luke 6:5) in my life, then there must be a regular Sabbath for me to keep.5

Both the teaching and practice of the Apostles was to keep the Sabbath. They taught that the Law was holy (Romans 7:12; Romans 13:8; 1 Timothy 1:8; 1 John 3:4) and not to be despised. The strong implication from James 2:10 is that all the Ten Commandments still stand and are not to be separated. Hebrews 4 bases its argument concerning heaven to come on the picture of heaven that the weekly Sabbath gives. As recorded in section 6.5.2(4), Acts 20:7 and 1 Corinthians 16:1–2 make it clear that the practice of the first believers was to meet on the first day of the week and keep one day in seven as a special day and one complete book (Revelation) was given to John one Sunday during his lonely exile on Patmos. Thus the authority of God's special day (first Saturday and now Sunday) stands as a landmark for *all* societies everywhere. It is the watershed separating the godly from the godless surrounding them. In our Western so-called liberated and permissive life-styles, we have gone well beyond the watershed and fallen to depths of behaviour which individually and nationally affront God's holiness. One step in the route back is to keep his day holy again.

Turning to the prophetic Scriptures, it is significant that Isaiah 66:23 predicts '… from one Sabbath to another, all flesh shall come to worship before me, says the Lord.' As Ryle has stated:6

The subject of this prophecy no doubt is deep. I do not pretend to say that I can fathom all its parts: but one thing is very certain to me—and that is that in the glorious days to come on the earth, there is to be a Sabbath, and a Sabbath not for the Jews only, but for 'all flesh'. And when I see this I am utterly unable to believe that God meant the Sabbath to cease between the first coming of Christ and the second.

Voltaire, the renowned French atheist, spoke of not ridding the world of the Christian church unless you rid the Christian of his day. Holyoake, the English atheist, wrote in 1857:

Whether Englishmen know it or not, it is the English Sunday that has made and keeps England great. If you would kill Christianity, you must first kill Sunday.7

The church by and large has conceded this day, by not keeping it. Because she had not kept the day, she has lost the privilege and has also caused incalculable damage to the cause of the gospel in England and many Western nations. The church itself is now today far weaker as a result.

6.5 The Christian Sabbath and the change of day

6.5.1 MAJOR PRINCIPLES

This issue is probably the most common area of debate and misunderstanding by believers today. Before considering the specific matter of the change of day, it is vital to reiterate two truths expounded in the last section:

i. The principle of one day of rest in seven is a *creation* ordinance, not a Jewish one. Genesis 2:3 was given at the beginning of all nations and Exodus 20:9–11 gives the reason for the Sabbath law as being God's rest in the creation week. Only later in Deuteronomy 5:13–15 is a connection made with the redemption from Egypt.

ii. The Lord himself gave his authority to the Sabbath (Luke 6:5; Mark 2:28). Rather than overthrow the Sabbath law as a part of the Ceremonial Law soon to fall away, he showed that in the past (a) it was made in the beginning for man (Mark 2:27) and (b) in the past and present, he is Lord of this day. It is to be a day with his name attached to it. We cannot escape the implication of Mark 2:27–28 together, that there is a Sabbath law applying to us today.

There is also a third principle which we must establish:

iii. The Sabbath principle as originally given was not attached to the seventh day. This is where the Seventh Day Adventists have misunderstood the original principle given at creation. The principle is best explained by Jonathan Edwards who wrote,

The words of the fourth commandment do not determine which day of the week we should keep as a sabbath; they merely determine that we should rest and keep as a sabbath every seventh day, or one day after six days ... the words in no way determine where those six days shall begin, and so where the rest or sabbath shall fall.[8]

Thus the Sabbath is not inseparably attached to Saturday. This is important and underlines the first principle above, that the Sabbath rest is not a Jewish ordinance. Furthermore, Christians now keep Sunday as a witness to Jews and to any who keep other days (see section 6.5.3).

Compare these three principles with the commonly held erroneous beliefs[9] that (a) the Sabbath was simply Jewish (b) the Lord's Day was a *new* institution brought in by the Apostles and (c) the seventh day of the week is the essence of the sabbatical institution. Such superficial reasoning has led many to lose the great benefit of a spiritual oasis which the Lord has for his people in the desert of ungodliness all around us. Hearts longing for spiritual life need a weekly Sabbath 'made for man'. Physically and mentally our bodies also require that one day in seven is a time of ceasing.

6.5.2 REASONS FOR THE CHANGE OF DAY

We can now turn to the question of the change of day. The best expositions of the principle of the change of day are the writings of Edwards,[10] Hodge,[11] Warfield[12] and Legerton.[13] In the main, we follow the succinct argument of Hodge.

I. CHRIST ROSE AGAIN ON THE FIRST DAY OF THE WEEK (JOHN 20:1–18)

Literally the phrase is 'first of the sabbaths' (used typically in Matthew 28:1; Mark 16:2; Luke 24:1; John 20:1) which, with the root of seven (shabua) from the Hebrew is the English equivalent of the literal rendering 'first day of the week of days'. It is no accident that Christ rose on this day and just as the last day of the week marked the completion of creation, the first day becomes the day of the completion of redemption. In the words of Hodge:

The fact of the resurrection consummates the process of redemption as far as it is objective to the Church. It is the reason of our faith, the ground of our hope, the pledge of our personal salvation and of the ultimate triumph of our Lord as the Saviour of the World.[14]

II. *CHRIST APPEARED TO HIS DISCIPLES ON THAT DAY*

Not only did Christ rise on the first day of the week (Matthew 28:1–10) but he made this day special by choosing to frequently appear on the two Sundays after the vital resurrection Sunday (John 20:19–20; John 20:26— notice '… after eight days …' which scholars agree is inclusive counting. indicating that the next appearance was again on a Sunday). As referred to in section (4) below, years later the vision of the Lord Jesus and the Apocalypse was given to the Apostle John on the Isle of Patmos on 'The Lord's Day' (Revelation 1:10). Because of the above resurrection appearances, there is every indication from John's usage of this term, that the first day of the week is being alluded to.

III. *THE HOLY SPIRIT WAS GIVEN ON SUNDAY*

From Leviticus 23:15–16 it is evident the day of Pentecost was always seven weeks later from the 'day after the sabbath' when the initial sheaf of the first fruits was given as a wave offering by the priest (a symbol which was fulfilled by Christ's own resurrection). Thus Acts 2:1–4 recording the Holy Spirit coming on the Church, happened again on the first day of the week.

IV. *THE PRACTICE OF THE APOSTLES*

A powerful testimony to the importance of the first day of the week is given by the apostolic practice of meeting on that day (Acts 20:6–7; 1 Corinthians 16:1–2) as a strong witness to the resurrection of Christ. Hodge states:[15]

The [New Testament] record is also full of evidence that the members of all the apostolic Churches were in the habit of assembling in their respective places at regular times for the purposes of common worship (1 Corinthians 11:17, 20; 1 Corinthians 14:23–26; Hebrews 10:25). That these assemblies were held on the 'first day of the week' is certain from the action of Paul at Troas (Acts 20:6–12) 'And we sailed away from Philippi after the days of unleavened bread and came unto them to Troas in five days; where we abode seven days. And upon the first day of the week, when the disciples came together to break bread, Paul preached unto them, ready to depart on the morrow; and continued his speech until midnight.' [i.e. Paul left the day after the first day, when the church evidently gathered.]

So also his orders to the churches of Corinth and Galatia (1 Corinthians 16:1–2), 'Now concerning the collection for the saints, as I have given order to the churches of Galatia, even so do ye. Upon the first day of the week let everyone of you lay by him in store, as God hath prospered him, that there be no gatherings when I come.' The change was then certainly made, as we can trace by an unbroken and consistent chain of testimonies from the time of the apostles to the present. The motives for the change assigned by the early Christian Fathers are known to have operated upon the apostles, and are perfectly congruous with all that is recorded of their characters, lives and doctrines. The change, therefore, had the sanction of the apostles, and consequently the authority of the 'Lord of the Sabbath' Himself.[15]

There can be little doubt that both days were kept for a while until gradually the Lord's Day took over as the day for Christians to keep. So in Acts 16:13 Paul and Silas speak to a prayer meeting at the riverside in Philippi on the Jewish Sabbath. It is important to bear in mind here the three principles (i)–(iii) established earlier which imply that there is a *creation* Sabbath principle obligatory upon *all* men for their benefit and sealed by Christ himself. On the basis that these principles must stand, then the overwhelming testimony of the early church was that the 'first day of the week' became 'the Lord's Day' (Revelation 1:10) and the Christian's Sabbath.

V. THE PRACTICE OF THE EARLY FATHERS

Hodge[16] shows by many quotations from the writings of the early fathers that (a) they regarded the first day of the week as special for believers and (b) they regarded it as part of the Sabbath principle. Those listed are Ignatius (martyred approximately *c.* AD 107), Justin Martyr (AD 140), Dionysius, Irenaeus (AD 177), Clement of Alexandria (AD 192), Tertullian (*c.* AD 190–200), Athanasius (AD 296–373). In AD 321 Constantine, the first emperor to acknowledge (at least outwardly) Christian belief, ordained that most work should cease on the first day of the week and from this point on there was a growing secular commitment to resting from work on this day. Some of the later Reformers did not hold to the perpetuity of the Sabbath. This was because they were seeking to resist another Roman Catholic error which came in the ensuing centuries, the teaching that the church has supreme authority. This was justified by some Reformers by wrongly appealing to the Apostles moving worship from the seventh day to the first. However, the main leaders of the Reformation clearly taught that the Sabbath was ordained for the whole human race from creation—see, for example, Luther, Calvin, Knox and Beza, who all held to the Sabbath as now being identified with the first day of the week, the Lord's Day.[17]

6.5.3 ALLUSIONS TO THE CHANGE OF DAY

Wilson[18] makes some interesting comments concerning a possible allusion to the change of day. There is some indication of a change of day to come in the Old Testament. Psalm 118:22–23 reads, 'The stone which the builders rejected has become the chief corner stone. This was the Lord's doing; It is marvellous in our eyes.' This is applied six times to Christ in the New Testament (Luke 20:17; Acts 4:11; 1 Peter 2:7; Ephesians 2:20; Matthew 21:42; Mark 12:10) and in particular to his death and resurrection. But Psalm 118 goes on to read in verse 24, 'This is the day which the Lord has made. We will rejoice, and be glad in it'. Thus Christ's resurrection is alluded to on the first day of the week and verse 24 marks out that day as special in the gospel age.

The Lord's Day is a witness that Christ has finished his work of redemption just as the seventh day was a witness that the work of creation was finished. As explained earlier, Hebrews 4:1–10 is a careful argument based on this comparison.

As the Sabbath day has changed, so Christians should seek to keep Sunday as a witness to Christ and his resurrection. The fact that the Sabbath principle is one day in seven does not mean that the church is free to change the day for convenience. We do not do well to disown Sunday by moving church worship to Fridays in Islamic countries and Saturdays in Jewish communities. Where it is at all possible, the Christians should meet on Sundays. The early Christians (such as the slaves in Caesar's household) were denied the privilege of keeping the whole day, but they met early in the morning of the first day of the week, before doing the duties demanded of them. As soon as it was allowed, Christians kept the whole day. So believers in every culture should aim to keep the first day of the week. This day is rightly called the Lord's Day.

6.5.4 A COMMON OBJECTION

In closing this section we refer to a common objection raised by some believers: 'Is not every day a sabbath?' This and other objections are ably dealt with by Legerton[19] in a booklet entitled *Yes … But*. Granted, every day should be lived as unto the Lord and no Christian should be just a Sunday believer. However, that important truth does not absolve the best saint from still keeping one day set apart since God, who never sins, never fails and who never strictly needs rest, himself 'blessed the seventh day, and sanctified it' [literally: 'set it apart'] (Genesis 2:3). Legerton quotes Bonar who, commenting very perceptively on this point, said that:

Should not every day have been a Sabbath to Adam? Yet he was commanded even in Paradise to keep a Sabbath to the Lord. Was not every day a Sabbath to the Lord Jesus when on earth? Yet He kept the Sabbath, and always made known His reverence for it by vindicating Himself from the charge of Sabbath-breaking, and showing that works of mercy might be done upon that day.[20]

Those who use the argument that every day is a sabbath rarely avoid the pitfall that 'they profess to bring up every day to the level of a Sabbath; but it is invariably found that, in reality, they bring down the Sabbath to the level of every day'.[21]

6.6 How should the Christian believer keep the Sabbath?

The fact that the Sabbath is a creation command has far reaching consequences. It means that we as Christians should keep a day of rest as (1) a testimony to our Creator and (2) a testimony to the Saviour.

For the believer it should be:

(a) A day of rest. The meaning of the word 'sabbath' is 'ceasing'. Each week, we should stop. It is good medically for our bodies, but it is vital for our souls. Nehemiah 13:15–22 teaches it is not a day for buying or selling, for commerce and trading. We are legitimately to take part in such things during the week, but this day is to be set apart.

(b) A day of holy rest. Exodus 20:10 teaches that the one day in seven is 'the Sabbath of the Lord your God'. The day is God's day, a day to meet him, a day to meet his people. This is a day for reading, meditating on the

Saviour and all that he has done—notably the glorious salvation he purchased for us at Calvary. This is why in Deuteronomy 5:15 in the second statement of the Ten Commandments, the Lord bids his people to remember that he brought them out of Egypt 'by a mighty hand and by an outstretched arm'. Thus on this day, we are to remember particularly how Christ died for us and with his crucified arms and feet made himself a once-for-all sacrifice for sin. We should use Sunday particularly to remind ourselves of this glorious truth.

(c) A day for the Lord. Isaiah 58:13 speaks of calling the Sabbath a delight, honouring him, not finding our own pleasure and not speaking our own words. This may seem an onerous task to some, but in fact the opposite is true in the experience of the author. In my work, I quite often have to travel to other countries and as a general rule I avoid travelling on the Sunday, for the very positive reason that there is immense strength obtained by meeting with his people and worshipping the Lord, particularly when away from home. Recently I visited Indonesia and benefited enormously from the fellowship with the believers in Jakarta before venturing into the business of the week. Indirectly you also pass on a great blessing to others as you testify to them of God's grace in your soul.

It is notable that the recently published book by Weir[22] on Christian sportsmen and sportswomen, which seeks to justify sport on Sunday, makes no reference to this verse in Isaiah. They argue that the stand of Liddell and others not to dishonour the Lord's Day was outdated. In the light of the previous section, the Lord's people should recognize that a principle is at stake and a principle which directly affects the growth of our spiritual lives.

(d) A day with consequences. Isaiah 58:14 goes on to tell of the glorious effect to a believer who honours God's day. (i) By keeping God's day and calling that day a delight (verse 13), *he enables* you to delight in him. It is all of grace, we cannot do it ourselves. Do you have problems drawing close to the Lord? Is it because you need to repent of misuse of his day? Maybe you are attending only one meeting of worship and are using the rest of the day for sport? This surely will bring spiritual poverty. (ii) He causes us to ride upon the high places of the earth. This is a wonderful promise. God will feed us with the heritage of Jacob—Jacob, the man who was far from perfect! A twister who by God's grace came the hard way to trust in God alone. This speaks of us. Conscious of our great sin, we feel we have no right to God's blessing. But God says, repent, keep my day and you will know great inner resources. You will have strength for all the week, of which the world will be envious. If we humble ourselves under God's mighty hand in this matter (1 Peter 5:6–10), he will settle and establish us in our family life, our work life and our church life.

(e) Employees and employers. A word to Christian employees. It is important that Christians, where they can exert any choice, avoid paid employment on a Sunday, unless they are involved in medicine (doctors, nurses), and the emergency services (police, fire and ambulance workers). The Word of God allows for this as Christ healed on the Sabbath day and specifically allowed acts of mercy (Mark 3:1–6; Matthew 12:11–12) on that day. It is quite a different matter to accept other types of paid secular employment on Sunday. This is to be avoided. However, work practices today are such that there are situations where a Christian has a stark choice of working on a Sunday or losing his employment entirely. In these days of rotating shifts, the problem is becoming more acute, particularly when there are also dependants to consider. The principle is that honouring the Lord is more important than financial gain. If it is possible, other work should be found by such a person, even if it means taking lower pay, for the Lord says that those 'who honour me, I will honour' (1 Samuel 2:30).

A word now to Christian employers. Is it possible that those of us who employ others, have not stood for the day ourselves? Have we, as managers, allowed the company to introduce changed working practices which may not immediately affect us, but which will have a large affect on others on the shop floor and on those of the next generation of workers? We should do all within our power to stop the erosion of the Sabbath day. The Sabbath command in Exodus 20:10 includes the manservant and the maidservant, that is, the people who work for us. Consequently we should do our utmost to avoid others working on our behalf. I often advise those in my research group at the university to take Sunday off (though I cannot legislate for them). I recommend that undergraduates do not work on the Sunday before examinations (or on any Sunday for that matter). If they have spent the other days revising thoroughly, they will be far more refreshed for a Monday exam if they do not work on the Sunday. Christians should seek if possible to avoid using buses and trains and shops on Sundays so that bus drivers, train drivers and shop vendors are not required, by us at least, to lose the rest they need. It is important for those Christians with their own transport to help those who otherwise would be reliant on public transport for church attendance on Sunday. In that sense we are all employers of others and we do well to examine whether all the tasks we require of others on Sundays are really necessary.

Chapter 6 notes

1 **V Wright,** *The Lord's Day—A medical point of view* (LDOS, 1993).

2 **WE Vine,** *Expository Dictionary of New Testament Words* (New Jersey: Barbour, 1952).

3 This view of Hebrews 4:1–11 is expounded thoroughly in **Daniel Wilson's** book *The Lord's Day* (republished LDOS, 1988), and has been held by notable Christian leaders, such as **John Owen, Jonathan Edwards and John Ryle**—see Ryle, *A Day to keep* (LDOS), p. 8.

4 The reader is encouraged to refer to the excellent book by **Daniel Wilson,** *The Lord's Day* published in 1827 and republished by LDOS in 1988. Many of the arguments used in this article are laid out more clearly in that book.

5 Consider further that the Sabbath is the key to the first four commandments from Leviticus 26:2, 'You shall keep My Sabbaths and reverence my sanctuary. I am the Lord'. Honouring his day is the key to learning to honour the Lord. The fourth commandment is thus the key to all the first four commands. That the tenth commandment is also the key to the last six is brought out in the New Testament when the Saviour instructs the rich young ruler (Luke 18:22) to 'Sell all that you have and distribute to the poor'. Covetousness is the root cause of social evil.

6 **JC Ryle,** *A Day to keep* (LDOS), p. 9.

7 **Mark Roberts,** *The Lord's Day, 100 Leaders speak out* (LDOS, 1989), quote 83, p. 13.

8 **J Edwards,** 'The perpetuity and change of the Sabbath' in *The Works of Jonathan Edwards,* Vol. 2 (Edinburgh: Banner of Truth, 1979), Sermon XIV, p. 96, quoted in **D Wilson,** *The Lord's Day* (1827; republished LDOS, 1988) p. 98. Sermons XIII–XV of in Vol. 2 of Edward's *Works*, pp. 93–103 are a brilliant exposition of the whole matter of the change of day.

9 See for example, **RW De Haan,** *Why Christians Worship on Sunday* (Grand Rapids: Radio Bible Class). Much of Radio Bible Class material (particularly the Bible notes *Our Daily Bread*)

is excellent. But on the matter of the Sabbath, they are not correct in their exegesis, and effectively teach that there are only 9 commandments today.

10 J Edwards, 'The perpetuity and change of the Sabbath', *The Works of Jonathan Edwards,* Vol. 2 (Edinburgh: Banner of Truth, 1979), Sermon XIV, p. 96.

11 AA Hodge, *The Day Changed and the sabbath preserved* (LDOS).

12 BB Warfield, *Foundations of the Sabbath* (LDOS).

13 HJW Legerton, *The Sabbath Day. Only a shadow? Abolished?* (LDOS).

14 AA Hodge, op.cit., p. 7.

15 AA Hodge, op. cit., pp. 9–10. Material in square brackets added.

16 AA Hodge, op. cit., pp. 10–15.

17 AA Hodge, Ibid, pp. 17–20.

18 D Wilson, *The Lord's Day* (1988, LDOS), pp. 103–104.

19 HJW Legerton, *Yes … But. 14 Problems about the Lord's Day* (LDOS, 1972).

20 H Bonar, *Earth's Morning.*

21 H Bonar, *Earth's Morning.*

22 Stuart Weir, *More than champions*—sportstars' secrets of success (London: Marshall Pickering, 1993).

Genesis and the gospel

As we have indicated in chapter 3, the Bible's authority stands or falls with the historicity of Genesis. But we shall see in this chapter that the very heart of the gospel is put in question once one gives way on evolution. This is hardly surprising, since evolution is really a religious philosophy. Consequently its worldview is bound to clash with that of Scripture, which revolves around man's fall and redemption.

7.1 The authority of Christ

It is often said that Christians don't really need to worry about the Old Testament—with the implication that the New Testament is more reliable. This is particularly stressed to people who have recently become Christians. They are told just to concentrate on the New Testament and the Good News of Christ. This sounds so plausible until we realize that Christ referred to all the key events of the early chapters of the Old Testament as real: Adam and Eve (Matthew 19:4); Abel (Matthew 23:35); Noah (Matthew 24:37) and the Flood (Matthew 24:38). Consequently the authority of Christ himself is inseparably connected to the trustworthiness of those early records. Because he referred to all these events and showed his authority by his resurrection for which there were eyewitnesses, it is a weighty matter indeed to doubt his Word on origins.

We are living in an age where everything is push-button, quick and easy. Thus it is tempting to reduce the gospel message to such an extent as to minimize the importance of the foundations it is built on. Indeed it has often been shown by missionaries that people cannot understand the gospel message until they have grasped Genesis and the Fall. Christ does not seem to be important until sin is made abundantly clear as an offence against a holy Creator.

7.2 The authority of the New Testament

It is not just odd isolated verses that refer to the early events recorded in Genesis, but as will be seen in the sections below, a number of crucial arguments in the epistles of Paul and Peter rely on the historicity of the Genesis record.

The Apostle Paul four times refers to Adam and Eve as real people. The argument of Romans 5:14–21 stands on the historicity of Adam and the Fall. Verse 14 explicitly refers to Adam. Verses 17, 18, and 19 repeat a direct comparison between Adam's sin in producing death and Christ's obedience producing righteousness. Thus, verse 19, '... as by one man's disobedience many were made sinners, so also by one man's obedience many will be made righteous.' The emphasis is that *one* man sinned and only the one great Man can save us. 1 Corinthians 15:22 is very similar: 'For as in Adam all die, even so in Christ all shall be made alive' and 1 Corinthians 15:45, '... The first man Adam became a living being. The last Adam became a life-giving spirit'. Both these chapters (Romans 5 and 1 Corinthians 15) rely on a literal Adam and Eve. A non-literal Adam makes Romans 5 a nonsense. What is the point of comparing Christ with a mythical Adam? The theology of headship of the human race (Adam) and the head of those redeemed (Christ) has no firm foundation if the progenitor of the human race is in fact a sub-human brute. The arguments of Romans 5:12–19 and 1 Corinthians 15:21–47 both rely on a *single* progenitor compared to the *only* Redeemer, Christ. Though Stott[1] rightly commands great respect for his long-standing Christian service, he is not correct to argue for a so-called 'Homo Divinus' after a long line of hominids. Eve came from Adam, *not* a hominid pair before him.

In 2 Corinthians 11:3 Paul refers to Eve being beguiled by the serpent and the danger that present believers would be easily led astray. If the first event is a figment of Paul's imagination, then the force of the warning to believers is lost. In 1 Timothy 2:13–14 the argument concerning the role of women depends heavily on not just the fact that Adam and Eve were real people, but that 'Adam was formed first, then Eve' (verse 13). All these scriptures would be quite false if Adam and Eve were not real persons. Interestingly there has been the suggestion recently from evolutionary scientists that all the human race indeed descends from one single Eve, just as Genesis 3:20 states, Eve 'was the mother of all living', but Scripture teaches clearly that in the beginning the female was made from the male, and *not* the other way round.

The authority of the New Testament is again at stake when the Genesis Flood is doubted, for 1 Peter 3:20, 2 Peter 2:5 and 2 Peter 3:5–6 refer explicitly to Noah and the Ark (which we have already noted was referred to explicitly by the Lord himself in Matthew 24:38). Indeed the whole argument of 2 Peter 3 relies on the Genesis 6–9 account of a *world-wide* flood, for it makes a comparison with the world then and the world leading up to Christ's return. Just as the world then was flooded, so the world in the future is 'reserved for fire until the day of judgement'. *All* the world will be judged in the future, just as *all* the world was flooded in the past. One cannot have a partial flood and not also bring serious doubt on the teaching of *world-wide* judgement and the authority of the New Testament itself.

7.3 The biblical teaching on death

The Scriptures teach that death came only after the Fall of man. This theological argument, in the author's view, is the most powerful of all. Romans 5:12 states '… just as through one man sin entered the world, and death through sin, and thus death spread to all men …' Genesis 2:17 teaches that (verse 17) in the day Adam or Eve ate of the tree of the knowledge of good and evil, that they would 'surely die'. There are two deaths here. Literally the Hebrew is 'dying, thou shalt die'. Dying spiritually immediately, Adam and Eve would eventually die physically— for Adam some 930 years later (Genesis 5:5). Spiritual separation from God followed the disobedience of eating the forbidden fruit, so that God calls out to Adam (but in him, to us all) the searching question (Genesis 3:9) 'Where are you?' Thus death is separation—initially spiritual—and if there is no repentance, the final eternal separation in Hell (Gehenna itself— 2 Thessalonians 1:9, Matthew 10:28). The authority of the great teaching in 1 Corinthians 15 on the resurrection to come is linked with that in Genesis on death directly, for it states in 1 Corinthians 15:21 '… since by man came death, by man also came the resurrection of the dead …' The first Adam was the cause of death in this world. The last Adam, Christ, brings life. Some, however, have argued that although death came upon man after the Fall, death of animals could have occurred before.[2] First, it should be pointed out that this view only allows time for supposed gradual fossil formation, if along with this, a day-age view (or the Gap theory) of creation is held. These theories have already been discussed earlier in this book. Let us, however, consider this point head-on. Does Scripture allow for the possibility of animal death before the Fall? The answer is 'No' for the following reasons:

i. Romans 8:21–23 teaches that (verse 22) '... the whole creation groans and labours with birth pangs together until now ...' The marginal translation is 'every creature groans together ...' The implication is the whole creation is 'out of joint' as a result of man's sin, rather like a wheel with the axle off-centre. We do well to recall that Genesis teaches the ground was cursed, delaying our deserved condemnation but bringing sorrow and pain on all men. Romans 8:21 teaches that the creature is in the bondage of corruption. Though it is not spelt out in so many words, the implication is that all creatures reeled under the effect of the Fall, and the death it brought.

ii. If animal death was known *before* the Fall, can this fit with Genesis 1:31 'And God saw everything that He had made, and indeed it was very good'? Animal death is ugly because it involves the shedding of blood. God's command in Genesis 2:9 was for Adam and Eve to feed on fruit and vegetables. The death of animals for food is only mentioned later in Genesis 9:3 *after* the Flood. These two passages show that the death of animals was not God's original intent. It was not the original 'very good' of Genesis 1. Furthermore the evidence from fossils (which many incorrectly insist were before man) is of disease and suffering, as well as sudden death. This cannot be consistent with the 'very good' of Genesis 1:31. Most fossils bear testimony to God's judgement at the Flood.[3]

iii. The significance of animal death is highlighted by all the Old Testament sacrifices looking forward to the one sacrifice of Christ at Calvary. Hebrews 9:22 says '... without shedding of blood there is no remission ...' When Adam and Eve sinned they sought a covering for their nakedness; 'they sewed fig leaves together' (Genesis 3:7). Yet God refused such a covering. Genesis 3:21 states 'Also for Adam and his wife the Lord God made tunics of skin, and clothed them.' God's covering involves the shedding of blood. Animals died so Adam and Eve should have a covering. The implication is that *God* made the first sacrifice, showing right at the start the need for substitution. Pictures of Christ and his great substitutionary atonement all begin in these important early chapters of Genesis. The 'seed of the woman' referred to in Genesis 3:15 *will* 'bruise the serpent's head'. The 'seed of the woman' speaks of the virgin birth and the serpent is the devil. God predicts the coming of Christ to conquer Satan. These matters are dealt with more thoroughly in chapter 10.

7.4 The biblical basis for redemption

This is really the focal point of the whole debate. Although many sincere Christians, last century and now, fail to see the importance of the creation/evolution issue, Huxley in his day recognized that the heart of the Christian gospel is at stake once you accept evolutionary thinking. In his essay 'The lights of the Church and the light of Science,'[4] he writes:

If the covenant with Abraham was not made; if circumcision and sacrifices were not ordained by Jehovah; if the 'ten words' were not written by God's hand on the stone tables; if Abraham is more or less a mythical hero, such as Theseus; the story of the Deluge a fiction; that of the Fall a legend; and that of the creation the dream of a seer; if all these definite and detailed narratives of apparently real events have no more value as history than have the stories of the regal period of Rome—what is to be said about the Messianic doctrine, which is so much less clearly enunciated? And what about the authority of the writers of the books of the New Testament, who, on this theory, have not merely accepted flimsy fictions for solid truths, but have built the very foundations of Christian dogma upon legendary quicksands?

The reader is referred to a recent article by Ken Ham[5] for a full discussion of Huxley's views, but the above makes it abundantly clear that the leading antagonists of the Christian faith have no doubts as to why they must disprove Genesis. Undermining Genesis undermines the whole structure of the Christian gospel. The Bible teaches that only Christ can redeem man from judgement to come. Many Scriptures connect the Fall with redemption. Thus the argument of Romans rests heavily on this. Key verses are:

Romans 5:15, 'For if by the one man's offence many died, much more the grace of God, and the gift by the grace of one man, Jesus Christ, abounded to many.'

Romans 5:19, 'For as by one man's disobedience many were made sinners, so also by one man's obedience many will be made righteous.'

Romans 6:23, 'For the wages of sin is death; but the gift of God is eternal life in Christ Jesus our Lord.'

Elsewhere in 1 Corinthians 15, the glorious future of the resurrection of Christ's Church is inextricably connected with the doctrine of the original sin and Fall of Adam. Thus 1 Corinthians 15:19–22, 'If in this life only we have hope in Christ, we are of all men the most pitiable. But now Christ is risen from the dead, and has become the first-fruits of those who have fallen asleep. For since by man came death, by Man also came the resurrection of the dead. For as in Adam all die, even so in Christ shall all be made alive.' Also 1 Corinthians 15:47, 'The first man is of the earth, made of dust; the second man is the Lord from heaven.' The whole essence of the apostolic teaching is that the whole of the human race is fallen through Adam, the first man, but that the second man from heaven, that is Christ, is the only Redeemer. Death came by sin. Rather than evolution, which teaches that death is not only *acceptable* but *necessary* to push life on earth to a 'higher plane', the Bible firmly teaches the opposite, that man is *sinful* and death has come *by sin*. Only through Christ can this be reversed. Just as Genesis speaks of literal thorns growing when the ground was cursed (and we note from Genesis 3:18 that Adam and his descendants were *not* at this juncture cursed), Christ is the one who is the divinely appointed substitute to take our curse for us. Thus Galatians 3:13 states, 'Christ has redeemed us from the curse of the law, having become a curse for us (for it is written, "Cursed is every one who hangs on a tree").' So the Divine Redeemer having laid prostrate on the already cursed ground in Gethsemane (Matthew 26:39), shortly afterwards bears the symbol of the curse as he wears the crown of thorns (Matthew 27:29) at the trial and later at the cross. The only Redeemer of sinners was nailed to the Cross where he took the punishment for sin in the sinner's place. 2 Corinthians 5:21 states, 'For He made Him who knew no sin to be sin for us, that we might become the righteousness of God in him'. God the Father punished his own Son in place of those who believe in Christ, as their substitute. Such is taught throughout Scripture, even in Genesis where God himself sacrifices an animal to clothe Adam, which spoke not only of physical covering, but of the vital need of the shedding of blood (Hebrews 9:22) for the remission of sin. Abel was only received by God in Genesis 4:4 because he brought a blood sacrifice whereas Cain was refused because he brought an offering *without blood* from the fruit of ground which had been cursed. The first thing Noah did after the Flood was to offer a blood sacrifice (Genesis 8:20–21). Later, Abraham, Isaac, Jacob and his descendants were instructed to bring a blood sacrifice for the cleansing of sin. There is no doubt that Christ fulfilled all the pictures in the Old Testament. John the Baptist cried of Christ (John 1:29), 'Behold! The Lamb of God who takes away the sin of the world!' Paul referred to Christ as, 'Christ our Passover, [who] was sacrificed for us' (1 Corinthians 5:7; cf. Exodus 12) and the writer to the Hebrews spoke of it being, 'impossible for the blood of bulls and goats to take away sins' (Hebrews 10:4) but that, 'This man [Christ] after he had offered one sacrifice for sins for ever, sat down at the right hand of God' (Hebrews 10:12).

So the connection of the gospel to the Old Testament and right back to Genesis in particular is impossible to sever without destroying the essence of redemption itself. Paul in 1 Corinthians 15:53–57 sounds a triumphant note:

For this corruptible must put on incorruption, and this mortal must put on immortality. So when this corruptible has put on incorruption, and this mortal has put on immortality, then shall be brought to pass the saying that is written, 'Death is swallowed up in victory'. 'O Death where is your sting? O Hades where is your victory?' The sting of death is sin; and the strength of sin is the law. But thanks be to God, who gives us the victory through our Lord Jesus Christ.

Remove a literal Genesis, a literal Fall, a literal death and curse for sin, and the mission of Christ in terms of redemption is lost. If there is death before the Fall then death arising from rebellion and sin and the vicarious nature of the death of Christ are undermined. Evolutionary teaching strikes right at the heart of the gospel itself.

7.5 Establishing the foundations

The Lord leads individuals step by step after conversion. Not all will become believers through the issue of creation/evolution, although a number have.

It would be wrong to stipulate that creation is a fundamental matter of salvation. It evidently is not. When a person is in danger of drowning in the sea and is saved by a passing ship, he knows only the immediate danger he is in and the kindness of the seamen who rescue him. He will not know necessarily about boats as regards their design, or operation. But if he is later in command of a vessel going to go out to sea again, he will certainly need to make sure the ship is well designed, that there are no leaks in the hull and that he understands the operation of the engine and the rudder. He will be sure to have charts of his proposed voyage with the dangers of hidden rocks and quicksands clearly marked. For the young Christian, if he is to grow and be established so that he is able to avoid shipwreck, he must similarly check that his vessel of belief is not holed by erroneous doctrines which seep in and may eventually overwhelm him. His charts are the Scriptures. If he is unsure about the first chart, he is hardly going to have confidence in the voyage of the Christian life, since shipwreck may follow very quickly. Christian firmness and growth come from an unshakeable belief in the authority of Christ, the Living Word, and Scripture, the Written Word, from Genesis to Revelation.

Chapter 7 notes

1 **John Stott,** *Understanding the Bible,* Scripture Union, 1984.

2 **DC Watts,** 'Fossils and the Fall' in *Biblical Creation,* 18, 1984 (20–21), published by the Biblical Creation Society in the United Kingdom. It should be pointed out that since then, the BCS has taken a much firmer stand against any death before the Fall.

3 This is not to exclude some post-Flood fossilisation, but not on the continental and world-wide scale of the Flood itself—see note 40 of Appendix B.

4 **TH Huxley,** chapter 6 'The lights of the Church and the light of Science', *Science and the Hebrew Tradition—Essays by Thomas H Huxley* (London: Macmillan, 1903). pp.201–238. The quote in the text is from pp 207–208.

5 **K Ham,** 'A child may see the folly of it', *Creation* 17(2), 1995, 20–22.

Genesis and outreach

8.1 Preaching with conviction

Edwards, in his definitive book on Revival,[1] makes it clear that a necessary condition before revival comes to the church of God is that Christians have a strong belief in the authority of Scripture. God blesses the preached Word in his own sovereign way. For preaching to be effective, the church itself must be obedient and submissive to the Word. God's blessing in some generations has led to vast numbers of people being saved. Whether that is to happen in our generation or not, we should be people obedient to the Book of books, holding firmly to its veracity and trustworthiness. When revival has come, the men God used in revival have always been men with an overwhelming conviction that *all* of Scripture is the inspired and infallible Word of God. Thus the Reformers: Huss, Wycliffe, Zwingli, Calvin, Tyndale, Latimer, Ridley; the Puritans: Owen, Baxter, Bunyan; those of the 18th century Awakening: Whitefield, Wesley, Cennick, Brainerd, Jonathan Edwards; those in the 19th century: Spurgeon, Ryle, M'Cheyne, Bonar; those in the 20th century much used of the Lord: Evan Roberts of the 1904 revival, Lloyd-Jones in Aberavon and London, were all men with a thorough and deep submission to the Word of God. Historically this has always been the hallmark of the Evangelical faith. Brian Edwards writes:[2]

He [God] will not trust revival to those who will not trust His Word. It has to be stated as a point of historical fact that revival never begins with the 'liberal' wing of the church; that is, those who deny the full authority and accuracy of Scripture. I am not aware of any exception to this.

This submission to Scripture includes an uncompromising stand on Genesis. As explained in chapter 7, the heart of the gospel is at stake if we give way on the authority of Genesis. Spurgeon fought against the liberals within the Baptist movement in the 'Down-grade controversy' in the nineteenth century and had no time for the Darwinism of his day. So a vital need for our evangelism today is a thorough conviction concerning the authority of all the Bible, including Genesis. The Lord put a vital importance on preaching in the New Testament. Thus Paul wrote in Romans 10:14 'And how shall they hear without a preacher', and in 1 Corinthians 1:21–23 'For since, in the wisdom of God, the world through wisdom did not know God, it pleased God through the foolishness of the message preached to save those who believe. For the Jews request a sign, and the Greeks seek after wisdom; but we preach Christ crucified, to the Jews a stumbling-block and to the Greeks foolishness.' Again Paul states in Titus 1:3 'But [God] has in due time manifested his word through preaching …'.

A preacher without deeply held convictions has little lasting effect on his hearers. Because Genesis deals with the beginning of sin and the desperate need of men and women to see how much they have rebelled against God, it is vital that a belief in a real Fall of a real Adam and Eve is adhered to. Unconverted men and women will not understand the seriousness of sin unless told by someone who himself realizes it. Imagine a fire-fighter telling people to leave their burning home with the words, 'It might be advisable to leave within the hour as it's going to get a bit hot soon.' There is no conviction in the words of many preachers because there is no sense of urgency. This lack of urgency can often be traced to a low view of Genesis and the Fall. Lot had little effect on his sons-in-law because he had already compromised with Sodom (Genesis 19:14). So we as believers should repent of our compromise and raise a clear clarion call to the unconverted, based on a firm belief in God's Word.

8.2 The stumbling block to faith

Having said that evangelism should be primarily by preaching (and witnessing) to men and women, this is not to say that it is by emotional rhetoric to by-pass the mind. On the contrary, believers themselves are to be transformed by the renewing of their minds (Romans 12:2), and to *reason* with unbelievers regarding the things of righteousness, temperance and judgement as Paul did before Felix (Acts 24:25) and with many who saw him in his last days (Acts 28:23). In 2 Corinthians 5:11, Paul states, 'Knowing, therefore, the terror of the Lord, we persuade men'.

Today we have moved away from appealing to the minds of men and women and the converts which the Lord may still graciously bring are often weak in the area of biblical teaching. We need at the outset to deal with the objections raised by unconverted people in our witness. There is no doubt that one of the major stumbling blocks is concerning origins. In the University where I work, if one raises the matter of the Christian faith, very quickly barriers are put up based on evolutionary ideas. Whether staff or students, in arts or science departments, the notion that evolution is a 'fact' and that the world has been here for billions of years is soon brought into a conversation. The cleverness of the enemy can be seen by a vagueness in peoples' minds as to where we have come from, and removes any sense of responsibility for a recent rebellion of man against God only a few thousand years ago. And this is not just true of our Universities. Try to speak to anyone in the streets or on their door-steps, and young people in particular will often raise these objections. They may not be well read on the subject and they do not necessarily expect you to be either. *But they do expect to have a clear answer as to where you stand.* Immediately you say that you believe in a six literal 24-hour-day creation and a global flood, that you are convinced of the authority of Genesis, you may be laughed at, by some. Indeed we should expect this for 2 Peter 3:3–6 predicts that there will be scoffers in the last days—those who '*wilfully* forget that by the word of God the heavens were of old'. We should expect false teachers within the professing church (2 Peter 2:1ff) and certainly should not be surprized by the outsider mocking at creation. However, at times, some people I have spoken to have a quiet respect for the scriptural arguments. It can help to know some of the scientific arguments to underline the reasonableness of the case for a recent creation. To say clearly that not only the Old Testament, but also Christ and the Apostles based their major teachings on creation will cause some to reconsider their position. We do not expect an immediate total acceptance of a view so foreign to most, but we can show that we have a clearly reasoned alternative. There is a thirst in some people for that which is real, genuine and solid, and when they see thinking Christians prepared to stand firm on all of Scripture and Genesis in particular, it removes one of the stumbling blocks to faith. Only the Holy Spirit converts people by changing the will of a man or woman, but he uses his people to reason with them. There are many smoke-screens that unconverted people will put up. The creation/evolution debate is but one of them, and it is our duty as faithful soulwinners to deal with this stumbling block to faith when it is raised, by showing them that it is not unreasonable and indeed not *unscientific* to have an uncompromising stand on Genesis.

8.3 The natural point to begin in our witness

Having shown that conviction in the area of origins is vital for dealing with a natural stumbling block to faith in others, I now seek to address the leading of a soul to the Saviour. It is vital in any matter 'to begin at the beginning'. This is certainly true in the matter of leading a seeking soul to faith in Christ. Some missionary societies have wisely recognized that if tribal people have never heard of Christ and the gospel, rather than jump straight into teaching directly on Christ, it is important to teach on origins first, thus laying a firm foundation for acknowledging God as Creator, the responsibility of man in rebelling at the outset, the awfulness of sin and the need of a Redeemer.

In a similar way it is important to realize that a whole generation of people now exist in our country who have very little, if any, knowledge of the Bible at all. Twenty years ago any child would have been able to say who was the mother of Jesus. Today there are some beach mission centres run by UBM, Scripture Union, CSSM and others in the summer where children, through no fault of their own, are ignorant of such basic facts from Scripture. In the inner city area of Leeds where I was working in a church for a number of years, it is customary to come across people who find it very difficult to read at all, let alone read the Bible. We need to wake up as believers to the situation around us. Although in some parts of the community there is great sophistication and technology, in many ways there is a growing divide in the area of 'moral understanding' (for want of a better term). In past centuries, Tyndale claimed that by his English translation of the Bible, the 'ploughboy would know more than the priest', which, by God's grace, took place. The artisan may not have read widely but he had a basic knowledge of the Bible. Today many working people are growing up with little learning of any kind and when, by the grace of God, their lives are touched, we need to take them from where they are, teaching carefully the authority of all the Bible, where we are from, the origin of sin and the great salvation we have in Christ.

Thus it is important first to teach who God is, how he created the world, how men first rebelled and sin came in, how the first world was flooded and how God planned from the beginning to send a Redeemer. By so doing, we not only unravel the grand account of God's love for fallen mankind and the climax of sending his Son, but we provoke minds previously deadened by the ungodly media to think for themselves as to where they fit into this world around them. This approach encourages them from the outset to have a totally different worldview and to recognize the radical step involved in putting their faith in Christ as Redeemer.

8.4 Storming the strongholds of Satan

The aim of evangelism is not only to see individuals won to Christ, but to see whole communities transformed. We long for revival and should pray God will touch our evangelical churches to bring a strengthening of the work he has begun. How is this to come about? Undoubtedly it is vital that first and foremost there should be repentance of unbelief.

Crack troops which storm enemy positions are trained to the highest degrees of preparedness and are taught carefully about all that intelligence has brought back concerning the number of troops the enemy has, what artillery they are using, where the ammunition is, supply lines are, etc. There is total commitment on the part of these front line troops; there are no secret agreements with the enemy. Today, without realising it, many churches are compromised. Leading evangelical church leaders in the UK are not agreed on the vital question of evolution. The trumpet is blown with an uncertain sound and for some churches, it is evident that secret agreements have been made with the enemy of souls. If you are a church leader and still not convinced, see the clear warnings of Paul as he left the Ephesian elders in Acts 20. Verse 30 reads 'Also, *from among* yourselves men will rise up, speaking perverse things, to draw away the disciples after themselves.' Peter writes in 2 Peter 2:1 '… there will be false teachers *among* you …'. It is the danger of evil doctrines *within* the church which is the greatest threat. Consider the illustration of this in Joshua 1–9. What opposition had the greatest and long lasting effect on Joshua and the children of Israel? Was it

Chapter 8

Jericho? No, despite its formidable and prestigious position, God brought the city to ruins. All Joshua's men had to do was encircle it thirteen times! Was it Ai and Achan's sin? This was serious and brought shame and defeat but when the children of Israel repented, there was victory. What of Gibeon in chapter 9? This was entirely different. The first two attacks were (a) frontal and (b) personal sin within. This last was (c) a clever deception of the enemy by passing himself off as a friend. Canaanite enemies of Israel made out that they were from a far away country. The telling verse, Joshua 9:14, '... the men of Israel took some of their provisions; but did not ask counsel of the LORD' sealed the trouble for years to come for the Israelites, as Joshua, '... made peace with them, and made a covenant with them to let them live ...' (Joshua 9:15). The solemn vow meant that the Gibeonites could now never be killed and their presence always weakened Israel. Although slaves for ever to Israel, they were a perpetual reminder that the enemy had come within. The lesson is clear. Compromise weakens the church of God. It may not necessarily stop God's blessing for he is gracious still to bless, despite our failure (see Joshua 10 where an enormous victory is still recorded even though Joshua had failed in chapter 9 over the matter of the Gibeonites). However, if we are to have lasting effect in building up communities where the Bible is honoured, there can be no letting up on its authority and relevance to those we are seeking to reach.

If we want to advance across the enemy's territories of indifference, immorality and the violent abuse of believers, then we must have full trust in the Sword of the Spirit, the Word of God. Paul said (2 Timothy 3:16), 'All Scripture is given by inspiration of God, and is profitable for doctrine, for reproof, for correction, for instruction in righteousness'. That *all* includes Genesis. The verse leads on into verse 17, 'that the man of God may be complete, thoroughly equipped for every good work'. We will not advance successfully against the enemy strongholds of immorality, vice, drugs and great wickedness unless first our base is securely founded on all of Scripture. Only a firm belief in Scripture as the Sword of the Spirit will bring down the other hidden, but equally evil strongholds of religious hypocrisy, pride, love of ease and intellectual arrogance. In the 19th century, Spurgeon referred to not needing to defend the Bible, rather to letting it loose like a lion to do its own work. Only when preachers and personal workers have a thorough going belief in the *totality* of Scripture will they see the Bible have its effect of bringing conviction of sin as it is used in evangelism. For it is the Bible itself which is 'living and powerful, and sharper than any two-edged sword, piercing even to the division of soul and spirit, and of joints and marrow, and is a discerner of the thoughts and intents of the heart' (Hebrews 4:12).

Chapter 8 notes

1 **BH Edwards,** *Revival!—a people saturated with God* (Darlington: Evangelical Press, 1994).
2 **BH Edwards,** op. cit., p. 64.

Chapter 9

Genesis and the nation

9.1 A nation without a sense of direction

When one flies long distances, it is now common practice to show to the passengers the route being flown, what height one is at, what the temperature is outside (usually a chilly minus 30°C!), how far it is to one's destination and the estimated time of arrival. Any good pilot has to know his present position and his progress from his original starting point in order to work out his route carefully, whether he has enough fuel, effect of headwinds, tailwinds, etc. The same must apply to any major journey we make. As a nation to have any sense of *direction*, it is imperative that we know *why* we are here and *where* we have come *from*. It would be foolish to think otherwise. No advance is made unless one has a clear goal and aim. Our own nation of Great Britain has a past history of Christian belief and much of its industrial progress and prosperity was built *originally* on honesty and trustworthiness from men and women brought up to honour God and to obey the Ten Commandments. Not only that, but because so many ordinary men and women knew the Lord Jesus as their Saviour and sought to serve him, when greed and vice corrupted the industrial revolution, Christians were prominent in those who fought against it. When many workers were brought to poverty and men cruelly sent women and children down the mines and young boys up chimneys, it was the leading Christian social reformer, Lord Shaftesbury, who championed them. The godly John Howard stood for the reform of prisons. In the 19th century, it was Wilberforce, converted through reading the Greek New Testament on holiday on the continent, who spent much of his life thereafter fighting against the slave trade.

But today? More £26,000 million is spent each year on alcohol in the UK, so it is hardly surprising that a very large amount of crime in our nation is drink-related. For instance, 45% of wounding and assault cases are due to drink. Coupled with this, 40% of all road deaths are caused by alcohol. Other soft drugs are now in the process of being legalized. The abortion rate was 400 per day in 1986 and 600 per day in 1994. Sexual practices once unthinkable are now justified, even by some leading members of the Church of England and the Methodist Church. Since the 1990s we have seen a revolution of evil ideas sweeping across the country. We see a nation which has lost its way from the top downwards. In the two years 1994/95 a right-wing government brought in legislation directly contrary to two of the Ten Commandments. The Shops Bill justified trading on Sunday and the Prime Minister openly endorsed gambling through the National Lottery. The left wing government of 1997 takes a liberal view on homosexuality. The nation is surely in a desperate state. When a ship is holed, drastic and urgent action has to be taken to avert worse disaster. It is no use painting the deck or reglazing the cabins! All hands to the pumps and seal off the damaged section. The fundamentals have to be given priority.

When we are lost, we must refer to a map to find our way out and to be certain of reaching safety, it is wise to trust someone who knows the way. Vital, fundamental changes are needed to bring the nation back on track. All credit to King George VI in 1940 who called the nation to a day of prayer in the darkest hours of the Second World War, when at that time we seemed small and alone against the impossible odds of Nazi Germany. But with striking similarity to the fall of Rome, what is becoming the undoing of Britain is corruption from within rather than invasion from outside. It is very noteworthy that at the height of the 1914–18 war, David Lloyd George is reputed to have said, 'When the chariot of humanity gets stuck ... nothing will lift it out except great preaching that goes straight to the mind and heart. There is nothing in this case that will save the world but that which was once called, "the foolishness of preaching".'[1] The only cure for our ills is to get back to Scripture, back to the Saviour, back to the old tried and tested paths. Jeremiah 6:16 states, 'Stand in the ways and see, and ask for the old paths, where the good way is, and walk in it: Then you will find rest for your souls'. And those who must first show the way should be Christian believers.

Just how much the errors of our day are due to incorrect teaching on origins has already been discussed in earlier chapters. Social standards of clothing, language, marriage and behaviour must all be derived from Scripture and they all find their roots in the Old Testament, and not least, Genesis. If we teach seriously that we came by accident and are really animals, then it is hardly surprising that some of our offspring grow up to behave as such. GK Chesterton said, 'When men cease to believe in God, rather than believing in nothing, they believe in anything'. The moral vacuum is a direct result of a failure to teach our true *origins*—that we are created by God; our true *purpose*—to glorify God; and our true *standard*—the Bible.

9.2 The Church and the nation: a clear signpost

When someone is lost he searches for a signpost. Our nation of Great Britain is in a very dire situation today and is crying out for direction. As believers it is vital we give a clear and convincing picture. This crying out for direction becomes particularly evident at times of national grieving (such as the death of Diana Princess of Wales in 1997). It is my considered view that the Lord may allow very grievous national disasters to shake us to our foundations and to wake us up as to our own great sin. One of the ongoing and most insidious difficulties faced by our nation has been the terrorism of Irish Nationalism and the retaliation of equally evil Loyalist extremists in Northern Ireland. It is significant that although the roots of these difficulties go back many centuries, the onset of the troubles in the last few decades came shortly after the passing of the 1967 Abortion Act brought in by David Steel. It is my personal conviction that the two are linked. As we slid down the road of infanticide on a vast scale, the Lord raised up a trouble we found difficult to handle. This principle is taught from Solomon's life. In 1 Kings 11 it is recorded that after Solomon's departure from the Lord, God stirred up adversaries to his authority (verse 14—Hadad, verse 23—Rezon and verse 26—Jeroboam). They were there before, but subdued. Now they became strong and Solomon could no longer control them.

Deuteronomy 28:43 states what will happen to Israel when she cuts loose from righteous living, 'The alien who is among you shall rise higher and higher above you, and you shall come down lower and lower.' This is surely an apt description of the state of England today. The swinging sixties led to the decadence and decay experienced by many in the nineties. It has been wisely stated that people today want permissiveness in the bedroom but not in the boardroom; but you cannot separate the two. Corruption of the inner life leads to a corrupt community and nation. What we sowed as a nation in the sixties we have reaped in the nineties and in the 21st century.

The church must first preach the gospel and be a signpost to who God is. She must preach the holiness of God, the origin of all men created in his image and the rebellion of man against his Creator. Only a person with firm beliefs in Genesis can preach such a message. But it is certain Britain needs such. It is said that Mary, Queen of Scots, feared far more the prayers of John Knox than the armies gathered against her. Oh for those who pray and preach in such a way that again a nation turns to them. Through mobs full of abuse, Whitefield and Wesley carried the gospel up and down our nation. These men of conviction and others like them became clear signposts for all to see and eventually they saw the nation turn.

9.3 The Church and the nation: standing for God's Book

Some people sincerely believe it right to have a national church bound up as an integral part of the state machinery. Others believe differently, but whatever one's view on such a question, there is no doubt that leadership in the nation will never go higher morally than that within the Lord's people. The Lord spoke of Christians being the salt of the earth (Matthew 5:13) and Paul taught that believers should shine as lights, 'in the midst of a crooked and perverse generation' (Philippians 2:15). Somebody wisely commented that 'when the church gets on its knees, the nation will get on its feet'. Thus we, as believers and church leaders, first need to repent and seek the Lord for forgiveness on areas of fundamental unbelief. The Lord upbraided his disciples often, not for lack of works, but for lack of *belief*. (Thus, 'O you of little faith'—Matthew 6:30; 14:31; 16:8 and Luke 24:25, 'O foolish ones, and slow of heart to believe in all that the prophets have spoken!') It is lack of belief in the totality of Scripture which has weakened the church and led to doctrinal and moral confusion and consequently led to a weak political leadership in the nation.

If in our own Christian homes, we are teaching our children the lie of evolution and not showing a firm belief in Genesis, we can hardly expect those that have no faith to teach their children to show a respect for God's Book. The Prussian general, Bismarck, aptly remarked, 'What you wish in the life of the nation, first put in the schools of the nation.' We may not be able to directly affect the school curriculum in this generation but we can indicate clearly our convictions and bring strong influence on our own children and Sunday Schools. Those of us who are governors, or on

Parent/Teachers associations, can put pressure to have evolution taught as only a theory, not fact, with creation taught as a viable alternative. Those who run Christian schools or who are involved in home schooling clearly have a golden opportunity to teach without hindrance the authority of Scripture and the relevance of Genesis. No examination board can penalize, even at GCSE or A-level Biology level, if the student shows that he or she knows what the evolutionists have written, whilst not personally accepting it. This is a very real battle ground and there are now texts available (see Bibliography) for those wishing systematically to teach science from a Christian perspective firmly based on creation and a strong belief in Genesis. The American Christian publishing houses have led the way on this and there is a great need to have British Christian publishers of repute to follow this lead. Above all, even if we have no immediate access to the wealth of scientific literature now available written from a creationist standpoint, we should teach our children to believe Genesis simply because it is God's Word. God always honours this attitude to Scripture.

Sir Winston Churchill, highly regarded as the great statesman of the 20th century, said:

We believe that the most scientific view, the most up-to-date and rationalistic conception, will find its fullest satisfaction in taking the Bible story literally ... we may be sure that all these things happened just as they are set out in Holy Writ. We may believe that they happened to people not so very different from ourselves, and that the impressions these people received were faithfully recorded, and have been transmitted across the centuries with far more accuracy than any of the telegraphed accounts we read of the goings-on of today.[2]

... Let the men of science and of learning expand their knowledge and probe with their researches every detail of the records which have been preserved to us from those dim ages. All they do is to fortify the grand simplicity and essential accuracy of the recorded truths which have lighted so far the pilgrimage of man.

We too easily forget that a strong belief in the Bible and its relevance lies at the very heart of our national heritage. We have many blots on our national history, and times when oppression ruled, but a full-blooded belief in the Bible is not one of these blots. Rather, where the Bible has been honoured, this has generally gone hand-in-hand with the raising of standards, of family values, care of the poor and a reduction in vice and crime.

9.4 The Church and the nation: standing for God's day

The Lord's Day is an ongoing witness of creation, so that hand in hand with the disbelief in a six 24–hour day literal creation is the growing disbelief in the authority of the Lord's Day. This is not surprising since the Sabbath rest every seven days is a creation principle. Once we water down a belief in creation, so also it follows that belief in the importance of Sunday as a day of rest diminishes. In the UK laws have finally been passed (November 1993) which allow much increased trade on Sundays, and this when for centuries the nation of Great Britain has stood firm on this important principle. To quote again Sir Winston Churchill:

Sunday is a divine and priceless institution, the necessary pause in the national life. It is the birthright of every British subject, our responsibility, privilege and duty to hand on to posterity.[3]

On the other side of the Atlantic, President Roosevelt said:

Experience shows that the day of rest is essential to mankind—that it is demanded by civilization as well as Christianity.[4]

And Abraham Lincoln in an earlier age stated:

As we keep or break the Sabbath we nobly save or meanly lose the last hope by which man rises.[5]

We do well to remember that the Scriptures clearly teach that 'Righteousness exalts a nation, but sin is a reproach to any people' (Proverbs 14:34) and 'If the foundations are destroyed, what can the righteous do?' (Psalm 11:3). Again Proverbs 22:28 states, 'Do not remove the ancient landmark which your fathers have set' (see also Proverbs 23:10).

Professor Verna Wright (until his death head of the Rheumatology department at the University of Leeds) has aptly commented:

In our country there are two major systems of philosophical thought. The first is built on revealed truth (the Bible). On this is placed the block of divine creation, then absolute morality, issuing in responsible man and a caring world. The alternative has humanist philosophy as its foundation. Atheistic evolution is placed on this, then situational ethics (or amorality), issuing in autonomous man and self-centred society. In pursuance of the latter scenario, the forces of evil have gathered to destroy the Lord's Day. What God has written in stone we do well to retain in the laws of our land. What God has forcibly set forth in the Bible should be a cardinal principle for our living.[6]

Christians should seek to do all within their power to keep this day holy. There may be exceptional circumstances when people are forced to have to work on Sunday as a matter of the only possibility of having work, now that laws have been passed altering the nature of the day. However, where we have control, it is inexcusable for Christians both to buy and sell and use the day for sport when the Bible clearly teaches against it. We cannot expect to affect our nation when we ourselves treat the day so lightly.

We end with the following very telling quotes: Robert Murray M'Cheyne (much used of the Lord in the 19th century in Scotland) said:

Did you ever meet with a lively believer in any country under heaven, one who loved Christ and lived a holy life, who did not delight in keeping holy to God the entire Lord's Day? *England without Sunday is England without God.*[7]

Dwight L Moody, the American evangelist stated:

No nation has ever prospered that has trampled the Sabbath in the dust. Show me a nation that has done this and I will show you a nation that has got in it the seeds of ruin and decay. I believe that Sabbath desecration will carry a nation down quicker than anything else. Adam brought marriage and the Sabbath with him out of Eden and neither can be disregarded without suffering.[8]

The British Prime Minister Disraeli during the 19th century said:

I hold the day of rest to be the most valuable blessing ever conceded to man. It is the cornerstone of civilization.[9]

Thus this great blessing of the Lord's Day to church and nation is built firmly on creation as recorded in Genesis. Remove Genesis and you remove the vital institution of a day of rest for the nation. The crumbling of our Western society is to a great extent due to the removal of this day.

9.5 The church and the nation: the only way back

Some years ago, the former Prime Minister, John Major, urged us to get 'back to basics'. He fell foul of human nature when not only members of his own Conservative party were poor examples of moral leadership, but also he himself, as it later transpired, had an extra-marital affair! He had no appeal to an absolute standard. Similar moral malpractice by political leaders has undermined the credibility of individuals in the Labour party's terms in power. The plea in this chapter and the whole book, is that there can be only one foundation—Scripture.

Margaret Thatcher once wrote:

For years when I was young and in politics with all my hopes and dreams and ambitions, it seemed to me and to many of my contemporaries that if we got an age where we had good housing, good education, a reasonable standard of living, then everything would be set and we should have a fair and much easier future. We know now that that is not so. We are up against the real problems of human nature. Why is it that we have child cruelty in this age? Why is it that we have animal cruelty? Why is it that we have violence? ... Why is it that people take to terrorism? Why is it that people take to drugs? These are much, much more difficult problems. ... Why, when you have got everything, do some people turn to those fundamental things which undermine the whole of civilization?[10]

That surely was a cry from the heart and echoed by many politicians across the political divide. Western civilization is not healthy. Corruption, violence and trouble is undermining the fabric of society. Without appearing trite and glib, Christians need to stand firm for what they *know* is the answer—the Scriptures in totality from Genesis to Revelation and the

Chapter 9

Saviour who alone can redeem us. Only when we raise the trumpet call of alarm first to the church, and then speak with conviction to the unconverted, will we see lasting changes in the nation of Britain. The Bible is as relevant today as in any age, and the foundation to all is Genesis.

Chapter 9 notes

1 **BH Edwards,** *Shall we Dance?* (Welwyn: Evangelical Press, 1984), p. 142.

2 **WS Churchill,** *Thoughts and Adventures* (London: Odhams Press Ltd., 1949) pp. 224–225. See also **David CC Watson,** *The Great Brain Robbery* (Worthing: Henry E Walter, 1975), chapter 18, 'Back to the Bible' where he uses the same quote.

3 **Mark Roberts,** *The Lord's Day, 100 Leaders speak out* (LDOS, 1989), quote 3, p. 3.

4 **Mark Roberts,** op. cit., quote 18, p. 5.

5 **Mark Roberts,** op. cit., quote 15, p. 4.

6 **V Wright,** p. xi of Foreword to **Daniel Wilson** *The Lord's Day* (1827; reprinted LDOS, 1988).

7 **Mark Roberts,** op. cit., quote 43, p. 8.

8 **Mark Roberts,** op. cit., quote 46, p. 8.

9 **Mark Roberts,** op. cit., quote 4, p. 3.

10 **M Thatcher,** *Thatcher tells of her vanished dreams,* article in *The Times,* front page, no. 63,510, 27 September 1989.

Genesis and the 21st century

Today in the 21st century we are faced with the ever-eroding nature of postmodernism. This philosophy is not just post-Christian in denying the gospel, but goes much further in denying absolutes altogether. The only rule allowed in our so-called 'politically correct' society is that 'my values must not impinge on yours'. This essentially is postmodernism.

10.1 The rise of militant Islam in the West—why?

Probably all of us can remember what we were doing on that fateful day of 11 September 2001 when news first came of the surprize attack in New York. As the events unfolded, it became clear that the world had suddenly been thrust into new, politically dangerous and uncharted territory.

10.1.1 THE RISE OF ISLAM IN THE WEST LINKED TO THE DEMISE OF CHRISTIAN ABSOLUTES

On one of the planes, a remarkable attempt was made by Todd Beamer, Jeremy Glick, Tom Burnett and a posse of other passengers on board the United Airlines Flight 93 to take back the controls of the Boeing 757 as it was heading on its suicide mission to Washington. All the other three planes had met their targets with dreadful precision. The delay in take-off at Newark of United 93 from 0800 to 0842 and the judicious use of an in-flight telephone by Todd Beamer to talk to a phone operator on the ground meant that a plan of resistance could be hatched against the hijackers. Todd and others quietly and deliberately spoke the Lord's Prayer and Psalm 23 together before, armed with boiling water from the galley, they charged forward to the cockpit to try and overcome the hijackers. Though they did not regain control of the plane, the testimony to their daring courage lay in the wreckage of the aircraft which, having flipped over onto its back due to the struggle in the cockpit, finally disintegrated on impact as it dived into an old deserted strip mine close to Shanksville, Pennsylvania.[1]

The battle on United Flight 93 that morning was won at the cost of 36 passengers and crew who had resisted the four hijackers. They had averted a further tragedy on the ground where possibly the White House or Capitol buildings would have been targeted with inevitable further high loss of life. Todd Beamer ended his last words to Lisa Jefferson on the ground with the now famous exhortation 'Lets roll!' A convinced Bible-believing Christian, Todd, with great courage, led others to withstand a great evil on that fateful morning.

So what evil was Todd Beamer opposing that day? And what fuelled the terrorism? Greed? Money? Asylum seeking? None of these, as we all know. The terrorists were driven by a false fundamentalism—a false over-arching world-view—a view which promotes murder and terrorism in order to obtain supremacy. Todd's fight was the conflict between the dying embers of a post-Christian culture and militant Islam. That evil system has arisen *precisely* because we have not won the battle in our culture against postmodernism—the denial of all absolutes. Since the Second World War Islam had been growing in its influence in the West.[2] Undoubtedly one of the main reasons for its growth was the vast wealth of oil found in the Arab nations which subsequently backed the spread of Islam worldwide. However, this, of itself, did not explain why some in the so-called Christian West should begin to embrace Islamic fundamentalism. That was because postmodern thinking had denied any ultimate right and wrong. Because the very essence of this thinking denies absolutes, it has created a vacuum and a hunger for the very thing it denies. Hence the way is made open for a *false* fundamentalism with a very definite over-arching world-view. As the West has turned its back on the true gospel and Biblical creation, Islam has strengthened.

10.2 Understanding the times: Postmodernism—where did it come from?

So how did we get to this point? Understanding the historical context of postmodernistic thinking exposes the error of this philosophy.

10.2.1 A HISTORY OF THOUGHT LEADING TO POSTMODERNISM

In an excellent booklet, the Christian conference speaker, writer and thinker Erroll Hulse carefully traces the origins of the present postmodern thinking.[3] Following the writings of Thomas Oden,[4] he suggests that the 'pre-modern' world before the French Revolution was dominated by feudalism and spiritual hierarchies. The monarchy imprisoned its political opponents, but this period came to an end and gave way to Modernism and the so-called Enlightenment with the storming of the Bastille in the French Revolution of 1789. The liberation of political prisoners heralded the exaltation of the Goddess of Reason and the Rights of Man. Christian thinking was relegated, the Huguenots fled France, and Man was thought to have come of age. For the next hundred years, though the gospel knew great advances in missionary work from parts of Europe and America, Europe as a whole was coming under the increasing influence of post-Christian thinking. The period of the late 18th century and the beginning of the 19th also saw the rise of the Romanticists such as Blake, Wordsworth, Keats and Shelley, with their powerful use of imagination to offset the dominance of reason and rank sensuality that came with the extremes of the Enlightenment. But, lofty as some of their ideals were, they too lacked a firm Biblical foundation, and in the midst of the growing storm of modernistic thinking, Darwin penned his famous *Origin of Species*, published in 1859. In the years of argument that followed, Thomas Huxley crowed his triumph over Bishop Samuel Wilberforce at the Oxford debate of 1861. In the fledgling states of America, post-Christian thinking had its effect on both sides of the American Civil War. The harshness of the abuse of slaves that took place in some areas (North and South) is well known. However, more subtle were the deist/humanist influences, particularly in the finally victorious North. These influences continued to erode the loosely 'Christian'[5] thinking on both sides of the Atlantic. This in turn led in Europe to the Russian Revolution of 1917, which opened the way mid-century to the enormous oppression and ruthlessness of Stalin. The brutality of the First World War, the immense struggle in the Second World War to defeat the advance of Nazi Germany and then the uneasy Cold War between the West and the Soviet empire, were all examples of evil ideologies in collision. Many think that the age of Modernity came to an end with the fall of the Berlin Wall on 1989. Before this time, competing post-Christian ideologies fought it out and material progress was identified inextricably with technological advance. The collapse of Communism in Eastern Europe led to a quite sudden advance of thinking which challenged the whole idea of any absolutes at all, even scientific ones. Erroll Hulse states[6]

Beginning in the 1960s and 1970s, the Western world had gradually moved philosophically from modernism to postmodernism. For about 200 years the Enlightenment shaped the world's thinking with its emphasis on human reason coupled with optimism for human ability and human achievement. In its arrogance, this modernist view bypassed God and his revelation, the Bible, which led to the collapse of morality. Postmodernism is fiercely antinomian (against law). Right and wrong is a matter of human opinion, and therefore my view is as good as yours or that of the next man. The result is the slide of Western society into the abyss of lawlessness. This is seen in the break-up of the family, rising divorce rates, and overcrowded prisons.

10.2.2 THE ACCELERATING MORAL LANDSLIDE

As the West threw off its Christian heritage, far-sighted Christian leaders such as Francis Schaeffer[7] predicted that there would come a time when not just a post-Christian, but a postmodern age would emerge when even reason itself would be demoted. All absolutes would be removed with euthanasia and abortion, homosexuality, bestiality and worse vices on demand. In chapter 1 of the very telling book *Whatever happened to the human race?* co-authored with C. Everett Koop (former Surgeon General of the United States), he states[8]

The thinkables of the eighties and nineties will certainly include things which most people today find unthinkable and immoral, even unimaginable and too extreme to suggest. Yet—since they do not have some overriding principle that takes them beyond relativistic thinking—when these become thinkable and acceptable in the eighties and nineties, most people will not even remember that they were unthinkable in the seventies. They will slide into each new thinkable without a jolt …

… In our time, humanism has replaced Christianity as the consensus of the West. This has had many results, not the least of which is to change people's view of themselves and their attitudes toward other human beings. Here is how the change came about. Having rejected God, humanistic scientists, philosophers and professors began to teach that only what can be mathematically measured is real and that all reality is like a machine. Man is only one part of the larger cosmic machine. Man is more complicated than the machines people make, but is still a machine, nevertheless ...

For a while, Western culture—from sheer inertia—continued to live by the old Christian ethics while increasingly embracing the mechanistic, time-plus-chance view of people. People came more and more to hold that the universe is intrinsically and originally impersonal—as a stone is impersonal. Thus, by chance, life began on the earth and then, through long, long periods of time, by chance, life became more complex, until man with his special brain came into existence. By 'chance' is meant that there was no reason for these things to occur; they just happened that way. No matter how loftily it is phrased, this view drastically reduces our view of self-worth as well as our estimation of the worth of others, for we are viewing ourselves as mere accidents of the universe.

Schaeffer here rightly connects the centrality of evolution as a major plank in the progress of atheistic humanism to the postmodern denial of any need for an over-arching ideology at all.

10.3 'If the foundations be destroyed ...'—the basis of reality

Postmodernism leads to confusion. By refusing absolutes it becomes an insanity, a contradiction within itself. As a good friend of mine[9] has rightly stated, 'If you want to disprove the nonsense of relativism or "truth according to me", simply punch a man on the nose. He will certainly say, "That was wrong." Answer him, "It was right for me!"' The conscience faculty we all have of making accusation or excuse is born of a sense of absolutes.

But postmodernism also leads to a loss of what is real and unreal in the world. Hulse[10] shows that a mark of such thinking is *deconstructionism* where meaning is separated from any form of language. So human language is not connected with an objective world and words carry no authority—in particular, the meaning of the Bible is not an objective certainty. This deconstructionist thinking (applied to Scripture) flowed from a number of scholars of whom Karl Barth is probably the most well known.[11] For these thinkers meaning is in the mind of the reader and not absolute.

10.3.1 THE BASIS OF REALITY

So postmodernism not only removes ideology (the idea of over-arching world-views), it asserts the right of individuals to hold their own 'truth'. This inevitably then leads to no objective Truth at all and denies the basis for reality itself, ultimately of experimental reality which is so necessary to scientific endeavour. The whole concept of how truth can be ascertained and verified is obscured. Instead of saying there is a Universe of facts and ideas to be explored and tested to lead me to truth, the basic philosophy of truth itself ceases to be objective but subjective. Thus there is no lasting Reality and even words fail to keep their meaning. Evolution now becomes the welcome handmaid to postmodernism, since at a stroke it conveniently removes any necessity for, and relevance of, a God distinct from a created Universe. It now becomes the final appeal for all thinking, for evolution is a philosophy that allows no facts that can be explored and tested. Everything is chance and has no meaning. Truth is what you want it to be, reality is in your own mind. Even the rise of computer technology with its concept of 'virtual reality' has added to this thinking. Reality is what you make it.[12] If you want to believe in God that is fine, but do not ascribe any relevance to him in the natural world. Keep your belief to yourself.

10.3.2 EXTREMISM, TOLERANCE AND THE NEW POLITICS
How does a government which cannot admit to absolutes deal with false fundamentalism within its borders? Such false thinking has not just come from the claim of militant Islam to be doing God's will by perpetrating terrorist acts. There are others (such as some anti-abortionists) who claim the same as they commit atrocities and murder. How does modern society cope with these extremes? With no recourse to absolute truth, the only way is for governments to try and accommodate all in a pluralistic society. So we must become tolerant of all, and regard all faiths as equal. Pragmatism reigns. The tacit assumption is that all faiths are just personal add-ons rather like the clothes we wear, just subject to personal choice. There is little actual connection to modern day reality. The watchword must be *tolerance*. One must only be 'intolerant of intolerance' (a phrase actually used by the UK chief inspector of schools in a prime-time radio broadcast recently[13]). No doubt there must be fairness towards those with whom we disagree, but political leaders have set a course, the logical conclusion of which will be that biblical Christianity cannot be taught at all. By doing this we destroy

foundations which have been the very basis of the freedoms of expression that so many have enjoyed and are so much prized.

From the political confusion, already an ominous consensus is emerging within postmodern society which is creating a culture of what is politically acceptable and what is not—a new order of so called 'tolerance', which in the end denies freedom of thought. Postmodern thinking must lead in the end to tyranny. There has to be an *imposed* politically correct legislation telling people what they are allowed to do and think. Aldous Huxley, the arch humanist of his day, may not have been far from the truth when he described[14] the emptiness of a world where men and women are trapped in a politically correct, mechanized paradise, but one which is meaningless.

10.3.3 POSTMODERNISM AND SCIENCE

Having anchored itself in evolution, postmodernism now redefines science. It does this by subtly relegating experimental evidence. It still plays a part but is no longer fundamental. If the evidence does not fit then the evolutionary framework is adjusted, for evolution is the only way to look at the evidence.[15] Naturalistic science (evolution) simply needs to state that 'This is all there is, this is the *only* game in town'. Remarkably this is essentially what Professor Richard Dawkins said in an interview with Melvyn Bragg and others on the BBC radio programme *In Our Time* broadcast on Thursday 23 September 2004, concerning the origin of life. The whole quote surrounding his statement is given here so that the reader can understand the context (**RD**: Richard Dawkins, **MB**: Melvyn Bragg) and the key phrase relevant to postmodernist thinking is italicized :

RD: 'Life is what you get when the ordinary laws of physics and chemistry which pervade the entire universe find themselves filtered through this remarkable process of natural selection. And natural selection will arise on any planet in the universe wherever you have true heredity, and true heredity means that you have entities which are self-replicating with high accuracy (but not with perfect accuracy) such that you get a population of such replicating entities which are not all identical. Therefore some of them are better at replicating than others. Some of them die away. Others increase in the population of replicators. And that is the starting point for natural selection; because once that starts, then everything else follows which we call life.'

MB: 'But the real question is "How does that start? How does the first replicator replicate? And how do we know that with any degree of accuracy?"'

RD: 'That's exactly what we don't know, and that's exactly what the whole field of origin of life research is about, in my view. It is how do you get from the ordinary laws of chemistry to—'

MB: 'Biology?'

RD: '—Well, to an entity which is self-replicating in this peculiar sense. *And that must have happened. It did happen, because here we are.* If it happened anywhere else in the universe, there will be another kind of life.'

A non scientist but brilliant lawyer who has applied his shrewd mind to the Creation/Evolution debate, has wryly commented on the replacement world-view of atheistic naturalism—[16]

In the beginning were the particles and the impersonal laws of physics.
And the particles somehow became complex living stuff;
And the stuff imagined God; But then discovered evolution.

In denying the existence of a meta-narrative evolution states its own, and in a postmodernistic environment it can get away without ever producing the evidence. That there is no evidence is not an issue, for as long as the high priests of this world-view *believe* there is, who should doubt their sincerity? The final arbiter of truth has shifted away from objective reality, since nothing is ultimately bound by any empirical test.

The consequences of such erroneous thinking do not bode well for the future of science itself as a rigorous discipline. Evolution as a paradigm has stopped biologists/zoologists/geologists following where the evidence leads, since they are forced to view the data from a world-view which at all costs must be shown to be true. Postmodernism downplays the role of evidence. Though technology will always be driven by the need to show that it works (consequently engineering is the last discipline likely to be affected), the power of genuine invention and discovery undergirding good engineering is suppressed.

The conflict between special creation and evolution is therefore not just that between Christianity and humanism, but it is in fact also at the watershed between objective truth and falsehood. Without an appreciation that objective reality is defined outside my own mind (and thus reality is at the whim of my imagination), I can have no real grasp of truth. The nature of science then loses its way as it shifts from firm empiricism (the investigation of the natural world based on experiment) to dogmatic assertions (simply stating unproved theories without evidence). Nancy Pearcey and Charles Thaxton brilliantly discuss these concepts in their book *The Soul of Science*.[17] They argue that the type of thinking we know today as 'scientific', with its emphasis upon experiment and mathematical formulation, arose in our society as a result of a Judeo-Christian world-view. Consequently, when this foundation is eroded, the whole basis of truth and reality is at stake.[18] The Creation/Evolution controversy is no side issue. It lies at the very heart of the battleground of the 21st century. It is part of a culture war that we as Christians must be engaged in, if we are to have any relevance to Western society. Reality itself is thus anchored firmly in the *external revelation* of *who* we are and *why* we are here. Not only scientific investigations, but economic and political thought are rooted in the profound Biblical statement (Genesis 1:27), 'So God created man in His own image; in the image of God he created him; male and female He created them.'

10.3.4 CRUMBLING FOUNDATIONS

In a bid for the equality of all religions and viewpoints, postmodern thinking has opened the way for the evil in man to grow without bounds. And ironically in a bid for freedom, we have not become free, rather we are imprisoned by the new ideology. The Bible states that all men are born with sin deeply rooted within them (Ephesians 2:1). Remove the boundaries and we will reap the consequences. Evil beyond our control becomes an inevitability as more and more safeguards are stripped away. These safeguards were originally in place because men of deep conviction (often finding its origin in Bible belief) raised up powerful institutions of government to restrain the worst in our society. We have to replace the erroneous foundational world-view which says that we are a worthless evolutionary accident, by showing that the Scripture not only has some relevance to the way we live our day-to-day lives, but that Christ has total ownership of the world in which we live, for he made it.

Psalm 11:3 asks, 'If the foundations are destroyed, what can the righteous do?' In answer, three things are stated in that short Psalm (verses 4–5): 'The LORD is in his holy temple, the LORD's throne is in heaven: …The LORD tests the righteous.' The three things to which we must be brought back as a church in the 21st century are that firstly our priority must be the glory of the Lord himself—he is holy and over all. Secondly he is enthroned in Heaven. It is his Universe made for his glory. And thirdly our departure from the Book of books has consequences and he will test the righteous (the true believers). Our compromise must be repented of, first of all within the church. The true foundation of Genesis and a literal six-day Creation needs re-establishing in all our seminaries and pulpits and then on that firm basis we need to reclaim the territory lost. A full-orbed view of Creation and God's ownership of the Universe needs to undergird our evangelism.

10.4 Speaking of truth in a postmodern world—meet the owner

10.4.1 THE EXCLUSIVENESS OF THE GOSPEL OF CHRIST

Once we have understood the change that has now taken place in the thinking of our society, we can more readily consider how to counter this. Clearly we ourselves have to be abundantly clear (i) that there is a true meta-narrative/over-arching world-view—the Biblical one, and (ii) that the individual does matter. Truth is intertwined with personal relationship and faith in Christ. The motive behind many embracing postmodern thought seems to be that in the past the individual has been sacrificed to a large impersonal cause. Two world wars in the last century have made many become cynical about over-arching ideals. So the church today has been right to stress the personal approach in its evangelism. It is important to get to know people in a non-confrontational, informal setting, before speaking to them of Christ. However, sooner or later in evangelism we have to face people with the question 'What is truth and where can it be found?' Clearly with statements such as John 14:6, 'I am the way, the truth, and the life', the personification of Truth all in one person is a striking bridge to a postmodern mind, he or she is immediately confronted with Truth inextricably involved in one individual and our relationship to him. The difficult part for a postmodern mindset is the exclusive statement: '… no-one comes to the Father except through me'. This is where there is a deep divide between Islam and Christianity—both of which speak boldly of a meta-narrative—only in Christianity is there a stress on relationship[19] since God has always from eternity been in relationship within the Trinity. Consequently, whereas in a postmodern world which refuses an over-arching definition of Truth, extreme Islam is forced to the sword and the bullet to stake its claim on territory and rights, Christian believers have a tremendous advantage, since their knowledge of Truth is both personal and based on a clear global timeline and 'meta-narrative' from the Bible. In that sense the gospel is always timeless and never needing to accommodate or change its message in any age. The Bible without alteration stands as the authority in every age.

10.4.2 EXPOSING PRESUPPOSITIONS

Clearly any conversion is a mighty work of the Lord himself, but it is good to have in our minds the following two aspects of approach when speaking today with people who think it is unnecessary to have absolutes. Increasingly we meet such people in open-air or any other form of evangelism. It can come across as apathy. However, though for some it will be sheer materialism which has cooled their interest in spiritual matters, for many it is not—they believe in a different set of 'values' which, they maintain, does not come from 'you insisting on telling me what is true'. That would be an affront to their postmodern 'right' to find their own 'truth' inside themselves. Unseating this deeply held belief requires two propositions. First we must propose that personal knowledge of Truth is possible in the only perfect man, Jesus Christ. Though not all would start with Christ before establishing the basis for Truth, in my experience this is a valid route, since it shows immediately that we are not dealing with something abstract but something experiential and tangible. This is important to people dominated by a touchy-feely mentality. Then we have to confront them with the whole basis of Truth. Left only at the experiential level, we do no better than the pick and mix mentality they are so used to. Such teaching will not unearth the root of atheistic humanism which still underlies the postmodern mindset. The anchor of that root is the belief that there is no Owner, no Creator, and that we are simply here by a cosmic accident. Even science itself may not have the true guide to what is right anymore.

Challenging the evolutionary belief system is vital for that person, since his whole concept of truth is warped by it. Even his whole concept of reality has to be reworked from the basis of the Creator/Owner who has made us and to whom we are answerable. Put any confusing notion that God used a process of evolution in making mankind, and this weakens his whole concept of truth to being something subjective. God then is not the omniscient, all-powerful God of the Bible. Showing the consistency of the message of Genesis (a Perfect Creation followed by the Fall, Death and Suffering, then Redemption) proposes reality defined outside of themselves. That science fits so well needs to be clearly demonstrated—the intricate design of living creatures, the digital programming of DNA at the micro level, the molecular motors of immense complexity, the stratified rocks which consistently speak of world-wide catastrophe, the history of nations which inexorably points back to the Babel dispersion. All these arguments and more are a powerful tool to show to a reasoning mind that there is an altogether consistent and logical reality. They also show that sin and suffering, which we all experience, is rooted in us. Such a person has to realize that he is made as a responsible creature, and thus he is brought to the nub of the issue—repentance. This is so since experience of the Truth in our lives is only possible when we have submitted to Christ himself and his authority, and have received him, John 1:12, 'But as many as received Him, to them He gave the right to become children of God, to those who believe in His name.'

10.4.3 CHRISTIAN GROWTH—THE NEED FOR A VITAL GRASP OF REVEALED TRUTH
Even after conversion there is still the danger of being heavily influenced by the experience-dominated society in which we live. Consequently, after a person has become a Christian from this background, it is important that he realizes that the Bible is Absolute Truth which is independent of the age

in which it is written and ultimately of the writers and people who first wrote it. It is not enough simply to teach the Bible by expounding passages with regard to how the people thought at the time it was written. This reduces truth to experience again and could weaken the foundations of new believers. Truth surpasses time and space. Where this particularly becomes important is when people argue that the Creation account was only put the way it was because that was all Moses at that point could understand. That is an example of an attempt to 'deconstruct' Genesis— and in the process debasing the value of language so that words lose their meaning. We must resist that strongly. Correct exposition, showing that Christ and the Apostles all believed in what Genesis clearly states, gives a deep sense of the power, authority and infallibility of Scripture. Reality and Truth go hand in hand with a high view of Christ and Scripture.

10.5 Origins and the future

Postmodernism with its denial of any over-arching world-view and with no external concept of reality and value, cannot give true meaning to an individual in the present—here and now. This also applies to the future. With a postmodernistic outlook, there is no sense of true purpose, identity or *destiny*. When things go wrong, such people can do no more than encourage counselling (which can no doubt satisfy an immediate need), but they have no fundamental answer to tragedies. However, the Biblical Christian world-view with a firm belief in Creation and the Fall of Man gives an accurate understanding of the past, present and future. It does not have all the answers, but it clearly teaches the goodness of God, the rebellion of man in his natural state, the redemption at God's instigation, and that there is an end in view when all will be brought to account.

All genuine Christians believe in the personal return of Christ. Christians who try to walk with an evolutionary view of Genesis quite often have a difficulty with the Biblical teaching concerning the last things as well. Having insisted on a slow process in Creation, there is a tendency to also take a non-literal view concerning the end. The place where these two areas are both described is in 2 Peter 3. The chapter speaks of the word that brought creation and the word that keeps the heavens and earth 'reserved for fire until the day of judgement' (2 Peter 3:7). Just as there was a world-wide cataclysm (the Flood) that wiped out all men from the earth save Noah and his family, so (2 Peter 3:10) 'the day of the Lord will come as a thief in the night, in which the heavens will pass away with a great noise, and the elements will melt with fervent heat; both the earth and the works that are in it will be burned up.' On 26 December 2004, approximately 280,000[20] were swept to their deaths in countries round the Indian Ocean by the tsunamis following the Richter scale 9 earthquake under the sea off the west coast of Sumatra in Indonesia. Dreadful as it was, this pales into insignificance against the magnitude of the Flood 4,500 years ago. According to Matthew 24:7–8 the current events—famines, pestilences (diseases such as Aids and Malaria which are decimating whole populations in Africa) and earthquakes—'are the beginning of sorrows'. With regard to the future, there is worse in store. Revelation 9:15–18 speaks of immense tragedies, such as one third of the world's population being killed at the sound of the sixth trumpet, leading up to the final return of Christ in judgement announced at the seventh. 2 Peter 3 urges us therefore to take Creation and the Flood seriously, and to look for the kingdom to come with Christ as King. We should always have in our minds, in the very uncertain days in which we live, the practical exhortation of 2 Peter 3:11–12:

Therefore, since all these things will be dissolved, what manner of persons ought you to be in holy conduct and godliness, looking for and hastening the coming of the day of God …?

Peter urges us, by our teaching, evangelism and manner of life, to show that Scripture is entirely trustworthy from Genesis to Revelation. This alone will stop the scoffer and the sceptic in the last days.

Chapter 10 Notes

1 **Lisa Beamer,** *Let's Roll: ordinary people, extraordinary courage* (Wheaton, Illinois: Tyndale, 2002).

2 The terrorist bombings of trains and a bus in London on 7 July 2005, and the earlier terrorists attacks on the trains in Madrid on 11 March 2004, emphasized the worldwide nature of this conflict.

3 **Erroll Hulse,** *Postmodernism* (Chapel Library, Pensacola, Florida, 2003).

4 **Thomas C Oden,** *Two Worlds: The Death of Modernity in America and Russia* (Downers Grove, Illinois: Inter Varsity Press, 1992).

5 By labelling pre-war Europe as 'Christian' it is not being proposed that Biblical Christianity held sway. Rather it is being stated that a loosely Christian outlook was being held in the sense of values essentially emanating from Christian thinking. However, in this period much liberalism had already led to great decay in adherence to these standards.

6 **Erroll Hulse,** op. cit., p. 5.

7 **Francis Schaeffer,** *The God Who Is There* (London: Hodder and Stoughton, 1968).

8 **Francis Schaeffer,** *Whatever Happened to the Human Race?* (Westchester, Illinois: Crossway Books, 1983).

9 Pastor **David Harding** of Milnrow Evangelical Church near Rochdale. He was a policeman earlier in his career, which may explain the illustration!

10 **Erroll Hullse,** op. cit.

11 **Karl Barth,** *The Word of God and the Word of Man,* translated by Douglas Horton (New York: Harper, 1957), p. 80. The relevant quote showing his erroneous view of Scripture and of truth is: 'What we find in the Bible is the world of God's incomprehensible being and acting, which drives us out beyond ourselves, beyond the Bible as the mirror of our own reflection, to the world of God. It is only when we arrive at this point that we encounter the crisis, the awakening to the relativity of all our thoughts and expectations. Only then are we prepared to hear of the last things which make known the truth that is hidden from the wise of the world. At that point only one possibility remains, but that lies beyond all thinking and all things—the possibility: Behold, I make all things new! The affirmation of God, man, and the world given in the New Testament based exclusively upon the possibility of a new order absolutely beyond human thought; and therefore, as prerequisite to that order, there must come a crisis that denies all human thought'. See also the web site: http://www.faithquest.com/modules.php?name=Sections&op=viewarticle&artid=23

12 Reality TV is all part of the paradigm shift in our culture to invent a new truth and reality. It attempts to redefine an artificial reality by, in this case, providing entertainment from watching others struggle when placed in extreme situations. All sense of right and wrong is subsumed to the one goal—survival. I am grateful for discussions with Mark Walsh Jno-Baptiste from Winchester, who is writing on the subject of the media; the modern emphasis on image and not substance in our society is strongly connected with the rise of postmodernism. In a private communication with the author, Mark Walsh Jno-Baptiste (1 March 2005) writes: 'There exists a long-standing tension between the image and the

word, the image always seeks to humiliate the word. Writing is the ideal medium to conceptualize the invisible God. God is intangible, invisible, all-knowing, transcendent, immortal, eternal spirit and most holy. Images, whether paint or pictures are just too inadequate to communicate such truths.'

13 **David Bell,** Chief Inspector of Schools (UK) speaking on 'Faith Schools' on BBC Radio 4's *World at One,* 17 January 2005. The full quote is: 'I would go further and say that an awareness of our common heritage as British citizens, equal under the law, should enable us to assert with confidence that we are intolerant of intolerance, illiberalism and attitudes and values that demean the place of certain sections of our community, be they women or people living in non-traditional relationships'. See web site:
http://news.bbc.co.uk/1/hi/education/4180845.stm

14 **Aldous Huxley,** *Brave new world* (Harmondsworth: Penguin, 1955).

15 **Nancy Pearcey** and **Charles Thaxton,** *The Soul of Science* (Wheaton, Illinois: Crossway Books, 1994).

16 **Phillip E Johnson,** *The Right Questions: Truth, Meaning & Public Debate* (Downers Grove, Illinois: Inter Varsity Press, 2002).

17 **Nancy Pearcey** and **Charles Thaxton,** op. cit., p. 17. In reviewing this book, Dr David Shotton, Lecturer in Cell Biology, Department of Zoology, University of Oxford, gave an excellent summary of the major thesis of this work: "I consider *The Soul of Science* to be a most significant book which, in our scientific age, should be required reading for all thinking Christians and all practising scientists. The authors demonstrate how the flowering of modern science depended upon the Judeo-Christian world-view of the existence of a real physical contingent universe, created and held in being by an omnipotent personal God, with man having the capabilities of rationality and creativity, and thus being capable of investigating it ...'

18 **Nancy Pearcey,** *Total Truth* (Wheaton, Illinois, Crossway Books, 2004).

19 **D Pawson,** *The challenge of Islam to Christians* (London: Hodder and Stoughton, 2003). Though I would not commend every aspect of this book, I was struck forcibly by the facts of the rising tide of Islam in Western society, and the very helpful way that Pawson shows that God always has been in relationship from eternity.

20 Final estimates of the death toll from this tragedy are difficult to make, but conservative figures are well over 200,000. See John Blanchard's booklet *Where is God when things go wrong?* (Darlington: Evangelical Press, 2005), p. 9 for not only a discussion of the facts of this disaster, which is one of the worst in living memory, but also for the stark issue it raises concerning the need to understand suffering from a Biblical perspective.

Genesis and the Saviour

In the previous chapters, it has been the intention to present a call to us all to reconsider our foundations for 'If the foundations are destroyed, what can the righteous do?' (Psalm 11:3).

In the *Independent* newspaper of 27 December 1995, Professor Peter Atkins (Chemistry Professor at Oxford) wrote an article called 'A desolate place to look for answers'. The subheading was 'The meaning of life in our universe is not as perplexing as it is depressing'. The article concluded:

Where did it come from? From nothing. Where is it going? To oblivion. How is it getting there? By purposeless decay into chaos. And the cosmic purpose? I leave you to draw your own conclusion.

What a contrast to the biblical thinking (referred to in section 2.4 'Scientific Endeavour') which drove men of science to great beneficial discoveries, men of state to government by principle, men of compassion to the setting up of hospitals and centres to care for special needs. The thinking of Professor Atkins and others is hardly likely to inspire another Florence Nightingale to go to the Crimea or Mary Slessor to undo the inhumanity of African tribes without the Saviour. Romans 11:36 states 'For of Him and through Him and to Him are all things …'. Here alone is the answer to every fundamental question—Christ and Christ alone. Nothing but Christ-centred thinking and preaching will ever counter the secular humanism which is the dominant religion of the day.[1]

Now, in this concluding chapter it is my intention to leave the reader with a deep respect for Genesis and to show in particular something of the beauty of this book as it reveals pictures of Christ himself. The following are some of the patterns and themes which show the greatness of this book of beginnings.

11.1 The seed of the woman

As referred to in section 4.4 earlier, Genesis 3 contains the first reference to the promised Redeemer. In verse 15, there is a promise of the bruising of the serpent's head by the *seed of the woman*. The prophecy concerns Christ's future coming finally to conquer Satan by the death he would achieve on the cross and his resurrection sealing the end of Satan's hold on men and women who turn to the Saviour. But notice also that Christ is referred to as the 'seed of the woman'. This refers to something supernatural, for the woman has no natural seed. Here then is a prophecy of Christ's birth from a virgin[2] even before that of Isaiah 7:14: 'A virgin shall conceive, and bear a Son'. It is not often realized that Isaiah was repeating the prophecy enunciated 3,300 years before him, that people would know the Messiah had come because he would be born of a virgin. An interesting sequel comes to this prophecy in Genesis 4:1, when immediately after the birth of Cain, Eve exclaims, 'I have acquired a man from the Lord'. The 'from' in the original Hebrew is a translation of 'et' in the Hebrew[3] which is often used as a substantive to emphasize the noun. Thus it is likely Eve was in fact exclaiming concerning the *first ever* birth 'I have acquired a man—*the* Lord'. She longed for an immediate fulfilment of the prophecy of a Redeemer against her enemy, Satan. But not so; Cain proved to be the bringer of sorrow as he 'went out from the presence of the Lord' (Genesis 4:16), having killed his brother Abel. The promise came 4,000 years later in Christ through the line of Seth. Adam and Eve died 'not having received the promises' (Hebrews 11:13)—both this first promise and many others to come, were to be fulfilled in Christ.

In being made the seed of the woman, the Lord showed also his raising the level of womanhood. Though sin came through the woman being deceived (1 Timothy 2:14), 'God sent forth his Son, born of a woman' (Galatians 4:4). Not only was lowly Mary privileged to bear the Saviour into the world, but God showed his inclusion of both man and woman in his redemptive plan. (However, the fact that Mary was sinful is borne out by her bringing the sacrifice for childbirth (Luke 2:24) and her referring to Christ as her Saviour (Luke 1:47). There is no justification for the Mary-worship of Roman Catholicism.)

Lastly, in prophesying that the seed of the woman would bruise the serpent's head, the Lord shows that man is powerless to save himself. No son of Adam can break Satan's power. 1 Corinthians 15:47 states 'the first man was of the earth, made of dust; the second man is the Lord from heaven'. The last Adam (Christ) is our only hope for salvation.

11.2 The first clothing

The first blood to be shed was undoubtedly by God himself when he killed the animals necessary to make the clothes of skin to cover Adam and Eve. Genesis 3:21 states 'Also for Adam and his wife the Lord God made tunics of skin, and clothed them.'

Notice first he killed an animal. Leaves, with which they had first attempted to clothe themselves were not adequate and lasting for them. No covering even from woven silk would have been acceptable. God, in the immediate aftermath of the Fall, demonstrated the vital principle that 'without shedding of blood there is no remission' (Hebrews 9:22). Sin, which had caused the nakedness of man before God, had only one cure—the shedding of blood. This shedding of blood symbolized the blood that Christ would shed upon the cross and which alone covers sin. Psalm 32:1–2 states 'Blessed is he whose transgression is forgiven, whose sin is covered. Blessed is the man to whom the LORD does not impute iniquity …' When Adam and Eve fell, they lost the glorious covering which was probably like the splendour of the transfigured Christ in Matthew 17:2 and the face of Moses which shone after he had been with the Lord in Mount Sinai (Exodus 34:29). Now this has gone, the only covering for sinful man is Christ—the only one who can redeem.

Notice that there is no record that God instructed man to kill the animal. The first mention of sacrifice is important and we note that it is recorded that the Lord God made coats of skin. The coats were fashioned by the Divine Lord himself. They were well-fashioned garments and the word used is the same as that used for the linen garments of the priests. God made the provision for our covering. Salvation is of the Lord (Jonah 2:9) and the covering was beautifully made, speaking itself of Christ's righteousness. To quote Henry Law concerning the skins:4

They were taken from the offerings for sin. Hence each sacrifice presents to the eye of faith the double sign of full salvation. Each altar casts a shadow, not only of the blood, which buys from Hell, but also of the Righteousness, which buys all Heaven.

Truly in the covering described in Genesis 3:21 we see in picture form the greatness of Christ. He is Jehovah Tsidkenu, 'The Lord our Righteousness' (Jeremiah 23:6; 33:16).

11.3 Abel—his offering and his death

Adam and Eve initially had two sons—Cain and Abel. Only the offering of one was accepted—Abel's. Cain's offering was not accepted—why? Because he offered of the fruit of the ground (Genesis 4:3) whereas Abel offered of the firstling of the flock (Genesis 4:4).⁵ In chapter 5, we explained how the first family is a lesson; within each family there is a war of flesh against the spirit. But in this also there are great lessons as to the Saviour and our relationship with him. Abel came with a blood sacrifice and was accepted. Cain brought of the ground which had been cursed and came with a jealous spirit. God requires us to come through the cross. This is the only way of acceptance with him. Genesis 4:7 can be translated '… if you do not well, a sin offering lies at the door'. The word for sin in that verse (Hebrews 'chattath') is the same as that for sin offering. God has provided the means of salvation and we must come his appointed way.

Then the tragedy unfolds and Cain murders Abel. It is ever thus; the flesh, typified by Cain, kills the spirit, typified by Abel. Romans 8:1–14 is the exposition and application to us of what we see in allegory in Genesis 4. Romans 8:7 teaches 'the carnal mind is enmity against God' and verse 14 states 'as many as are led by the Spirit of God, these are the sons of God'. The first person to die, is not only righteous, but dies a martyr's death. Abel's death foreshadows the Martyr who would die on our behalf. Matthew 23:35 refers to the blood of righteous Abel as the first martyr. It is full of significance when God in Genesis 4:10 says, 'The voice of your brother's blood [lit. bloods] cries out to me from the ground …'. The blood cried judgement to God but secondly the blood typified the blood of Christ which not only was spilt on the cursed ground, but according to Hebrews 12:24, 'speaks better things than that of Abel'. What comfort to us that we have the 'voice' of the blood in heaven speaking for those who believe in him, on their behalf. Hebrews 9:24 states 'Christ has … [entered] into heaven itself, now to appear in the presence of God for us.'

Lastly, consider the name of Abel. It means 'vapour, transitoriness'. He typifies the believer who knows that he is not here for long. Indeed this earth now cursed, will not remain for ever, as stated in 1 Corinthians 7:31

The gospel before the Flood

Adam	'Man
Seth	appointed
Enosh	mortal
Kenan	sorrow
Mahalaleel	the God who is to be praised
Jared	shall come down
Enoch	teaching
Methuselah	his death shall bring
Lamech	despairing
Noah	rest'

*'Man [is] appointed mortal sorrow; [but] the
God who is to be praised, shall come down
teaching [that] his death shall bring
[the] despairing rest.'*

Figure 10

'The form of this world is passing away'. Abel, like Abraham, 'looked for a city whose builder and maker is God' (Hebrews 11:10: AV). The true believer has loose associations with this world.

11.4 God's long-suffering before the Flood
It was a blessing to the author to have it pointed out that the names of the patriarchs compose a message which points to the Saviour:[6]

Adam	=	Man
Seth	=	appointed
Enosh[7]	=	mortal
Kenan[8]	=	sorrow
Mahalaleel[9]	=	the God who is to be praised
Jared	=	shall come down
Enoch	=	teaching
Methuselah[10]	=	his death shall bring
Lamech[11]	=	despairing
Noah	=	rest.

(See also figure 10 where these names have been repeated so that the interested reader can readily refer to the information.)

Thus these names put together testify to God's grace in sending his Son—'Man (is) appointed mortal sorrow; (but) the God who is to be praised shall come down teaching (that) his death shall bring (the) despairing rest'.

As the names of the patriarchs unfolded over the centuries, there was a testimony to those early generations of God's purposes in redemption as well as the direct warning of impending judgement from the name of Methuselah. His name on its own spoke, 'When he is dead, it (the Flood) will come', but with the rest of the names, there was a declaration of hope and redemption. God never leaves the world without a testimony and here in these names is a record of God's purposes. We know that the world was full of wickedness and violence in the time leading up to the Flood (Genesis 6:5) and that God's Spirit was actively restraining the corruption of mankind (Genesis 6:3). It is specifically recorded this was 120 years before the Flood, so we can find encouragement that God is *active* in the very corrupt world we live in now which is prefigured in Noah's days. 1 Peter 3:20 teaches God was long-suffering while the ark was being prepared. He will judge sin, but he is 'slow to anger, abundant in kindness' (Nehemiah 9:17).

11.5 The testimony of Enoch

We also know that in the generations leading up to Noah, there was at least one very godly leader—Enoch. We read of him in Genesis 5:22, Hebrews 11:5 and Jude 14. He towers above others of his day and we know: (i) he was the seventh from Adam (Jude 14). This is not a chance comment that Jude records here. *All* Scripture is significant. Seven is God's perfect number (the seven-branched candlestick (Exodus 37:17–25, seven-fold sprinkling of blood and washing), Leviticus 14:7; 16:14–15, Numbers 19:4; 2 Kings 5:10, 14) so it fits that the seventh from Adam was a godly man; (ii) he walked with God. All the others in Genesis 5 are described as those who 'lived after he begot …', but with Enoch (verse 22), 'After he begot Methuselah, Enoch *walked with God*'; (iii) not only did he walk with God but he pleased God. (Hebrews 11.5). In all these matters he is a remarkable picture of Christ. His life of communion with God was pleasing because (iv) he walked *by faith* (Hebrews 11:5a). Hebrews 11:6 clearly states that '… without faith it is impossible to please HIM [God]'. Faith is trust, leaning upon God and what he has said. Hebrews 11:1–2 links our confidence in the future with our belief in creation in the past. We will not show the trust which pleases God—the walk of faith of Enoch—if we deny God's Word concerning creation. The power of the Spirit-filled life is always linked with a belief in God's Word (compare the effect of the Spirit indwelling the believer in Ephesians 5:18–19 and the effect of the word of Christ indwelling the believer in Colossians 3:16); (v) Enoch was also a prophet. In Jude 14, he prophesies of the second coming of Christ, for Enoch prefigures him. The subject of the second coming is often linked in Scripture with the early judgement of the Flood (Matthew 24:36–39, 2 Peter 3:5–10). Here is a vital principle. Evolution states the present is the key to the past. Scripture teaches the reverse. The past (which is revealed in the Bible and in Genesis in particular) is the key to the present and furthermore to the future also. In

Christ we are complete for he is our Priest, King and *Prophet*. Lastly (vi) Enoch was translated (Genesis 5:24; Hebrews 11:5). He was taken up supernaturally, just as Christ ascended into heaven (Acts 1:9–11). Enoch prefigures also the glorious day when all believers will be changed and translated to heaven for ever (1 Corinthians 15:51–57).

11.6 Noah and the ark

We have already seen how vital it is to have a clear view of the historical accuracy of Genesis (see chapter 3, Genesis and History) and the revolution in our world-view this gives when we suddenly see the rocks and the world around us in a different light. But the wonder of Genesis, is that not only does it give a firm, solid foundation to thinking in every sphere of life, but it holds treasures and pictures of the way of salvation. Probably the clearest of all these is concerning the Flood. The Lord Jesus drew the clear parallel himself. '… as the days of Noah were, so also will the coming of the Son of Man be' (Matthew 24:37).

First, the Ark is a clear picture of Christ himself. It probably took over a century to build, from the time when Noah was about 500 years old to his 600th year. This comes from Genesis 5:32–6:6 and Genesis 7:11. The reference to 'his days [i.e. man's days] shall be one hundred and twenty years' in Genesis 6:3, is taken by most scholars to refer to the time left till the Flood, and thus the beginning of God's plans for the ark which are expressed in Genesis 7:14 ff. It was 150 metres (450 feet) long, 25 metres (75 feet) wide and 15 metres (45 feet) high (Genesis 6:15 with 1 cubit approximately 0.5 metres or 1.5 feet). There was ample room for all the animals (no doubt some of the dinosaurs, although very large as adults, were taken on board as very young animals). Herein though lies a great encouragement to us all. There is ample room for all. None need be left behind. Christ has room for everybody many times over. The Scriptures teach the command to *all* men to turn to him. '[God] commands all men everywhere to repent' (Acts 17:30), 'Look to me, and be saved, all you the ends of the earth!' (Isaiah 45:22). There is even a command to the servants of the gospel to press them to come in. I am always encouraged in evangelism by the parable of the Great Supper (Luke 14:15–24). The Lord says to the servant to bring in the poor, maimed, halt and the blind to the feast, and the servant says (verse 22), 'Master, it is done …

and *still there is room*'. Then the Lord says to his servant (verse 23), 'Go out into the highways and hedges and *compel* them to come in, that my house may be filled'. It is undoubtedly true that none can ever come unless the Lord touches men and women to turn from sin; thus John 6:44, 'No man can come to Me, unless the Father who sent me draws him'. Nevertheless, we should plead with, pray for and long for others to come. Paul spoke of being made all things to all men 'that I might by all means save some' (1 Corinthians 9:22), and with scoffers all around, Noah urged men to enter the ark (1 Peter 3:20). He is called a preacher of righteousness (2 Peter 2:5). If, as seems likely, there were many workers which he employed, there would also be a deep concern to see them saved as well. The Lord in this time was long-suffering to all men (see again 1 Peter 3:20) and the comparison drawn by the Apostle Peter to our own day from the days of the Flood, teaches that he is similarly today 'not willing that any should perish but that all should come to repentance' (2 Peter 3:9). The size and capacity of the ark shows God's immense love and grace that should compel us to reach out to a lost world.

Notice also that there was a week when all was complete. The mighty ark was finished and a sceptical crowd looked on. The hammers had now stopped, the noise of saws had ceased, the rigs were removed. The stage was set; Noah and his family were called in with the animals, but God gave a week's grace (Genesis 7:4) before finally the door was shut by the Lord himself (Genesis 7:16). A solemn witness to all. Maybe some of the workers had planned to come on board and dithered, with family pulling them away from what they regarded as 'Noah's Folly'. The Lord sees the folly of a world today running to imminent judgement and Hell and before Christ comes again, like in the days of Noah, men will mock and scoff. Christ may well come soon but Grace is never in a hurry to bring the end.

The Ark was covered 'inside and outside with pitch' (Genesis 6:14). God sealed the final occupants from the storms and enormous upheaval outside with pitch. What was this? The root of the Hebrew noun translated as 'pitch' may be 'koper' which means 'ransom, atonement'. The verb in the same verse is linked to 'kapar' which also means 'to make an atonement'.[12] Was the pitch made using blood? We do not know, but the verb indicates that blood may have been used in some way. The picture of security in Christ crucified is evident. Those within God's family are ever reminded of the cross, but separated from the world by the same cross. Paul spoke of 'the cross of our Lord Jesus Christ, by whom the world has been crucified to me, and I to the world' (Galatians 6:14).

11.7 Abraham and Isaac

There are many pictures in the lives of these two people of the Saviour. Suffice to consider just one of the most striking—Genesis 22. Here Abraham is commanded to go to Mount Moriah and offer his own son as a sacrifice. The type of Christ is remarkable, for it shows:

i. The Father and Son both planned redemption. Genesis 22:8 'the two of them went together'. Abraham and Isaac went together to the place of sacrifice, typifying perfect agreement in the Deity concerning the way of Calvary to redeem us.

ii. Christ carried his cross. Genesis 22:6 ' So Abraham took the wood of the burnt offering and laid it on Isaac his son'. The Lord, bleeding from the scourging of the soldiers, then carried his cross to Golgotha (John 19:17).

iii. 'Where is the lamb?' Genesis 22:7–8 records this question and the answer, 'God will provide for Himself the lamb'. This is the first mention of the lamb in Scripture, and thus it is highly significant. At this point Abraham's faith was being tested. He was prepared even to go to the extent of sacrificing Isaac, for Hebrews 11:19 records that Abraham believed 'God was able to raise him up, even from the dead, from which he also received him in a figurative sense'. But as they went to Moriah, he was confident God would provide a lamb and in stating this, there was a prophesy of Christ. John the Baptist would eventually say, 'Behold! The Lamb of God, who takes away the sin of the world!' (John 1:29).

Notice also that Mount Moriah, where Abraham erected the altar, was the future site of the temple and the city of Jerusalem, which would surround it. There, in that same city, 2,000 years later, Christ would redeem his people. The significance of this altar is borne out by Abraham's calling it 'Jehovah Jireh', 'God will provide'.

11.8 Joseph

We turn to Joseph whose life and testimony have a marked effect not only on Jacob and Joseph's brothers, but also on the Gentile nations. There is no record of Joseph's failure (as there is with other patriarchs). There seems to be every reason for this, since of all the pictures of Christ, Joseph is one of the brightest. Below we list the likenesses:

	Joseph	Christ
Beloved of his father	Genesis 37:3	Matthew 3:17
Sold into the hands of his enemies	20 pieces of silver	30 pieces of silver
	Genesis 37:28	Matthew 27:3
In favour with God and man	Genesis 39:2, 21–23	Luke 2:52
His garment taken	Genesis 39:12–13	John 19:23–24
Falsely accused	Genesis 39:7–20, 40:15	Mark 14:56
Numbered with the transgressors	Genesis 39:20	Isaiah 53:8–12
		Matthew 27:38
Left in his hour of need	Genesis 40:14,23	Psalm 105:18–19
		Matthew 27:46
Two companions -	Genesis 40:1,4	Luke 23:39–43
One saved, the other lost	Genesis 40:20–23	
	Genesis 41:13	
Restored / Resurrected	Genesis 45:28	Luke 24:6,7
Aged thirty at start of public ministry	Genesis 41:46	Luke 3:23
Repentant forgiven	Genesis 50:15–21	Matthew 9:13
Fellowship with one's brother is required		
in order to be accepted	Genesis 42:34, 43:3	Matthew 5:23–24
Bread provided	Genesis 41:55–56;	John 6:35–51
	Genesis 45:23	

Godly Joseph by faith 'gave instructions concerning his bones' (Hebrews 11:22; Genesis 50:25) because he saw in the future, Israel's deliverance from Egypt when 'God will surely visit you'. Likewise, God will visit us and Christ will return 'a second time, apart from sin, for salvation' (Hebrews 9:28).

11.9 The foundation of all

Christ is the key to all things both inanimate and living for he upholds all things 'by the word of His power' (Hebrews 1:3). Thus Genesis is not just vital to the scientific study of origins but to every area of human endeavour and existence. All theology finds its roots in Genesis. The matters of sin, the Fall, death and redemption by blood all begin there.[13] The study of people (Anthropology) can only be properly understood by grasping the principle surrounding God's dealings with nations and the dispersal at Babel (Genesis 11) because of great wickedness rising up again under the leadership of Nimrod. God is *active* in the peoples of the world restraining sin by government (Romans 13). Even corrupt regimes are under his power and the nations are as a drop in the bucket (Isaiah 40:15). In Isaiah God refers to the Gentile peoples as the 'isles of the Gentiles' (Isaiah 51:5; 60:9; 66:19 AV), but all his purposes flow from the principles of Genesis 10 and many of these nations (such as Babylon) are referred to in prophecies of events to come (Ezekiel and Revelation). Let the reader have a high view of Scripture in this regard. God controls and rules all. He is the Sovereign God of the nations. As a consequence, the law of God is important for the governing of society. We have shown that all such laws flow from Genesis—the rules of marriage, clothing, the Sabbath, and the laws against hatred and murder all begin in this vital book. Society itself is rooted in Genesis, the book of beginnings.

11.10 Unto him

We end this short anthology of pictures of Christ in Genesis by a telling verse at the end of Jacob's life (Genesis 49:10) 'The sceptre shall not depart from Judah, nor a law-giver from between his feet, until Shiloh comes. And to Him shall be the obedience of the people'. The central theme of Scripture from Genesis to Revelation is Christ. Shiloh here is not the northern city in Ephraim's territory but is linked in a prophetic manner to Shiloah (Isaiah 8:6; Nehemiah 3:15 and in Greek 'Siloam', John 9:7) where there was a fountain and pool in Jerusalem from which flowed a little brook past Mount Zion. God's people are rebuked in Isaiah 8:6 for refusing 'the waters of Shiloah' and in John 9, the man born blind is told to wash in the same pool, where we are told it means 'Sent'. Shiloh also means 'his son' and 'prince of peace'.[14]

The prophecy in Genesis 49:10 refers to the one sent, his Son who will come. Christ, the Lion of Judah (Revelation 5:5) is the hope of all, the Desire of Nations (Haggai 2:7). So men must look to Christ. He alone is our Redeemer and Peace-maker. Moses writes again in the same vein in

Deuteronomy 18:15, 'The LORD your God will raise up for you a Prophet like me from your midst, from your brethren. *Him* you shall hear'. Jesus says in John 12:32, 'I, if I be lifted up will draw all peoples *to Myself*'. Christ attracts the lost to him. He came to seek and to save that which was lost (Luke 19:10). He himself and his cross are central to the message of all Scripture. The day will come when Christ returns,

And every creature which is in heaven and on the earth and under the earth, and such as are in the sea, and all that are in them ... (will say) ... Blessing, and honour, and glory, and power, be to Him who sits on the throne, and to the Lamb for ever and ever (Revelation 5:13).

And why is this? Because '... You created all things, and by Your will they exist and were created' (Revelation 4:11) and '(you) have redeemed us to God by Your blood out of every tribe and tongue and people and nation' (Revelation 5:9).

The message of Genesis is, 'In the beginning God created', and that same message is deeply relevant to us today, 'For of *Him* and through *Him* and to *Him*, are all things: to whom be glory for ever. Amen' (Romans 11:36).

Chapter 11 notes

1 See for instance, the very informative article by **Roger Carswell** which shows the enormous effect that secular humanism as a religious philosophy has had on Europe. *Europe—a huge mission field* by **Roger Carswell** (Open Prayer letter January-March 1997).

2 **H Law,** *Christ is All—The Gospel in Genesis* (London: Banner of Truth, 1961), p. 32. Originally published 1854, this excellent study by the one time Dean of Gloucester gives greatinsight into the pictures of Christ in Genesis. Many of the headings and thoughts in this chapter originate with Law's exposition.

3 **R Laird Harris, Gleason L Archer, Jr** and **Bruce L Waltke,** *Theological Word book of the Old Testament* (Chicago: Moody Bible Institute, 1980), Vol. 1, p. 83.

4 **H Law,** op. cit., p. 48.

5 Some have argued that Cain was **not** in error to bring the fruit of the ground, on the basis that the sacrificial laws in Leviticus allowed grain offerings. Leviticus chapters 2,6,9,14 all mention such offerings. However, grain is never used as a sin offering. It is associated with the

main burnt offering of a lamb (e.g.: the cleansed leper of Leviticus 14:9–32), but not as a separate sin offering. The principle is stated clearly in Hebrews 9:22 'without shedding of blood there is no remission'. The sin offering must be a blood sacrifice.

6 For this point, I am indebted to **Dr David Rosevear** of the Creation Science Movement who published this in the March 1995 edition of the monthly *CSM journal*(CSM Journal 8 (9) p.1.) One is not arguing here for a literal Hebrew sentence, but a progression of thought from Man through Sin and the Fall into sorrow, then hope from God Himself in the promised Redeemer to come, and who is typified by Noah.

7 Sometimes written as *Enos*.

8 Sometimes written as *Cainan* and thus the meaning has been linked to Cain, 'acquired', but there is some evidence it is linked to the word 'qin' meaning 'lament, sorrow'.

9 **Mahalalel** means 'praise of God' or 'he who praises God'. **R Laird Harris, Gleason L Archer, Jr** and **Bruce L Waltke,** *Theological Wordbookof the Old Testament* (Chicago: Moody Press, 1980), Vol. 1, pp. 217–218, have the literal translation 'the God who is to be praised.'

10 **Methuselah** is not regarded by all scholars to mean 'his death shall bring' because the Masoretic pointing gives an 'e' to the 'Meth' part of his name, which does not translate then as 'death'. However since the Masoretic pointing is later than the original, there is a case for 'muth' (death), particularly as Methuselah does indeed die just before the Flood.

11 **Lamech** is usually translated *overthrower*. As such his name typifies man in his natural rebellious state. The word in its root form is linked to the word *despair*. This Lamech is of course different to the bragging Lamech of Genesis 4:19–24 in Cain's line considered earlier in chapter 5. We do not know the type of life Lamech, the father of Noah, lived. It may be that like his counterpart in Genesis 4, he rejected God's way despite, in this case, godly ancestry.

12 This perceptive observation came from a most profitable conversation with **Mr Philip Utley,** pastor of Bethel Evangelical Church, Ripon, Yorkshire.

13 The theme of redemption by blood runs right through Genesis: God sacrificing an animal to clothe Adam and Eve (Genesis 3), Abel offering a blood sacrifice (Genesis 4), Abraham offering a ram in place of Isaac (Genesis 22), the altars of the patriachs Abraham (Bethel Genesis 12:8—and others), Isaac (Beersheba Genesis 26:25) and Jacob (Bethel again Genesis 35:7), Zarah and Pharez (Genesis 38:27–30) (Scarlet thread typifying redemption by the greater descendant of Pharez—Christ). These are some examples.

14 **H Law,** op. cit., pp. 176, 179, 180.

Bibliography

The following books are recommended for further reading:

JK Anderson, and **HG Coffin,** *Fossils in Focus,* Christian Free University Curriculum (Grand Rapids, Michigan: Zondervan, 1977). (A useful guide, although written from an evolutionary perspective.)

EH Andrews, W Gitt, and **WJ Ouweneel** (eds), *Concepts in Creationism* (Darlington: Evangelical Press, 1986.

J Ashton (ed.) *In six days: why 50 Scientists choose to believe in Creation* (London: New Holland, 1999).

MJ Behe, *Darwin's Black Box—The Biochemical challenge to Evolution* (New York: Free Press, Simon and Schuster). (Behe is no creationist, but brilliantly answers Dawkins' anti-design stance).

Beka Educational Text Books (invaluable for reference). (Beka Book Publications, Pensacola Christian College, Box 18000, Pensacola,Florida 32523):
History of the World in Christian Perspective
    Vol. I—*Since the Beginning*
    Vol. II—*The Modern Age*
Science: Order and Reality
Science: Matter and Motion
Science of the Physical Creation
Chemistry: Precision and Design
Biology: God's Living Creation
Physics: Foundation Science
(All available through Tabernacle Bookshop, Metropolitan Tabernacle, Elephant & Castle, London SE1 6SD.)

Stuart Burgess, *Hallmarks of Design—Design in the natural world* (Epsom: Day One Publications, 2000).

Bibliography

DC Burke (ed.), *Creation and Evolution,* Book of series *When Christians disagree,* series editor, **OR Barclay** (Leicester: InterVarsity Press, 1986). Contributions from **EH Andrews, OR Barclay, RJ Berry, DC Burke, AG Fraser, DT Gish, DG Jones, V Wright.**

W Cooper, *After the Flood: The early post-flood history of Europe traced back to Noah* (Chichester: New Wine Press, 1995).

R Dawkins, *The Selfish Gene* (2nd ed., Oxford: Oxford University Press, 1989).

R Dawkins, *The Blind Watchmaker* (London: Penguin, 1991).

R Dawkins, *Climbing Mount Improbable* (London: Viking, 1996).

(The above three books by Dawkins are extreme in their anti-design viewpoint, holding to a fiercely evolutionary approach. Again, the religious, philosophical aspect of the viewpoint adopted is very evident.)

M Denton, *Evolution: A Theory in Crisis—New developments in Science are challenging orthodox Darwinism* (Bethesda, MD: Adler and Adler, 1985). (A very scholarly book. Denton is not a creationist, but shows from the complex engineering of birds and animals that this cannot adequately be explained by evolution).

H Enoch, *Evolution or Creation* (London: Evangelical Press, 1967).

FA Everest, *Dust or Destiny* (Chicago: Moody Press, 1949). (This book was used in film/video of the same name.)

K Ham, *The Lie: Evolution* (Colorado Springs: Master Books, 1988).

DR Humphreys, *Starlight and Time: Solving the puzzle of distant starlight in a young universe* (Colorado Springs: Master Books, 1994).

M Lambert, *Fossils: A Kingfisher guide* (London: Ward Lock, 1978).

JE Lovelock, *Gaia—a new look at life on Earth* (Oxford: Oxford University Press, 1987). (Heavily evolutionary in bias, Professor Lovelock FRS, gives an insight into the religious nature of the Creation-Evolution debate.)

ML Lubenow, *Bones of Contention: A Creationist Assessment of Human Fossils* (Grand Rapids: Baker Book House, 1994). A scholarly examination of human fossils showing that there is much evidence against the supposed ape-connection proposed by the Leakey family and others.

R Milton, *The Facts of Life—Shattering the Myth of Darwinism* (London: 4th Estate, 1992).

AJ Monty White, *What about Origins* (Kingsteignton, Newton Abbot: Dunestone, 1978).

HM Morris, and **GE Parker,** *What is Creation Science?* (Colorado Springs: Master Books, 1987).

HM Morris, *The Genesis Record* (Grand Rapids: Baker Book House).

HM Morris, *Science and the Bible* (Amersham-on-the-Hill: Scripture Press, 1988).

JD Morris, *The Young Earth* (Colorado Springs: Master Books, 1994).

MA Noll, *Scandal of the Evangelical Mind* (Grand Rapids: Eerdmans/IVP, 1994). (This book gives a good summary of the historical perspective to the evangelical/liberal debate. His non-creationist stance shows that creation is now a major issue on both sides of the Atlantic.)

D Rosevear, *Creation Science—confirming that the Bible is right* (Chichester: New Wine Press, 1991).

H Ross, *Creation and Time* (Colorado Springs: Navpress, 1994) (the main proponent of the Progressive Creation view which tries to join evolution and Genesis. The book below by **Van Bebber** and **Taylor** (1995) clearly answers this.)

LD Sutherland, (1988), *Darwins' Enigma: Fossils and other Problems,* Master Books, California.

MV Van Bebber, and **PS Taylor,** *Creation and Time—a report on the Progressive Creationist book by Hugh Ross* (Mesa, Arizona: Eden Communications, 1995, 2nd edition) (a carefully written answer to the Progressive Creationist position of Hugh Ross).

Bibliography

David CC Watson, *The Great Brain Robbery—Studies in Evolution* (Worthing: Henry Walter, 1975).

David CC Watson, *Myths and Miracles—A new approach to Genesis 1–11* (Worthing: Henry Walter, 1976).

JC Whitcomb and **HM Morris,** *The Genesis Flood—The Biblical Record and its Scientific Implications* (London: Evangelical Press, 1969, 1st British Edition).

JC Whitcomb, *The Early Earth* (London: Evangelical Press, 1972),

JC Whitcomb, *The World that Perished* (London: Evangelical Press, 1973).

C Wieland, *Stones and Bones* (Acacia Ridge, Queensland: Creation Science Foundation, 1994).

AE Wilder-Smith, *The Natural Sciences know nothing of evolution* (Colorado Springs: Master Books, 1981).

Biblical Creation Society, PO Box 22, Rugby, Warwickshire CV22 7SY. Magazine *Origins* produced 4 times a year.

Answers in Genesis (UK). PO Box 5262, Leicester, Leics., LE23 XU, UK. Head Office in Brisbane, Australia. Publishes *Creation Magazine* four times a year and *Creation Technical Journal* three times a year.

Creation Science Movement, 50 Brecon Avenue, Cosham, Portsmouth PO6 2AW. Newsletter produced monthly with regular articles.

Creation Resources Trust, Mead Farm, Downhead, West Camel, Yeovil, Somerset BA22 7RQ, UK. Regular children's broadsheet, 'Our World' Student's broadsheet, 'Original View' and newsletter approx. 4 times a year.

M uch of the content of these appendices appears in the following books to which the author is much indebted (see Bibliography for full references):

DC Burke, *Creation and Evolution.*

M Denton, *Evolution: A Theory in Crisis.*

DR Humphreys, *Starlight and Time.*

ML Lubenow, *Bones of Contention.*

R Milton, *The Facts of Life.*

AJ Monty White, *What about Origins?*

JD Morris, *The Young Earth.*

The **Beka Educational Text Books** of Pensacola Christian College, Florida.

JC Whitcomb, and HM Morris, *The Genesis Flood.*

AE Wilder-Smith, *The natural sciences know nothing of evolution.*

Fundamental scientific evidence concerning order and design

In this appendix we discuss in more detail the concept of order and design, firstly from the point of view of the basic laws of thermodynamics and then concerning the detailed structure of the cell from which all living creatures are made. In the opinion of the author, the arguments concerning order and design are (and always have been) the most unassailable by the evolutionist. Richard Dawkins in his books, *The Blind Watchmaker*[1] and *The Selfish Gene*,[2] has tried to remove the teleological argument (the argument that design implies a designer) put forward so succinctly by Paley[3] over 150 years ago. Although the ideas of Dawkins seem clever, there is nothing new in terms of mechanism in his works. There is no new discovery as to how the complicated living organisms were supposedly made by chance. Dawkins' approach to Paley's arguments is to make dogmatic assertions that God must be out of the picture. Thus he states:

The only thing he [Paley] got wrong—admittedly quite a big thing!—was the explanation itself. He gave the traditional religious answer to the riddle, but he articulated it more clearly and convincingly than anybody had before. The true explanation is utterly different, and it had to wait for one of the most revolutionary thinkers of all time, Charles Darwin.[4]

He then goes on to state what is 'the true explanation':

Natural selection, the blind, unconscious, automatic process which Darwin discovered, and which we now know is the explanation for the existence and apparently purposeful form of all life, has no purpose in mind. It has no mind and no mind's eye. It does not plan for the future. It has no vision, no foresight, no sight at all. If it can be said to play the role of watchmaker in nature, it is the blind watchmaker.[5]

As Poole[6] brings out, there is a playing with words here. A creating God is denied, but the goddess of creating chance and natural selection is affirmed!

In the 1991 Royal Institution Christmas lecture, *The Ultraviolet Garden* concerning bees and their role in plant pollination, Richard Dawkins states that natural selection 'designed' plants to be pollinated this way. The facts demonstrated in that lecture shouted planned, purposeful design as he went on to show a bucket orchid being pollinated by a bee; the bee is attracted by the pool of nectar, but then falls into the nectar bucket trap with only one exit near the pollen sac. The bee thus pollinates this species of orchid as it flies to other bucket orchids. The tortuous arguments using the goddess of chance sounded more like a visit to Alice in Wonderland than the straightforward explanation that intricate design has been put there from the beginning.[7] As Dawkins rightly states, chance has no purpose, so how can one say natural selection *designed* anything? Such reasoning is not science. There are no new ideas, no new model to fit the facts, no better explanation than Paley had ever given! To appeal to chance is effectively to say, that there is no 'mechanism' in living organisms, which evidently is not true. One is tempted to say that the observer appealing to chance may himself be blind, rather than natural selection.

To give credit where it is due, Dawkins was right when he stated:

The kind of explanation we come up with must not contradict the laws of physics. Indeed it will make use of the laws of physics, and nothing more than the laws of physics.[8]

So it is from those very laws concerning order that we can make powerful arguments against the possibility of chance producing both the material world and living organisms. I would urge all my readers to read Dawkins chapter 1 'Exploring the very improbable' in *The Blind Watchmaker*,[9] then summarize what new argument he has invoked to change amoeba to men, other than waving the magic wand of chance mutations and natural selection. Most reasonable, thinking people would agree there is no new argument. It is ironic that in his brilliant description of the human eye[10] he virtually torpedoes his own argument since the complexity of such a device shouts 'design!' If I found a camera on a desert island, would I seriously be led to believe that natural forces had gradually built such a sophisticated marvel? How then can one state any differently concerning the human eye which has a lens which changes in size to accommodate seeing near and far objects, has an iris which automatically changes size to accommodate changes in the amount of light available and has 125 million photocells in the retina to translate live pictures along nerve lines to the brain? I think it would be better to agree with Darwin on this point who said:

To suppose that the eye with all its inimitable contrivances for adjusting the focus to different distances, for admitting different amounts of light, and for the correction of spherical and chromatic aberration, could have been formed by natural selection, seems, I freely confess, absurd in the highest degree.[11]

Order and the second law of thermodynamics

There is a fundamental law in the universe to which there is no known exception. That is, that when there is any work done due to energy conversion, there is *always* some dissipation of useful energy. In purely thermodynamic terms, this means that, for a closed system, the measure of energy no longer available for useful work is increasing. This is called entropy. Thus in a closed system, the overall entropy is increasing. However, the law applies not only to the area of mechanics and engines. It applies to any system, since entropy is effectively a measure of the disorder in that system. In overall terms, disorder increases, cars rust and machines wear out. No spontaneous reversal of this process has ever been observed for a closed system. If one lifts the restriction of a closed system, so that energy can come in from the outside, the evolutionist is no better off. Energy (such as from the Sun) may increase the local temperature difference (and thus increase the *potential* for useful work that can be done locally), but without a *machine* (that is, a device which is made or programmed to use the available energy), there is still no possibility of the self-organisation of matter. There has to be previously written information or order (this is termed 'teleonomy' in the text books) for passive, non-living chemicals to respond and become active. Thus the following summary statement applies to all known systems:

Energy + Information → Locally reduced entropy
(or teleonomy)   (Increase of order)
with the corollary:
Energy on its own ⇏ Decrease in Entropy

(The symbol ⇏ means 'does not imply that'). Another way of saying the same thing is that energy must be *directed* to be of any use. Water coming from a dammed river, even in a controlled way (Energy) is of no use unless it is guided to a previously made turbine (teleonomy) which then generates electricity. Similarly heat and light from the sun are no use without solar cells to convert the energy into a useful form. Electricity itself, though a controlled form of energy, is of no use to boil water without a kettle (information/machine/know-how) which has been previously designed to transfer electric power to heat the water.

For living systems, this law still applies. That which is dead (such as a stick or leaf from a tree) has no information or teleonomy within it to convert the sun's energy to useful work. Indeed it will simply heat up and entropy will increase. However, a living plant has information within such that the energy from the sun is absorbed (along with carbon dioxide and water) by its leaves through photosynthesis. The chlorophyll of the leaf acts as a catalyst to the biochemical reaction:

Carbon Dioxide	Water	Sunlight		Sugar	Oxygen
$6CO_2$	+ $6H_2O$	+Radiant Energy With chlorophyll catalyst	→	$C_6H_{12}O_6$	+ $6O_2$

Effectively the plant is a living machine coded to absorb sunlight and carbon dioxide/water, then to grow and produce oxygen and sugar. The entropy locally is lower because of the information acting with the energy absorbed. Indeed, the plant sustains a slightly lower temperature than the dead stick or fallen leaf due to the very fact that it is alive and that, locally, entropy (disorder) is decreased.

The theories propounded for self organisation are largely due to

Manfred Eigen [12,13] and a critical review of this subject is given in the work of Wilder-Smith.[14] To quote Wilder-Smith, p. 59,

raw matter within a closed system, plus a teleonomic machine, might yield auto-organisation derived from endogenous [that which comes from within] energy. Raw matter within an open system, plus a teleonomic machine may yield auto-organisation derived from endogenous and/or exogenous [that which comes from without] energy. *Within both open and closed systems, however, a mechanism (machine, teleonomy, know-how) is essential if any auto-organisation is to result.*

One evolutionist at least acknowledged the seriousness of this problem. After arguing that auto-organisation by random processes[15] may be possible in non-equilibrium systems (and see the later work[16]) Prigogine states:

Unfortunately, this (self-organisation) principle cannot explain the formation of biological structures. The probability that at ordinary temperatures a macroscopic number of molecules is assembled to give rise to the highly ordered structures and to the co-ordinated functions characterising living organisms is vanishingly small.

More detailed arguments concerning the whole concept of meaning and order at the fundamental level in the biological world are to be found in the excellent books by ReMine[17] and Gitt.[18]

Entropy, information and the living world

The major obstacle to evolutionary theories as to origins is that information cannot be defined in terms of physics and chemistry. The ideas of a book are not the same as the paper and ink which constitute the book. Indeed those same words and thoughts can be transmitted through an entirely different media (such as a computer floppy disk or a tape recorder). The chemicals do not *define* the message they carry. Meaning *cannot* spontaneously arise since meaning presupposes intelligence and understanding. One of the greatest discoveries was that of DNA (deoxyribonucleic acid) by Francis H Crick (UK) and James D Watson (USA) in 1953 (see Figure A1 above). This molecule was found to be the universal storage medium of natural systems. A length of DNA is formed in such a way that two deoxyribose sugar-phosphate strands together form a double helix 2nm (10^{-9}m) in diameter with a pitch of 3·4nm. Between these two strands are hydrogen bridges across which four types of nucleotides are placed: adenine (A), thymine (T), cytosine (C) and guanine (G). Effectively these four nucleotides are the chemical alphabet for writing 'words' on the chemical 'paper' which is the two sugar-phosphate strands. The helix enables a 3–dimensional storage of information formed by the patterns of the chemical letters used. The DNA string is like a sequence of dots and dashes in a coded message. The sequence of nucleotides in the DNA is a code which determines the organisation of amino acids in proteins. For a particular amino acid, the order of three adjacent nucleotides determines which amino acid it is. There are 64 ways of arranging the four different nucleotides above (A,T,C,G) in groups of three so that this more than covers the twenty amino acids found in proteins.

DNA molecules range from a few thousand to many millions of nucleotide pairs on the double strand of the helix. The length of DNA will vary according to the information it is carrying. In every cell of a living creature there are a certain number of lengths of DNA and proteins called chromosomes in the nucleus. For human being cells there are 46 chromosomes composed of 23 pairs. The chromosomes involve a combination of DNA strands and protein molecules which form the material chromatin at the nucleus of each cell. One or more molecules of protein and a strand of DNA will compose a 'gene' of information concerning a characteristic of the living creature. Sometimes two genes are required to express a characteristic (for instance, two genes are used to code for the eye colour in humans). Thus each of the 46 chromosomes in human being cells carry millions of genes representing all the information concerning the individual. It is a remarkable fact that *every cell* in a living creature carries *all* the information about the individual.

Ever since the DNA structure was first discovered by Watson and Crick in 1953, this area of science has become one of the fastest growing areas in biology and chemistry. The DNA from just *one* chromosome (out of 46) in *one* of the billions of cells in our bodies would stretch to about sixteen inches long. It has been estimated that if the coded information carried by the DNA were spelled out in English sentences, there would be 600,000 pages of print

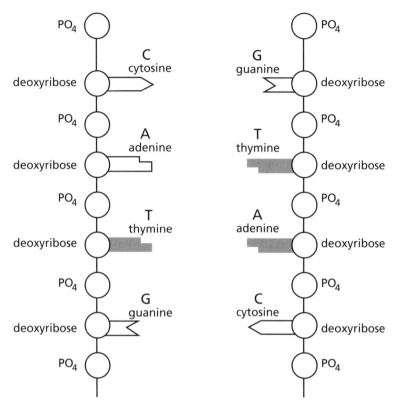

Fig. A1: The double strands of the deoxyribonucleic acid (DNA) molecule. Schematic section showing four bases (**A** = adenine, **T** = thymine, **G** = guanine, **C** = cytosine) bound by sugar molecules (deoxyribose) which in turn are bound by phosphate molecules (**PO_4**). Weak hydrogen bonds between the base molecules form bridge-like links between the two strands, such that adenine always combines with thymine (A–T or vice versa) and guanine always combines with cytosine (G–C or vice versa).

averaging 500 words per page. This would be equivalent to a library of 1,000 books. Because this information is so important, the DNA at the centre of each cell has a carefully laid self-checking mechanism such that on cell division (which is particularly evident in foetus development, but also occurs throughout life), the DNA of the daughter cell is an exact copy of the DNA of the parent cell. This is why the DNA is a double helix. As duplication is needed, the DNA is unwound and then either side separates revealing the four types of nucleotides (adenine, thymine, cytosine and guanine), the order of which is vital for maintaining the character of the living creature. These base nucleotides are effectively opposites to each other. Thus adenine on the left strand pairs with thymine on the right strand; guanine on the left strand pairs with cytosine on the right strand and vice-versa. Thus the bridges across the strands of DNA are effectively A—T, G—C, T—A or C—G. Under self-replication the two strands separate and extra nucleotides (which have been made in the cell for the purpose) are added to the parts which have separated. Thus for example, if the A—T bond has separated, then the adenine from the left strand is joined to a new thymine nucleotide brought in for the purpose and the thymine from the right strand is joined to a new adenine nucleotide. This is done for every single nucleotide pair until one has two identical DNA strands. In that the order is vital and the number of nucleotide bridges runs into about three billion (three thousand million) per cell, it is a feat of engineering and information technology, that only rarely is there ever a copying error (mutation) to any of the genetic material.

But there is more! Because the DNA represents a master plan which should only be copied when absolutely necessary (cell division), there is a mechanism for generating a different string molecule ribonucleic acid (RNA) which is *not* double-stranded and is only as long as required for making a certain type of protein. This is similar to an architect keeping hand drawn plans of a building at his office but allowing a contractor (say a carpenter) to copy *part* of the plans (make a blueprint) for his part of the building work. The RNA molecule is only single-stranded and is put together as follows. The necessary part of the DNA unzips to reveal the relevant genetic material to be copied. However, unlike the self-replicating mechanism described earlier, the nucleotide bases which have separated out, are mated with a new relevant pair only on one side of the DNA. One other difference is that a different nucleotide, uracil (U) is used in place of thymine (T). Thus a free adenine (A) on the DNA strand is paired off with a uracil (U) nucleotide made for the purpose. A free guanine (G) is again paired with a cytosine (C) nucleotide made from the nucleus material. Similarly a free thymine (T) is paired with a new adenine (A) and the free cytosine (C) is paired with a new guanine (G) made for the purpose. Thus the sequence *as transcription takes place* will be in various combinations of the bridges A—U, G—C, T—A and C—G. The next stage is remarkable, for the RNA molecule formed of ribose sugar—phosphate 'anchors' (with its appropriate sequence of nucleotide bridges), now *detaches* from the DNA which then closes up again in its original double helix form. Thus the genetic information (i.e. the ordering of the four nucleotide bases in the DNA) has been transferred onto a somewhat different (but related) chemical structure. It is these RNA molecule strands which then build the various parts of the cell according to the ordering of the nucleotides— uracil (U), cytosine (C), adenine (A) and guanine(G). It is found that the nucleotides U, C, A and G group in triplets to form 'letters', e.g. possible RNA triplets might be ACG, GUC, CAU, CAG, GAC and so on. Each triplet represents the code for a specific amino acid which are the basic building blocks of proteins. Thus RNA molecules are the 'worker' molecules for building the various proteins needed in each cell. The information as to which protein is coded by the triplets is derived from the ordering of the nucleotides which in turn were obtained by transcription from the DNA. The DNA is a replica of the original DNA formed when making the 23 pairs of chromosomes at the conception of the living creature (23 each from the sperm and egg of the parent for human beings). The DNA information for human beings goes right back to our original ancestors Adam and Eve at Creation.

What is vital in the above description of DNA, is to recognize that the coded information using the letters (ACG, GUC, CAU, etc.) rides on the complicated chemical molecules, but is *not defined by it*. Information does not equal energy or matter. In radio signals there is a carrier wave of higher frequency than the information signal which rides on the back of the carrier wave. Once received, the carrier wave is not important and the message is converted to sound and speech. In exactly the same way, the information concerning one cell could have been written using entirely different coding, that is, a different ordering of the nucleotides. As long as the rules stay the same, it is unimportant. Alternatively, completely different chemistry could be involved, that is, a different 'alphabet' leading to a completely new language structure. What is paramount in this discussion is that *information* (that is the setting of the rules, the language, code etc.) has been there from the beginning. To argue that this came by chance is scientifically preposterous. As Professor Gitt has stated:

Meanings always represent mental concepts. They are distinct from matter and energy. They originate from an intelligent source.[18]

To show the impossibility of chance events ever producing a living cell, consider the proteins which are the fundamental parts of a cell. The proteins are composed of amino acids.[19] These can be produced by an electric discharge passed across a reducing (ammonia-rich) atmosphere (as Miller[20,21] demonstrated in the 1950s). It was then thought that this was the basic building block for life from a primeval soup of methane, water and ammonia. All one needed was the normal, unguided, random chemical reaction:

Methane Water Ammonia	Radical NH_2 Amino Group
$CH_4+H_2O+NH_3$+Energy $\rightarrow$ (e.g. Lightning)	R – CH–COOH Carboxy Amino Acid Group

and one had it—biogenesis! However there is a big difficulty. The amino acid molecule is similar to a tetrahedron in structure. There are four vertices to which the four valencies of the carbon atom (and thus the four chemical bonds) are directed. Consequently there are geometrically two types of amino acid structures—right-handed or left-handed. These are chemically the same but structurally are fundamentally different. The structure affects the properties of the proteins built from amino acids. In living protoplasm (the material of a living cell) left-handed amino acids predominate with very few exceptions. However the random experiment of Miller for producing amino acids leads to left *and* right-handed amino acids being produced in roughly equal proportions. Thus they are of no use! This is even before DNA comes on the scene which has information implanted on it and cannot be derived from the chemicals.

Evolutionists are forced to appeal to chance to justify first the appearance of DNA and RNA to begin with, and then to the idea of random mutation to change the DNA sequence carefully put together for one species, into that for another. The key problem in all such speculation is that one never obtains *extra* information from the coded material that one starts with. Hence the auto-organisation of molecules from non-living material to form DNA has never been observed.

Neither has it ever been shown that mutations can alter one species to another. Nearly all have harmful effects. What all such pseudo-scientific explanations fail to explain is that no mutation has *ever* produced more information than that which was there in the gene pool already. Mutant fruit flies can be bred which are blind and with legs in odd places, but there is *no new information*. Indeed, if these mutants are made to breed, in about 10 generations, the mutation is removed. Blind flies are able to produce sighted offspring. Thus selection works against change and there is in fact a strong *stability* in every species.[22] Thus even Crick (the Nobel prize-winning discoverer of DNA) admits:

An honest man, armed with all the knowledge available to us now, could only state that in some sense, the origin of life appears at the moment to be almost a miracle, so many are the conditions which would have had to have been satisfied to get it going. But this should not be taken to imply that there are good reasons to believe that it could not have started on the earth by a perfectly reasonable sequence of fairly ordinary chemical reactions.[23]

Thus he backs off from the obvious implication of his words (creation!) to circumvent this alternative (which Huxley said is unthinkable); Crick[24] adopts a view similar to Hoyle[25] that somehow the information to form the first cell came from outer space (see also ref. 26). Thus Crick's only ground for optimism is that there *is* life on earth (a view echoed by the evolutionist David Attenborough in his famous 'Life on Earth' television series and book[27]) and the *presupposition* that it came about by natural means leads to chemical evolution being the only acceptable option. But just as equally (and with far more probability) an open mind can conclude *design*! But this thinking is deemed 'out of court', and not allowed in today's world. The religious nature of the debate is evident. Dawkins fully admits the complexity of the workings of the cell, but cannot avoid the attempt here to justify his religious views:

To explain the origin of the DNA/protein machine by invoking a supernatural Designer is to explain precisely nothing, for it leaves unexplained the origin of the Designer. You have to say something like 'God was always here', and if you allow yourself that kind of lazy way out, you might as well just say 'DNA was always there', or 'Life was always there', and be done with it.[28]

So Dawkins turns to the goddess of random mutations to produce DNA and the information encoded with it! Creation is a singular event and the Christian believer openly admits it is beyond the reach of scientific observation. Dawkins and others would tell us to replace it with chance producing DNA from non-living material. It has happened (because it is here!) but is unrepeatable (these chances do not happen that often!). Is that science? As Milton[29] has rightly argued, the chance required for each evolutionary step is gigantic because at every stage of the so-called amoeba-to-man ladder there is a need not only for an 'upward' change, but an upward change *in the right sequence*. Is it not more reasonable to adopt the view that a Creator is behind this vast complexity with the quiet humility of Newton who stated:

I seem to have been only like a boy playing on the seashore, and diverting myself in now and then finding a smoother pebble or a prettier shell than ordinary, whilst the great ocean of truth lay all undiscovered before me.[30]

Wilder-Smith has summarized the position of Dawkins and others well when he writes:

Evolutionary theory attempts to attribute the problem of biogenesis and of the origin of species to chance and to natural selection in the struggle for survival. It attributes the generation of teleonomy [design] to random non-teleonomy [disorder], which is sheer non scientific nonsense. Today, it is simply unscientific to claim that the fantastically reduced entropy of the human brain, of the dolphin's sound lens, and of the eye of a fossilized trilobite simply 'happened', for experimental experience has shown that such miracles just do not 'happen'. By attributing such marvels to happenstance, we are simply throwing in the scientific towel. Attributing the production of the well-nigh inconceivable concept of a brain or an eye to chance is not only scientifically unacceptable—it is simply naive, and because it amounts to an often religious philosophy; it is superstitious as well. It is a fact of experience that superstitions die hard.[31]

Appendix A notes

1 **R Dawkins,** *The Blind Watchmaker* (2nd Edition; London: Penguin, 1988).

2 **R Dawkins,** *The Selfish Gene* (2nd edition; Oxford: Oxford University Press, 1989).

3 **W Paley,** *Natural Theology on Evidence and Attributes of Deity* (18th ed.; Edinburgh: Lackinton, Allen and Co., and James Saivers, 1818).

4 **R Dawkins,** *The Blind Watchmaker,* op. cit., p. 4.

5 **R Dawkins,** op. cit., p. 5.

6 **M Poole,** 'A critique of aspects of the philosophy and theology of Richard Dawkins', *Science and Christian Belief,* 6, 1994, 41–59, p. 54. Poole would not accept a young earth creationist position, but here argues convincingly against Dawkins. The reader is also referred to **R Penrose,** *The emperor's new mind: concerning computers, minds and the laws of physics* (London: Vintage, 1990), p. 151, where Penrose, who is no friend to the creationist position, nevertheless skilfully argues that not all truth (in particular mathematical) can be explained mechanistically.

7 **G Lambert,** 'Design in Nature—The Bucket Orchid-orchard bee relationship', *Biblical Creation* 5 (15), 58–64, 1983.

8 **R Dawkins,** *The Blind Watchmaker,* op. cit., p.15.

9 **R Dawkins,** op. cit., pp. 1–18.

10 **R Dawkins,** op. cit., p. 17.

11 **C Darwin,** *The Origin of Species* (1859, 6th edition London: Odhams, 1972), chapter 6. p. 185. However see also pp. 186–192 where Darwin (who was frank enough to admit that chance building the eye is absurd), goes on to say that the eye appeared by gradual stages nevertheless! Darwin was more honest about the difficulties than Dawkins, but in the end both deny obvious common sense, that intricate mechanisms never happen without external thought and purpose. Neither has disproved Paley's original argument.

12 **Manfred Eigen,** 'Self Organisation of Matter and the Evolution of BiologicalMacromolecules', *Naturwissenschaften,* 58. 1971.

13 **M Eigen** and **R Winkler**, *Das Spiel: Naturgesetze steuern den Zufall* (R Piper Verlag, München/Zürich, 1975); English version **Manfred Eigen** and **Ruthild Winkler,** *Laws of the game: how the principles of nature govern chance,* trans. Robert and Rita Kimber (London: Allen Lane, 1982).

14 **AE Wilder-Smith,** *The Natural Sciences know nothing of evolution* (San Diego: Master Books, 1981). See particularly chapter 4 'The Genesis of Biological Information'. Quote from p. 59 has bracketed material added. See also **EL Williams** (ed.), *Thermodynamics and the development of Order* (Creation Research Society, 1992) (ISBN 0 940384 01 9), for a thorough treatment of the 2nd law and its implications for evolutionary ideas.

15 **I Prigogine, G Nicolis, and Babloyants,** 'Thermodynamics of Evolution', *Physics Today,* 25 (11), 1972, 23–28. See also **P Coveney** and **R Highfield** *The Arrow of Time* (London: Flamingo, 1991). They also argue for a reversal of the second law of thermodynamics by 'Creative evolution' (see chapter 6, pp. 182–219) from chaos theory. The weakness in all such thinking is that *pattern* is *not* the same as *intelligent design* which is necessary for useful, purposeful machines to emerge. Similar debates about entropy and the second law are taking place in Astronomy–see **R Penrose,** *The emperor's new mind: concerning computers, minds and the laws of physics* (London: Vintage, 1990), ch. 7, 'Cosmology and the arrow of time'.

16 **G Nicolis and I Prigogine,** *Self organisation in non-equilibrium systems* (New York: Wiley, 1977).

17 **WJ ReMine,** *The Biotic Message—Evolution versus Message Theory* (St Paul, Minnesota: St Paul Science, 1993).

18 **W Gitt,** 'Information: the third fundamental quantity', *Siemens Review,* Vol. 56, Part 6 pp. 36–41, 1989. See also **W Gitt,** *Information: the third fundamental quantity*, CSM Pamphlet, Creation Science Movement.

19 **AE Wilder-Smith,** op. cit., ch. 2.'Biogenesis by chance',p. 9.

20 **SL Miller,** *Science,* 117, 1953.

21 **SL Miller,** Journal of the American Chemical Society, 77, 1955, 2351.

22 **D Rosevear,** in *Creation,* Journal of Creation Science Movement, 9(4), p.12, Jan. 1996.

23 **F Crick,** *Life Itself, Its Origin and Nature* (London: MacDonald, 1982), pp. 87–77.

24 **F Crick,** and **LE Orgel,** 'Directed Panspermia', *Icarus,* 19, 341–346.

25 **F Hoyle,** *The Intelligent Universe* (London: Michael Joseph, 1983).

26 **JW Oller,** 'A Theory in Crisis', ICR Impact Article No. 180, June 1988.

27 **D Attenborough,** *Life on Earth* (London: Collins & British Broadcasting Corporation, 1979).

28 **R Dawkins,** *The Blind Watchmaker*, op. cit. p. 141.

29 **R Milton,** *The Facts of Life* (London: Fourth Estate, 1992), pp. 143–144.

30 Sir Isaac Newton, *Mathematical Principles of Natural Philosophy* (1687).

31 AE Wilder-Smith, op. cit., p.146. Bracketed material added.

Summary of scientific evidence for creation and the Flood

In this appendix, there are listed the main reasons why many scientists cannot accept the theory of evolution. These scientists do not necessarily reject it because of Christian convictions. Some, such as Sir Fred Hoyle, do not profess Christian belief but reject the major tenet that life formed by chance out of non-living matter. Others are biologists such as Michael Denton whose book *Evolution: A Theory in Crisis*[1] has powerful arguments against any notion of gradual biological change from one species to another. An excellent book which gives a detailed list of evidence for a young earth and a recent creation is the book *The Facts of Life* by Milton.[2] Again, this author has no professed religious beliefs. However, his book and others are recommended for further reading. The appendix here is meant only to be a summary of the main arguments since there is a growing wealth of creationist material now available.

Astronomy

There are a number of methods for considering how old the solar system is which indicate its youth rather than its great age. It is very easy to overlook these matters as being only for those interested in non-mainstream science. However a good scientist should always take notice of detail and if with a number of independent methods, calculations of age in fact indicate a young solar system, then there needs to be an admission that something is very wrong with the traditional theories, and a fundamental re-evaluation of the evidence needs to take place.

Short period comets

In 1997 many observed the brilliance of the Hale-Bopp Comet which passed across the night skies. There are a number of comets which circumvent our sun in long elliptical orbits coming from beyond Pluto and eventually within the orbit of the earth. It has been shown that comets are made primarily of water, ammonia and a few other elements. The description of comets as 'dirty snowballs' may be correct, but others suggest rather that there is gravitationally bound mass and dust with frozen volatiles in orbit, around a primary nucleus. All agree that the nucleus can be as small as a few kilometres across. When Halley's comet came by in 1910 the diameter of the nucleus was only about 5km. When it came last in 1986, it was not so bright and there was some evidence that it broke up completely. This is because every time a comet comes close to the sun, much of the material boils off, forming a glowing halo ('coma') which can be 400,000km in diameter. During this period, the 'solar wind' of myriads of particles and radiation from the sun in turn blow gas and dust particles off the coma leading to a tail forming from the comet, such that whichever way the comet is travelling the tail is always pointing away from the sun. Thus, even as the comet moves away from the sun, the tail is in fact ahead of it pointing in the direction of travel.

It is this loss of material every time a comet passes the sun, which gives an upper limit for the age of the solar system, for in the end, a comet disintegrates entirely. The lifetime of short period comets has been estimated[3] to be no more than about 10,000 years on the basis of the approximate amount of mass lost every cycle. For short-period comets of a hundred years or less, there is no doubt that even after a million years (and that is much less than the current 4 thousand million talked of), 10,000 cycles would be quite sufficient to remove all such short period objects. But the evidence is otherwise. From a Biblical point of view, Halley's Comet was coming to an end of its life at less than 100 orbits, and there are a number of comets still orbiting with cycles much less than a hundred years (such as Encke's comet (3·3 years) and Holmes' comet (7 years.) The existence of these short period comets is consistent with a solar system far younger than a million years, let alone 4 billion years, with some now speaking of yet greater ages. This is the most obvious explanation, but in order to make the evidence consistent with a very great age for the solar system, evolutionists propose a vast cloud of billions of comets, not seen but only believed to exist, just outside the

Solar System which now and then a passing star disturbs by its own gravity, so as to cause the odd comet to be dragged into motion around our sun. This cloud is called 'Oort's cloud' after the author of the original idea. As stated by Wieland,[4] the speculation by JH Oort of a 'resupply from the cometary "deep freeze" conveniently solves the problem why we still have rapidly decaying comets in a 4·5 billion year old solar system.' However, not only is observational evidence of its existence entirely missing, but also the calculated motions of comets do not agree with predictions made by the Oort cloud theory.[5]

Wieland has aptly commented:

Far from being an 'orbiting museum of evolution', the splendour of Halley's comet is actually caused by its disintegration and decay, reminding us of the fact that the universe is 'groaning in bondage to decay', not building up in complexity.[6]

The age of the stars

It is impossible to do justice to this enormous topic here, but the reader is referred to two excellent books on astronomy from a creation perspective. AJ Monty White, *What about Origins?* (Newton Abbot: Dunestone Printers, 1978), pp. 50–76 and Russell Humphreys, *Starlight and Time* (Green Forest, AR : Master Books, 1994).

It has often been argued that, given the large distances (millions of light years) of the stars from earth, and the known speed of light, then the age of the universe has to be measured in millions of years for there to be meaning to the images we see. However, as pointed out by Lubenow:

it is little known that the farthest *direct* age/distance measurement we can make in the universe is limited to about three hundred light years, done by triangulation using the diameter of the earth's orbit as a baseline. All age/distance measurements beyond that are *indirect*, and are based on assumptions which may or may not be valid.[7]

The direct measurement technique is called the parallax method. Consequently, for distances well beyond our own solar system, we have no absolute measure of distance. This fact may be surprising to some since we are indoctrinated from a very early age with the idea of vast distances. This principle of observation and theory has been well expressed by Eddington in 1958 who wrote:

There are no purely observational facts about the heavenly bodies [i.e. those well beyond our solar system]. Astronomical measurements are, without exception, measurements of phenomena occurring in a terrestrial observatory or station; it is only by theory that they are translated into knowledge of a universe outside.[8]

Consequently the large distances and the age of the universe are a *deduction* from a major (unproved) assumption that the Big Bang cosmology (the fashionable view today) is correct. In other words, we get out what we put in. Parts of that cosmology do seem plausible. The redshift of stars would seem superficially to be explained by the idea of expansion away from us (with the consequent implication of vast distances) but it is an odd fact that there is significant quantisation of redshift, that is the redshift of galaxies clusters around *definite values*.[9] This points to the possibility of some intrinsic cause for redshift. Redshift can be due to the Doppler effect (where the light is shifted in wavelength due to the relative speed of source and observer). Redshift means, in this case, that the star or galaxy is moving away from us. Blueshift (as with M31, the Andromeda Galaxy, our closest neighbour to the Milky Way) means the object is coming towards us. Other causes are the Cosmological Redshift effect discovered by Hubble and due to the expansion of Space-Time itself. However it has also been argued that this type of redshift may not necessarily be due to expansion.[10] The reader is encouraged to study not just the most popular works on the subject, for there are interesting details which can easily be overlooked. The following do not *prove* that the current red shift theory is definitely incorrect, but raise vital issues which cannot be ignored. We mention two such facts here:

i. The quasars have redshifts so strong as to indicate great distance from us. However Monty White states:

Changes in brightness of quasars have been observed to occur in the space of one day. This means that they cannot be larger than about one light day (about 16,000 million miles) across. But if they are as far away as their 'red shift' indicates, it is impossible for an object of such size to radiate energy at so great a rate. To overcome this problem, some astronomers believe that quasars are much closer than the 'red shift' indicates. But if this were so, then the 'red shift' is not a reliable indicator of distance.[11]

Further evidence has recently confirmed the weakness of the redshift distance theory.[12] Arp in his book *Quasars, Redshifts and Controversies*[13] has shown that quasars are often physically connected to other galaxies by bridges of material. Thus the quasar Markarian 205 with a 'red shift velocity' of 21,000km sec^{-1} is connected by a bridge of material to the galaxy NGC 4319 with a red shift velocity of only 1800 km sec^{-1}. According to the expanding universe hypothesis, this implies that the quasar is 1–2 billion light years distant and NGC 4319 is about 0·1 billion light years removed from us. This is but one example of many quasar-galaxy systems where the foundational assumption of the modern Big Bang hypothesis is shown to be false. Few astronomers yet admit this, but eventually the community will have to face the fact that there are too many astronomical observations which clearly show that redshift is *not* a measure of distance. A very fair discussion of this matter is to be found in the excellent book on redshift and its interpretation by Clark.[14]

Other notable problems with the idea of an old expanding universe concern missing supernova remnants, spiral galaxies which can only survive a few rotations, but are still clearly seen, and the dearth of Red Dwarf stars (the remnants of old stars)—many should exist after the alleged billions of years since the Big Bang supposedly took place.[15,16]

ii. The Cepheid variable star distance scale.[17] This is the method by which the distance of stars is measured by their apparent brightness. To quote Kofahl and Segraves:

Studies of the Cepheid variables in certain star clusters revealed a regular relationship between their periods of variation (1 to 100 days) and their apparent brightness in any particular cluster. Astronomers then reasoned that if the correct distances to some closer Cepheids should be measured, and if it could be assumed that the period-brightness relationship was universal for Cepheids wherever found, the result would be a known relationship between the period and the absolute brightness. Thus the distance to any Cepheid could be determined by measuring the period of variation and its apparent brightness, then performing a simple calculation.

Unfortunately, no Cepheids are close enough to have measurable parallaxes [the method used for nearby stars closer than 300 light years away—stars such as Sirius, 8·65 light years away], so astronomers made statistical studies of the apparent relative motions of the nearer ones. All stars are moving in random directions and speeds, and the apparent motion of any star in one year as viewed from the earth is called 'the proper motion' of that star. By measuring the proper motions and radial velocities over a period of years of some Cepheid variable stars and analyzing this information statistically, scientists determined the relationship between the period and the absolute brightness of the Cepheids, so that they could be used as astronomical distance markers. ...

... The initial studies were made with the assumption that all of the Cepheids had the same intrinsic brightness versus period relation, which is not really the case. In addition, the adsorption of their light by intervening dust in our galaxy was not correctly estimated. As a result it is believed that a major error was made. It was not until the early 1950s that it was decided that the Cepheids are actually four times brighter than originally thought. This meant that they were twice as far away as originally calculated. Consequently the accepted size of the universe suddenly doubled, a fact which made newspaper headlines.[18]

Thus the correlation of the brightness versus period relationship to real parallax-measured distances is not clearly established, raising doubts as to the Cepheid variable star distance scale.

Even if the scales are accepted (and there are noted creationist scholars who do accept them—such as Russell Humphreys, Sandia Laboratories nuclear physicist), there are important assumptions which have been criticized recently within the Big Bang cosmogony. In his recent work, Humphrey[19] starts with the basic ideas of General Relativity upon which the Expanding Universe ideas are based and alters two major assumptions. Firstly, he considers an initially *bounded* cosmos (present theories make this unbounded) and secondly he places *the earth near the centre* (the traditional big bang hypothesis had no natural 'centre'). The *same* mathematics is used, yielding startlingly different conclusions. These have to do with the gravitational time dilation predicted by the general relativity theory. It has been proved experimentally that clocks designed to the same standard, tick 5 microseconds a year slower at the Royal Greenwich Observatory, England, than at the National Institute of Standards and Technology (NIST, previously National Bureau of Standards, NBS) at Boulder in Colorado, USA, which is situated 5,000 feet up in the Rocky Mountains. Consequently when the assumption of a *natural centre* of a *bounded* expanded cosmos is made in the general relativity model of the universe, there is a very large disparity in the rate of physical processes (i.e. rates of clocks) at points well away from the centre, and points near the centre. This leads to processes which would normally take millions of years (such as light travelling from stars very far away) taking a very short time (hundreds of years) when measured by an observer near the centre. This is a possible explanation of how starlight from our perspective could travel large distances to us from the far reaches of the universe over a period of time measured on earth in thousands (not millions) of years.

So much of scientific enquiry is today dictated by an unquestioning acceptance of the theories of the 'experts' in any particular field; it is refreshing to have someone dare to challenge the assumptions used in the 'sacred cow' of astronomy. At the very least, Humphreys has demonstrated clearly that conclusions from the Big Bang theory are heavily dependent on unproveable assumptions.

Magnetic field changes

Dr Thomas Barnes of the University of Texas[20,21] has shown that over the last 100 years there has been a significant and measurable change in the earth's magnetic field. The first 'modern' measurement in 1829 by Erman Paterson[22,23] yielded a Dipole moment of $8 \cdot 454 \times 10^{22}$ joules/tesla with a steady decline to $7 \cdot 906 \times 10^{22}$ joules/tesla measured by the satellite Magsat in 1980. The decay was thought to be following a simple exponential decay by Barnes, but there is strong evidence also of oscillations in the Earth's magnetic field.[24] Dynamo theories (based on the idea that heat energy is converted into electrical energy) for the origin of the earth's magnetic field do not really fit the facts of the well-measured decay which is much more consistent with a freely decaying field. So what of the observed oscillations (measured by examining the magnetism of the rocks buried in sediments on the earth's surface)? Humphreys[25] has shown conclusively that the *energy* (as against the magnetic moment) of the earth's magnetic field has certainly decayed by as much as 14% since the 1829 measurements but that the dipole moment could well have reversed in the past. This is by no means inconsistent, and points strongly towards a freely decaying magnetic field which was severely distorted (possibly by a collision). There are thus two factors involved. (1) The energy of the field and (2) the moment of the field. The decay of the energy of the earth's field is indisputable and leads to the conclusion that the field has only decayed over at the most 10,000 years. There is, in fact, a maximum possible energy level. This is when *all* the molecules of the earth are lined up magnetically which would be highly unlikely, but sets an upper bound for the magnetic energy available, proportional to the planetary mass. The period of decay in the magnetic field implies that the reversals of the magnetic moment then have to take place over a very short period of time which suggests a collision of some kind[26] whereby the rotating molten magnetic core would be made to oscillate unevenly, thus causing the field intensity of the earth's surface to fluctuate up and down for thousands of years afterward. This model of the earth's magnetic field is called the dynamic-decay model. An interesting confirmation of this type of theory was the prediction made by Humphreys[27] of the magnetic field strength of Uranus before this was measured by the Voyager II spacecraft in January 1986. The dynamo theories predicted a very small magnetic field because there was little heat outflow from the planet's surface (and dynamo theories are based on heat energy converting to magnetic energy). Using dynamic-decay theory, the mass of Uranus indicated that a magnetic moment of between 1×10^{23} and 1×10^{25} joules/tesla should be expected. In the event, Voyager II measured a value of 3×10^{24} Joules/Tesla.

This evidence is very compelling, particularly as the *energy* of the field shows conclusively that it has always been gradually running down.

The moon and its distance from the earth

There is a certain distance from the earth's centre (about 11,500 miles) which is know as 'the Roche Limit'. Although the moon is slowly receding from the earth, it could never have been closer than the Roche Limit in time past because tidal forces would then have broken it up.[28] This presents a major problem for the supposed evolutionary origin of the moon. Because the recession rate is known, the supposed 4 billion years old age of the earth-moon system would lead to a distance of the moon from the earth far greater than the present 239,000 miles (centre to centre). Schlichter,[29] one time Professor of Geophysics at the renowned Massachusetts Institute of Technology, acknowledges 'the time scale of the earth-moon system still presents a major problem'. There is no strong evolutionary counter-argument. The only somewhat weak argument which can be put, is to say that the recession rate has changed. However given the mass of the two objects (earth and moon), recession rates can be predicted from Newton's laws of gravity and there is no known mechanism which could cause the rate to be different in the past. These and similar facts are rarely discussed in the literature but are in fact the Achilles heel of the modern day view of an ancient solar system.

Mountain building

Though undoubtedly there is much to be gained from the study of the slow movement of the continental plates (tectonics), the rate of movement of 1 to 10 centimetres per year is deemed inappropriate for the building of the Rockies, Andes, Himalayas and the Alps. Human artefacts at heights well above normal human habitation indicate human beings once lived in these regions but at much lower levels. Take for example, the cavern near the top of Drachenberg in the Alps at 8,000 feet above sea level. The implication is then of fast mountain building at some stage, since the human remains are in the recent past, thousands of years ago rather than millions.[30] A further example is of the well-preserved city of Tiahuanacu now 12,500 feet up in the Andes where corn will not ripen and its altitude is too high to support life for a city. The logical explanation is that the mountains rose considerably after the city was built.[31] The supposed slow rates of mountain building are not consistent with the archeological finds.

Large depths of volcanic lava

A region of 200,000 square miles in Idaho, Washington State and Oregon in the USA known as the Columbia Plateau is covered by lava to a depth of about 5,000 ft. Lava flows of current volcanoes could not account for this enormous depth, neither that of the Deccan traps in India or the lava beds of the Pacific Ocean. The indications are of catastrophism on a massive scale.[32]

Mass extinctions

From Loch Ness in Scotland to the Orkneys northwards is a rock formation of about 8,000 feet made from Old Red Sandstone. In this area 100 miles across, there are buried countless fish, contorted and contracted, as though in convulsion. There is all the evidence of catastrophic burial.[33,34] There are fish fossils that are also found on high mountains such as the Alps in Europe and the Rockies in the USA. Some fossil fish have been found in the process of eating one another.[35] In the middle of Siberia in the frozen wastes there are graveyards of mammoths[36] and other creatures which have been buried suddenly. Because of the extreme cold, soft tissue has also been preserved with evidence of recent digestion of food before sudden calamity overtook them. Thus the evidence again points to catastrophic burial with an original warm, even tropical, climate.

These evidences of catastrophe agree with the implications of soft bodied fossils which occur—e.g. jellyfish which can only be fossilized by quick, sharp burial.[37] These cannot be produced slowly.

In the Siwalik Hills north of Delhi, India, there are rich fossil deposits. They are in fact 2,000–3,000 feet high and several hundred miles long and are the foothill of the Himalayas. In hundreds of feet of sediment there are the jumbled bones of scores of extinct species. To quote Milton:

Many of the creatures were remarkable, including a tortoise twenty feet long and a species of elephant *with tusks fourteen feet long and three feet in circumference.* … Most of the species whose fossils are found are today extinct, including some thirty species of elephant of which only one has survived in India.[38]

The evidence again points to catastrophe. Milton[39] goes on to describe deposits of a very similar nature in Burma where amongst remains of mastodon, hippopotamus and ox, are large quantities of fossil wood, '…thousands of fossilized tree trunks and logs scattered in the sandstone sediments. In total the deposits may be as much as 10,000 feet thick and there are two distinct fossiliferous horizons separated by 4,000 feet of sandstone.' Further examples can be given of dinosaur burials with skeletons all on top of one another in New Mexico, Wyoming, Canada and Belgium.

These are no isolated instances. There are many and they challenge fundamentally the uniformitarian concept of rock formation. Thus it has been rightly stated:

… few modern geologists are prepared to accept that major features of the Earth's crust could have been caused by singular events, because such an admission seems to open the door to some kind of geological anarchy which threatens the orderly arrangement of exhibits in their glass cases.[40]

Living fossils

In Hagen, Germany, there is an excellent museum recently opened called Kuratorium Lebendige Vorwelt (Museum of Living Fossils) put together by Dr Joachim Scheven. The work is described in an article by Wieland[41] and is a remarkable testimony to the *unchanging* nature of creatures over time. He has very painstakingly put together, as far as can be done, exactly the same species, modern and (supposedly) ancient. Thus leaves, ants, turtles, scallop shells and other creatures are compared side by side.[42] Butterflies stay as butterflies, bats stay as bats. No changes are in evidence, except in size. Notable examples of 'living fossils' in the wild are the Tuatara which are found in Cretaceous and 'older' rocks (on the classic geological time scale) but none in 'recent' strata higher up the geological column. Yet they are still living today and show no change despite the supposedly 135 million year gap.[43] This is testimony against any evolutionary change. The Coelacanth (mentioned in Appendix C) was supposed to be a transition creature for fish to amphibians since fossils of these creatures are found in what is supposedly very old rock (but not in upper 'earlier' strata). Yet the finding of an exact modern counterpart in 1938 is another embarrassing example of a 'living fossil'. The record in the rocks is not one of transition, but of death and at times, extinction—such as the woolly mammoth and the pterodactyls, for which there are no modern counterparts. Rather than an *increase* in the number of species over the years, the records show each species stays the same and there is a *loss* of some species.

Sequoia and other ancient trees

An intriguing piece of evidence that suggests a young earth is the tree ring analysis of the renowned *Sequoia Gigantea* Trees.[44] The study of tree rings (dendrochronology) which generally occur once a year gives a rough method for estimating the ages of trees. The method is rough since ring patterns are affected by annual temperature and rainfall variations. The Californian Redwood[45] and Sequoia trees are known to be some of the oldest in the world. In particular, when this method is applied to the Sequoia which are known to be resistant to all disease, the tree ring estimates are of the order of 3,000–4,000 years. As Schulman has observed:

Perhaps the most intriguing of the unanswered questions regarding longevity in conifers has to do with *Sequoia Gigantea* Trees, which, some believe, may enjoy perpetual life in the absence of gross destruction, since they appear immune to pest attack. ... Pertinent also is the well-known fact that standing snags of this species, other than those resulting from factors of gross destruction, are unknown. Does this mean that shortly preceding 3,275 years ago (or 4,000 years ago, if John Muir's somewhat doubtful count was correct) *all* the then living giant sequoias were wiped out by some catastrophe?[46]

Thus, though Schulman was no believer in catastrophic geology, he acknowledged the dilemma of the old-earth position. 'Where have all the Sequoias gone?' was his lament! Further details are in an article by Robbins.[47] The position becomes even more difficult when one considers the bristlecone pines of the White Mountains of California. Again Schulman records:

Only recently we have learned that certain stunted pines of arid highlands, not the mammoth trees of rainy forests, may now be called the oldest living things on earth.

Microscopic study of growth rings reveals that a bristlecone pine tree found last summer at nearly 10,000 feet began growing more than 4,600 years ago and thus surpasses the oldest known sequoia by many centuries ... Many of its neighbours are nearly as old; we have now dated 17 bristlecone pines 4,000 years old or more ...[48]

Later, in the Guinness Book of Records, 1983,[49] it is recorded that a bristlecone pine called 'Methuselah' growing in the same locality that Schumann investigated (10,000 feet up in the White Mountains of California) was dated at 4,600 years old. Some have sought to maintain that the potential life-span cannot be greater than 6,000 years but this is simply speculation. There is no evidence of any known disease which kills them.

As Whitcomb and Morris rightly state, this is a very good evidence for the recent occurrence of world-wide catastrophe:

Since these, as well as the sequoias and other ancient trees, are still living, it is pertinent to ask why these oldest living things apparently have had time to develop only one generation since they acquired their present stands at sometime after the Deluge. There is no record of a tree, or any other living thing, being older than any reasonable date for the Deluge.[50]

Mechanisms in living creatures

A major reason for belief in the creation model of origins is the amazing mechanisms which are in any living creature. Rather than itemize many here, the reader is encouraged to study the book, *Biology: God's Living Creation* (published by Beka Books as part of the Pensacola, Christian College Course—see Bibliography) and Drickamer and Vessey's book *Animal Behaviour: Concepts, Processes and Methods* (Wadsworth, California) which show clearly the intricate design in the living world.

Lastly, a more recent book by Behe entitled *Darwin's Black Box* (New York: Free Press, 1996) brilliantly shows that the argument of design is becoming more and more insurmountable as minute complexity is discovered at the biochemical level. His description of the tiny bacterial flagellum[51] with a bacterial rotary motor shows that the gradualist explanations of Dawkins do not instruct the scientists in any new mechanism or principle which can remotely account for the compexity of living organisms. Behe shows the dry emptiness of the Darwinian failure to show experimentally any of the supposed evolutionary transitions.

Flight

One of the major mechanisms which, in the opinion of this author, is impossible to derive by small graduations is the fact of flight. Flight occurs in four types of creatures: pterodactyls (now extinct); birds, butterflies/moths/other insects, and bats. In each case, the wings are substantially different and there is no evidence whatsoever of any connection between the supposed evolutionary development of any of these creatures. The very detailed study by Lighthill[52] on animal flight still concludes this evolved, despite intricate design. Yet the evolutionist is faced with not just one impossible hurdle—that some reptiles developed feathers and began to fly—but two other hurdles. These are that flight evolved again when some rodents (mice? shrews?) evolved a skin-like surface and developed into bats and then *quite separately* some insects grew very thin scales to become flies, bees and butterflies!

Just consider the flight of a bird,[53] Aerodynamically the wings must be flexible to produce lift[54] and of lightweight engineering.[55] Though light, wings made of feathers are very wind resistant. This is because there is a clever system of barbs and barbules. The main barbs coming out of the central quill have barbules with hooks on one side and ridged rod-like barbules on the other. These connect rather like Velcro attaches to brush nylon. Thus, an ingenious mechanism exists for keeping the surface flexible and yet intact.

Gradual changes are impossible to explain such a marvellous feat of mechanical engineering. Unless the barbules are all one type (hooks) to the left, say, of a barb, and on the right the barbules are ridged rods, then the feather will not function. There is no advantage until *all* the barbules on one side are hooks and *all* the barbules on the other are ridged rods.

But there is more—as with any moving joint, oil is needed to prevent wear due to friction.[56] This comes from a bird's preening gland which is at the base of its spine. How does the bird get that to its feathers? By rotating its head 180° and putting some oil on its beak so that preening the feathers spreads the oil. And all this must be right first time for feathers to work!

The wing flapping motion of a bird requires a bird to have two main wing muscles[57] (unlike in most land based creatures which have one main muscle operating the limb near the body). The muscles need a high source of energy intake to operate them so that normal respiration is not good enough. Human beings breathe about 12 times per minute whereas small birds breathe about 250 times per minute. To achieve this, the air is fed straight into air sacs[58] which are connected directly to the bloodstream, with airflow going in both directions in the lung. As one air-sac inflates, another deflates—quite unlike other land-based creatures.

Further to this, a bird's bones have to be light,[59] so they are *hollow* with a truss arrangement of spars inside still to give load-bearing strength. A reptile's bones are not hollow, so for birds to 'evolve' from reptiles, hollow bones + feathers + preening gland + ability to turn head 180° + breathing mechanism + muscle development, must all develop simultaneously.

Flight alone demolishes any concept of evolution.

Further comment on mechanisms

The above example of flight illustrates the fundamental problem of Darwinian thinking, which we discussed in Appendix A. *Natural selection never builds a machine with a new blueprint.* All it can do is select *out* defective versions of an existing machine which, given a particular environment, will not survive—rather like the hated quality control inspectors at the end a production line! Thus, natural selection can operate in a limited way within species boundaries (that is, in terms of information, within a given 'gene pool'), but it is scientific nonsense to say that it ever produces new information. A 'new' component like a bird's wing considered above, requires a vast new pool of encoded information for thousands of 'parts' to this new 'machine' which *on their own* add *nothing* to the 'improvement' of the original living creature. Dawkins, in his book, *Climbing Mount Improbable*,[60] has failed to answer this point. Rather he has, through discussing mechanism after mechanism in his well-illustrated book, shown that the further one peels away the layers of complexity, the more complex things become. Sometimes Dawkins side-steps major difficulties. When discussing the giraffe for instance,[61] and its long neck, he assumes it is just a matter of adding vertebrae, rather like a stretched Airbus A340 airliner. The reality is much more complicated, for, as explained by Hofland,[62] the giraffe requires a very large heart to deliver sufficient oxygen-rich blood three metres up to the brain and yet it must also have by-pass and anti-pooling valves to stop the brain flooding with blood when the head is drooped for drinking. Even when Dawkins does consider the detail of supposed transitions, as he attempts to do with the eye,[63] he ignores the rules of compound probability. He insists that the probability of *each stage* occurring in the supposed evolution of this amazingly complex sense organ, is the same, because there is no 'knowledge' of the event before or after. In correspondence with the author,[64] he has drawn an analogy with finding the right set of figures to undo a faulty combination lock. Given enough time, the right number on one row will produce a 'click'. The same is then done for the next row and so on until all the numbers are found. Thus he propounds an unproven assumption, that there *always is* an obvious preferred route in evolution (corresponding to the 'click' in the analogy). This is the fundamental tenet of his book *Climbing Mount Improbable*, suggesting that there always is a *gradual path* to improvement. The reality is that, even for the 'simplest' cup-eye,[65] there is great complexity—it is essential to have the photocell, which converts light to minute bursts of electricity through the nucleus,[66] a connecting 'wire' to the brain, layers of photon-catching pigment for catching photons of light as well as a special receiving part of the brain to process the image. Dawkins goes on to argue that the layers of pigment are an example of the gradual route up Mount Improbable. He writes:

… ninety-one membranes are more effective in stopping photons than ninety, ninety are more effective than eighty-nine, and so on back to one membrane, which is more effective than zero. This is the kind of thing I mean when I say that there is a smooth gradient up Mount Improbable. We would be dealing with an abrupt precipice if, say, any number of membranes above forty-five was very effective while any number below forty-five was totally ineffective. Neither common sense nor the evidence leads us to support any such discontinuity.[67]

Yet a child can see the fallacy of this reasoning! *Any* number of pigment layers are useless without the connecting nerve 'wire' to carry current to the brain, which are bundled together in human eyes to form the optic nerve, and without a part of the brain to process such information. It is only the combination of *all* components which makes 'sense' of the integral whole—the entire machine.[68] The slick presentations of

Dawkins seem attractive, but his reasoning is false. At every stage, complexity increases. Thus what *appeared to be* a gradual route from stage A to stage B, always turns out to be a series of precipices when examined in fine detail. [In my own area of science it is well known that apparently smooth surfaces have a rough, 'fractal' nature when viewed under the microscope—clouds, coastlines or flames!] Indeed Dawkins fails to realize that the whole subject area of stability theory is relevant. To go from state A to state B may well involve a most *unstable* state in-between which *cannot be sustained*. This would certainly be true for a cup eye which suddenly found a blob of material meant to be a lens. The hillside of Dawkins' Mount Improbable does *not* have smooth and gradual slopes—it is fractal in nature—full of vertical precipices and discontinuities. In mathematical terms, he cannot avoid the laws of compound probability. Only if a series of stages, say A—M, are in place, will the new 'organ' or additional 'device' work correctly. The probability that event A takes place is written mathematically as $P(A)$ with $P(A)$ less than unity. (Unity denotes certainty.) The probability then that A to M are all in place is $P(A) \times P(B) \times \ldots \times P(L) \times P(M)$, which means that the compound probability becomes much less than one and the likelihood of these events all taking place *diminishes* rapidly. This point shows the problem of one scientist from a discipline (Dawkins is a zoologist) making generalisations about the supposed evolutionary changes which use probability arguments from another discipline (mathematics). In reality information from *all* branches of science is needed in order to understand what is going on. The same problem occurs when attempting to argue for the evolution of the bombardier beetle.[69] This beetle stops predators by exploding hydrogen peroxide and hydroquinone into the face of its enemy. Rightly stating that these do not react without a catalyst, he then states:

It is true that it squirts a scaldingly hot mixture of hydrogen peroxide and hydroquinone at enemies. But hydrogen peroxide and hydroquinone don't react violently together unless a catalyst is *added*. This is what the bombardier beetle does. As for the evolutionary precursors of the system, both hydrogen peroxide and various kinds of quinone are used for other purposes in body chemistry. The bombardier beetle's ancestors simply pressed into different service chemicals that already happened to be around. That is how evolution works.[70]

If I applied that sort of logic in my combustion research, the combustion would quickly be out of control! Has Dawkins studied carefully how the combustion chambers of modern gas turbines (such as the Rolls Royce Trent 800) are designed to ensure the combustion takes place in exactly the right location and is controlled to correctly transfer the energy to the turbine/compressor system? The addition of a catalyst to the hydrogen peroxide and hydroquinone is of no use for the bombardier beetle, if there is no combustion chamber[71] for then the beetle will uncontrollably blow itself up! The exhaust nozzle is also essential to direct the gases and to ensure the explosion takes place outside the creature. The precision of the aiming mechanism has only recently been uncovered by new research.[72] Experiments have shown that the creature can aim with pinpoint accuracy at a predator behind—as though it had eyes in the back of its head! By exposing the irreducibly complex nature of living creatures, Dawkins has shown the more thoughtful of his readers that smooth Darwinian change is impossible. 'Climbing Mount *Impossible*' might be a more apt description of his latest book.

Population growth and ancient genealogical records

As noted by Baker,[73] the world population figure of nearly 6000 million is not consistent with the view that man has existed for millions of years. United Nations published data (see for instance ref. 74) implies that it requires only about 5000 years to reach this figure. An attempt can be made to refute these arguments on the basis of there being wars and famines, but the effect on overall population would only be at the most a 2% change. Thus, for instance at the time of Christ, the world population is estimated to have been 500 million and a 2% fluctuation would represent a deviation of 10 million which would be very much an outside figure for premature death due to disease. In the second World War the premature death due to the conflicts around the globe were certainly less than 50 million[75] (2% of the total world population of about 2500 million in 1940). Indeed Osborn has stated:

It must be remembered that the numerical loss of human life in the last two great wars was relatively inconsequential when measured against the total populations of the countries at war. In fact, the wars of the last century have had virtually no influence in restraining population increase in the countries engaged.[76]

These points are further discussed in the authoritative creationist text *The Genesis Flood* by Whitcomb and Morris[77] The population graph is in fact then *very stable* and predictable once one gets to millions. Are old earth evolutionists really advocating a gigantic tail to when 'modern' man appeared—a tail extending to 2 to 5 million years ago (depending on which side of the fence you are over uniformitarian interpretations of KNM-ER1470[78])? Population statistics are not consistent with such a belief.[79,80] They point to a modern population beginning at the most 10,000 years ago.

If we turn to written records of genealogies and early population movements there is remarkable confirmation again of a recent start to mankind. In his unique study of early post-Flood history of Europe, Bill Cooper[81] has traced the records of many European kings back to a common descendancy from Japheth, son of Noah. What is remarkable is that though much of the source material has been heavily criticized by mainstream historians (e.g. the records of Geoffrey of Monmouth are discounted by many as made up myths and legends) the corroboration with scores of other records from Ireland, Denmark, Norway, Iceland and other countries concerning the major facts relating to recent descendancy from Japheth indicates that either there was collusion and fabrication on a large scale, or that they are, in the main, a testimony to the true recent origins of the European races.

When all these facts are considered along with the very many flood accounts that exist all around the globe, it is hard to escape the conclusion that we have a recent common ancestor in Noah.[82,83,84,85,86,87]

Appendix B notes

1 **M Denton,** *Evolution: A Theory in Crisis* (Bethesda, MD, Adler and Adler, 1986).

2 **R Milton,** *The Facts of Life—Shattering the myth of Darwinism* (London: 4th Estate, 1992), pp. 50–52.

3 **Lyttleton, RA,** *Mysteries of the Solar System* (Oxford: Clarendon Press, 1968), p. 110.

4 **C Wieland,** *Creation Magazine* 8(2), 1986, pp. 6–10.

5 **RA Lyttleton,** 'The non-existence of the Oort Cometary Shell', *Astrophysics and Space Science,* 31, 1974, 385–401.

6 **C Wieland,** *Creation Magazine,* 8(2), 1986, pp. 6–10.

7 **ML Lubenow,** *Bones of Contention* (Grand Rapids, Michigan: Baker Book House, 1994), p. 201.

8 **Sir Arthur Eddington,** *The Expanding Universe* (Ann Arbor: University of Michigan Press, 1958), p. 17 [italics his] quoted in **ML Lubenow,** *Bones of Contention* (Grand Rapids: Baker Book House, 1992), p. 201.

9 **HC Arp,** *Quasars, Redshift and Controversies* (Cambridge: Cambridge University Press, 1987).

10 **RE Kofahl,** and **KL Segraves,** *The Creation Explanation* (Wheaton, Illinois: Harold Shaw, 1975), p. 153.

11 **AJ Monty White,** *What about Origins?* (Newton Abbot: Dunestone Printers, 1978), p. 62.

12 **G Chapman,** *Quasars and Redshifts,* Factsheet 34 of Creation Resources Trust, 1992.

13 **HC Arp,** *Quasars, Redshift and Controversies* (Cambridge: Cambridge University Press, 1987) and **HC Arp,** *Seeing Red* (Montreal: Apeiron, 1998). Two reviews of these books are available in *Creation Technical Journal,* 14 (3), 2000: **Michael Oard,** *Doppler Toppler,* pp. 39–45, and **WJ Worraker** and **AC McIntosh,** *A different view of the Universe,* pp. 46–50.

14 **S Clark,** *Redshift* (Hatfield: University of Hertfordshire Press, 1997). See chapter 5, 'Unconventional interpretations of Redshift', pp. 151–187. It is by no means certain that redshifted starlight is necessarily to be taken as an indication of distance. Even if one does, the separation velocity may not be directly proportional to distance (as proposed by Hubble). The quadratic law proposed by Lundmark (for instance) would lead to a dramatic foreshortening of these distances and the Big Bang theory would be invalidated (see Clark, *Redshift,* p. 184). There is enough evidence to warrant a healthy scepticism of the Big Bang hypothesis.

15 **G Chapman,** *Hubble's Young Universe,* Factsheet 45 of Creation Resources Trust, 1996.

16 **J Sarfati,** 'Exploding Stars Point to a Young Universe', *Creation,* 19(3), 46–48, June 1997. See also **Clark** and **Caswell,** *Monthly Notices of the Royal Astronomical Society,* 174, 267, 1976.

17 **AJ Monty White,** op. cit. p. 62.

18 **RE Kofahl,** and **KL Segraves,** *The Creation Explanation* (Wheaton, Illinois: Harold Shaw,

1975), p. 150, quoted in **AJ Monty White,** *What about Origins?* (Newton Abbott: Dunestone Printers, 1978), pp. 63–64.

19 DR Humphreys, *Starlight and Time* (Green Forest, AR: Master Books, 1994).

20 TG Barnes, *Origin and destiny of the Earth's magnetic field,* ICR Technical Monograph No 4 (San Diego: ICR, 1973).

21 Barnes, TG, *Depletion of the Earth's magnetic field,* ICR Impact Article No. 100 (San Diego: ICR, October 1981).

22 KL McDonald, and **RH Gunst,** *An analysis of the Earth's magnetic field from 1835 to 1965.* Environmental Science Services Administration Technical Report, IER 46–IESI (US Deptartment of Commerce, 1967), p. 15.

23 RA Langol, RH Estes, GD Mead, EB Fabiano, and ER Lancaster, 'Initial Geomagnetic field model from Magsot vector data', *Geophysical Research Letters,* 7(10), 1980, 793–796.

24 RT Merril, and **MW McElhinney,** *The Earth's Magnetic Field* (London: Academic Press, 1983), 101–106.

25 DR Humphreys, *The Earth's magnetic field is young,* Impact No. 242, Inst. Creation Research, Aug. 1993.

26 M Bowden, *The recent change in the tilt of the earth's axis,* Creation Science Movement, Article No 236, July 1983.

27 DR Humphreys, *Beyond Neptune: Voyager II supports Creation,* ICR Impact Article No. 203, Institute of Creation Research, May 1990.

28 TG Barnes, *Young age for the moon and the earth,* ICR Impact Article No. 110, Institute for Creation Research, August 1992.

29 LB Schlichter, 'Secular effects of tidal friction upon the earth's rotation', *Journal of Geophysical Research,* 8(14), 1964, 4281–4288.

30 R Milton, op. cit., p. 84.

31 R Milton, op. cit., p. 85.

32 Ibid

33 R Milton, op. cit., pp. 85–86.

34 NH Trewin, 'Mass mortalities of Devonian fish—the Achananas Fish Bed, Caithness', *Geology Today,* March/April 1985, pp.45–49.

35 JL Amos and **D Jeffery,** 'Annals of Life written in rock: Fossils', *National Geographic Magazine,* 168(2), 182–191, August 1985, particularly p. 190.

36 *The Economist,* Science and Technology Section, 7 May 1983, p. 91.

37 G Chapman, *Creation Magazine,* 17(3), June 1995, p. 31.

38 R Milton, op. cit., p. 88 [italics mine].

39 Ibid., pp. 88–89.

40 Ibid., p. 89. Some creationists hold the view that there is evidence of much post-Flood fossilisation. Whilst there is room for some settling down after the Flood and thus the burial of creatures as a result, to suggest that all the fossils from the Cretaceous onwards are post-Flood, puts a question mark over the Rainbow promise (Genesis 9:11–12) and leads to doubt being placed on the post Flood genealogy of Genesis 11 which proponents of this view must stretch to allow for massive activity between the Flood and Abraham. This whole matter is discussed in the following articles: **AC McIntosh, T Edmondson** and **S Taylor,** 'Flood models; the need for an integrated approach', *Creation Techical Journal,* 14 (1), 52–59,2000, **AC McIntosh, T Edmondson** and **S Taylor,** 'Genesis and Catastrophe: the Flood as the major biblical cataclysm', *Creation Techical Journal,* 14 (1), 101–109, 2000, P Garner, M Garton, S Robinson and D Tyler 'Flood Models', *Creation Techical Journal,* 14 (3), 79–80, 2000 and **AC McIntosh, T Edmondson** and **S Taylor,** 'Reply to "Flood Models"', *Creation Technical Journal,* 14 (3), 80–82, 2000.

41 C Wieland, 'Mr Living Fossils', *Creation Magazine* 15(2), March 1993, pp. 14–19.

42 J Scheven, *Living Fossils: Confirmation of Creation,* 90 minute video, available from Creation Science Foundation (UK), PO Box 1427, Swenhampton, Swindon, Wilts., SN6 7UF.

43 JC Whitcomb, and **HM Morris,** *The Genesis Flood* (London: Evangelical Press, 1969), p. 177.

44 JC Whitcomb, and **HM Morris,** op. cit., pp. 392–393.

45 S Baker, *Bone of contention* (2nd edition; Welwyn: Evangelical Press, 1986), p. 24.

46 E Schulman, 'Longevity under adversity in conifers', *Science,* 119, 399– , 23 March 1934.

47 D EK Robbins *Can the Redwoods date the Flood?,* ICR Impact Article No. 134, Institute Creation Research, August 1984.

48 E Schulman, 'Bristlecone Pine, Oldest living thing', *National Geographic Magazine,* 113, 1958, 355.

49 N McWhirter (ed.), *Guinness Book of Records* (London: Guinness, 1983), p. 57.

50 JC Whitcomb, and **HM Morris,** op. cit., p.393.

51 M Behe, *Darwin's Black Box* (New York: Free Press, 1996), pp. 69–73.

52 Sir JE Lighthill, **FRS,** *Aerodynamic Aspects of Animal Flight,* Royal Institution Lecture 20th June 1974, Published by BHRA Ltd., Cranfield, Beds.

53 'Created to Fly', *Creation Magazine,* 9(2), March 1987, 18–20.

54 Sir JE Lighthill, FRS, op. cit.

55 WE Filmer, *Feathers—Wonders of Creation,* Creation Science Movement, Pamphlet 255, November 1987.

56 J Foucher, *Birds—a special Creation,* Creation Science Movement, Pamphlet 271, July 1990.

57 RM Alexander, 'Muscles for the Job', *New Scientist,* 15 April 1989.

58 M Denton, op. cit., see chapter 9 pp. 199–232 and in particular pp. 210–213 on the avian lung, pp. 202–203 on feathers.

59 J Foucher, op. cit.

60 R Dawkins, *Climbing Mount Improbable* (London: Viking, 1996).

61 R Dawkins, op. cit., pp. 91–93.

62 L Hofland, 'Giraffes—Animals that stand out in a crowd', *Creation,* 18(4), 10–13, September/November 1996.

63 R Dawkins, op. cit., chapter 5, 'The forty-fold path to enlightenment', pp. 38–40,

64 R Dawkins, private communications March-May 1996.

65 R Dawkins, *Climbing Mount Improbable*, p. 135.

66 R Dawkins, op. cit., p.132

67 R Dawkins, op. cit., pp. 132–133.

68 C Wieland, 'Seeing back to front', *Creation,* 18(2), 38–40, March/May 1996.

69 RA Crowson, *The Biology of the Coleoptera* (London: Academic Press, 1981), p. 981, chapter 15.

70 R Dawkins, *The Blind Watchmaker* (London: Penguin, 1991), pp. 86–87.

71 MJ Behe, *Darwin's Black Box* (New York: Free Press, 1996), pp. 32–33.

72 T Eisner, and **DJ Aneshansley,** 'Spray aiming in the Bombardier Beetle: Photographic evidence', *Proceedings* of the National Academy of Science, 96, 9705–9709, August 1999.

73 S Baker, op. cit. pp. 27–28.

74 United Nations, *Prospects of World Urbanization,* 1988, United Nations Publication, Deptartment of International Economic and Social Affairs, 1989.

75 Modern English Dictionary (London: Longman, 1976), p. 1271. 'The war (Second World War), which cost more than 36 million lives, was the most destructive and widespread in history …' This is still only a very small fraction (about 1½% of the total world population of about 2500 million in the war years).

76 F Osborn, 'Our Reproductive Potential', *Science,* 125, 531, 22nd March 1957.

77 JC Whitcomb, and HM Morris, op. cit., pp. 26–27.

78 ML Lubenow, *Bones of Contention* (Grand Rapids: Baker Book House, 1994), Appendix: 'The Dating Game', pp 247–266 and see charts pp 170–171. See also Appendix C of this book, 'Fossils and the Rocks'.

79 Nicholls, *Population Growth and the time-span of human history*, Creation Science Movement, Pamphlet 301, Portsmouth, UK.

80 HM Morris, *Evolution and the Population Problem,* ICR Impact Article, no.21.

81 Bill Cooper, *After the Flood—the early post-flood history of Europe traced back to Noah* (Chichester: New Wine Press, 1995).

82 JC Whitcomb, and **HM Morris,** op. cit., pp. 38–40 and pp. 47–49.

83 A Heidel, *The Gilgamesh Epic and Old Testament Parallels* (2nd ed.; Chicago: University of Chicago Press, 1949), pp. 224–258.

84 Sir JG Frazer, *Folk-lore in the Old Testament* (London: Macmillan, 1918), Vol I, pp. 104–361.

85 R Andree, *Die Flutsogen* (Brunswick, 1891).

86 BC Nelson, *The Deluge Story in Stone* (Minneapolis: Bethany Fellowship, 1968), p. 169.

87 J Urquhart, *Modern Discoveries and the Bible* (Marshall, 1898), pp. 163–191, chapter 9 'Traditions of the Deluge'. See also, chapter 14, pp. 285–310 which brings out remarkable testimony to the Tower of Babel and the post-Babel dispersion. As mentioned earlier in section 3.7, there is evidence that the foundation of the tower of Babel still stands today at Birs Nimroud south west of Hillah in Iraq. This evidence is little reported in modern Christian literature because of the tendency no longer to regard Genesis as literal history. See also **A Parrot,** *The Tower of Babel* (London: SCM Press, 1955).

The fossils and the rocks

Missing links in the fossil record

Gould advocates the theory of 'punctuated equilibrium' which says that changes in species arrived suddenly without gradual transition (that is, 'a dinosaur laid an egg of a creature with wings—the ancestor of a bird'). Though this theory is no better than classical gradualism advocated by Darwin, at least Gould acknowledged the lack of transitional forms in the fossil record when he wrote:

The family trees which adorn our text books are based on inference, however reasonable, not the evidence of fossils.[1]

A pamphlet is published by Chapman[2] which very clearly demonstrates that leading evolutionists acknowledge the very serious lack of transitional forms: from single-celled life to invertebrates, from invertebrates to fish, from fish to amphibians, from amphibians to reptiles, from reptiles to birds and mammals, from land animals to sea mammals, from non-flying mammals to bats, and lastly from apes to human beings. The gaps are so vast that experimentally the evidence is stacked against Darwinian evolution.

There are a few contenders. At one time it was thought that the coelacanth was a fish beginning to grow stumps which would become legs and that at last, this was the missing link of fish to amphibians. Not to be, for a living version was found exactly like its fossil counterpart, swimming quite happily near the sea floor (where it generally resides) near East London, off the coast of South Africa in 1938. You could say this transitional form had no leg to stand on!

Then there are the Archaeopteryx fossils long acclaimed as a transitional reptile to bird. The creature evidently had feathers and yet it seems to have been reptilian with teeth and claws on the wings and with a bony tail. However the feathers were in no transitional state, but fully formed, like modern bird's wings. Neither are the claws extraordinary, for the ostrich and hoatzin have claws on their wings, but this does not make them part-reptile/part-bird. The death-knell to any notion that Archaeopteryx was a transitional form came with the discovery of fossils of modern type birds in rocks which, according to the evolutionists' own dating system are 75 million years *older* than those with the archaeopteryx fossil![3] Milton, concerning the supposed evidence of progressive change of fossils in the rocks, has rightly stated:

But this simple relationship is not what is shown in the sequence of the rocks. Nowhere in the world has anyone met this simple evidential criterion with a straightforward fossil sequence from successive strata. Yet there are so many billions of fossils available from so many thousands of strata that the failure to meet this modest demand is inexplicable if evolution has taken place in the way Darwin and his followers have envisaged. It ought to be relatively easy to assemble not merely a handful but hundreds of species arranged in lineal descent. Primary school children should be able to do this on an afternoon's nature study trip to the local quarry: but even the world's foremost palaeontologists have failed to do so with the whole earth to choose from and the resources of the world's greatest universities at their disposal.[4]

A number of evolutionists (e.g. SJ Gould, N Eldredge, C Patterson and D Raup) recognize the lack of transitional forms in the fossil record which originally Darwin and others had expected.[5] Richard Goldschmidt, in his time a leading geneticist at the University of California, stated:

In spite of the immense amount of the paleontologic material and the existence of long series of intact stratigraphic sequences with perfect records for the lower categories, transitions between the higher categories are missing.[6]

Some (like SJ Gould) now propose a model of evolution where massive changes took place but with no evidence left of transition in the fossil record (the so-called 'Punctuated Equilibrium' theory[7]). Thus 'it all happened too fast to be recorded'. It is only because of Professor Gould's standing that he has got away with little ridicule.

What this all certainly shows is that noteworthy authorities on fossils are now changing their views.[8] However, this is also alarming since *gradual* transition was the main plank of evolution. As Professor Wright, a leading medical authority at the University of Leeds, has put it:

It is rather similar to the village clock striking thirteen—one distrusts all its previous pronouncements.[9]

No missing link from apes to men

The classic book reviewing the supposed evidence of human evolution is the book by Lubenow[10] who has researched this issue for 25 years and writes with authority. With masterful scholarship and using the evolutionists' own dating scheme he exposes the impossibility of any connection of modern Homo Sapiens to the Australopithecines (Southern Apes). As one evolutionist has recorded of his work,

He does his homework so thoroughly that he makes someone like me who would carry on a dialogue with him ... also do his homework ...[11]

He shows (using the evolutionist time scale and their own writings) that:

i. Fossils that are indistinguishable from modern humans can be traced all the way back to 4·5 mya (million years ago) which is before Australopithecines appear in the fossil record.[12]

ii. So called ancestors to modern Homo Sapiens such as Homo Erectus are concurrent with Australopithecines and modern Homo Sapiens fossils.

iii. The Homo Habilis fossils which are supposed to have evolved into Homo Erectus are found to be all contemporary with Homo Erectus.

iv. There are no Australopithecine fossils in the right time period to serve as evolutionary ancestors to humans.

v. More disturbing still is the independent check that at the *same* location and in the *same* level stratigraphically are found two different types of human fossils supposed to be set apart by enormous time spans. Thus, for instance, in Kenya at the East Lake Rudolf site (now East Lake Turkana), called Koobi Fora, the KNM-ER 813 skull, which is essentially modern looking, has been found with KNM-ER 803, 820, 1507 and 3883, which are supposed to be that of Homo Erectus, the ancestor of archaic and modern Homo Sapiens, *altogether*.[13,14,15]

The more recent Neanderthal fossils (supposedly about 50,000—100,000 years ago) have again been found *with modern Homo Sapiens* fossils at the same site. One of the most glaring examples of this is at the Tabun Cave in Mount Carmel in Israel,[16],[17] where four Neanderthal fossils were found with two fossils anatomically like modern Homo Sapiens.

I suspect that investigations are no further than in 1970 when Lord Zuckerman, MD, DSc, stated:

… if man evolved from an ape-like creature, he did so without leaving a trace of that evolution in the fossil record.[18]

—this despite the media attention given by David Attenborough and others to the work of Mary and Louis Leakey and more recently, Richard Leakey. The religious fervour of the search for supposedly ape-like ancestors is bound to continue, so long as men insist on scorning the obvious reasonable alternative—that men were created Homo Sapiens *from the beginning.*

Sir Ambrose Fleming, one time President of the Victoria Institute and Philosophical Society of Great Britain, Fellow of the Royal Society, stated:

Whatever may be the effect on the religious opinions of adults or of scientific men of an adherence to this evolutionary theory of human origin, it is unquestionable that it is disastrous to the ethical development or spiritual life of the young or uneducated to lead them to believe that men are 'descended from monkeys' or that 'the chimpanzee or gorilla are man's nearest relations', which is the form in which this theory takes expression in the minds of the general public.

The reckless popularization of the theory of organic evolution without regard to the strong arguments which can be urged against it, constitutes a serious danger.

Biblical teaching is not inconsistent with any definitely ascertained facts with regard to early mankind, when carefully interpreted.[19]

The dating of the rocks

If there is one matter which the evolutionist regards as sacrosanct, it is the geological column of rock strata. Although there is no place on earth where *all* the rock strata of the geological column can be observed, the view is strongly adhered to, that all the strata were laid down slowly. The massive amount of water-borne sediments across the globe from a creationist standpoint are entirely consistent with the biblical account of a world-wide flood. As will be shown in this section, contrary to the general view, there are *no* absolute methods for dating. So where does the ancient dating used by the evolutionist come from? It is important to grasp what, to many, are some very surprising facts.

FOSSILS IN SEDIMENTARY ROCK CANNOT BE DIRECTLY DATED USING RADIOISOTOPE TECHNIQUES

Radioisotope techniques (such as potassium-argon, uranium-lead methods) can only be used on *igneous* rock (such as lava from previous volcanic activity or granite). Since 75% of the world's land area is composed of sedimentary rock, and virtually all of the fossils are in sedimentary rock, this leads to an impasse for direct dating techniques. Generally, the way sedimentary rocks are dated is to consider some key fossils they contain. These are called 'index fossils'. The assumption of gradual deposition is made on the basis that the oldest rock is generally at the bottom (Cambrian) and recent rock is near the top (Quaternary). Because of buckling of the Earth's surface the rocks are not always in the same order, but the index fossils are used to identify the various rock layers. When William Smith[20] first began his study of the rock layers in the 1800s, it was most helpful in identifying where certain types of rock could be found (particularly for building contractors looking for new sources of stone), but the dating of the rock was not proven, and indeed was incidental to his study which simply recognized that certain types of rock generally contained certain (index) fossils.

Thus respected palaeontologists and geologists can unwittingly show up their real lack of certainty concerning the strata when they write:

A trained palaeontologist can identify the relative geologic age of any fossiliferous rock formation by a study of its fossils almost as easily and certainly as he can determine the relative place of a sheet of manuscript by looking at its pagination. Fossils thus make it possible to correlate events in different parts of the world and so to work out the history of the earth as a whole.[21]

Or an even greater admission:

The only chronomatic scale applicable in geologic history for the stratigraphic classification of rocks and for dating geological events exactly is furnished by the fossils. Owing to the irreversibility of evolution, they offer an unambiguous time scale for relative age determinations and for world-wide correlations of rocks.[22]

The cyclical nature of the reasoning now becomes apparent from the above quotes when having dated the rocks by the index fossils they contain (against a geological column which nowhere occurs in totality on the earth's surface), one then proceeds to date other fossils by the rocks in which they are buried!

As Morris has pointed out:

Instead of proceeding from observation to conclusion, the conclusion interprets the observation which 'proves' the conclusion. The fossils should contain the main evidence for evolution. But instead, we see that the ages of rocks are determined by the stage of evolution of the index fossils found therein, which are themselves dated and organized by the age of the rocks. Thus the rocks date the fossils, and the fossils date the rocks.[23]

Thus it is vital to recognize that *sedimentary rock of itself cannot be dated directly and neither can the fossils they contain*. Even indirect dating of sedimentary rock is impossible when it contains no fossils.

RADIOMETRIC DATING—CARBON 14

However, there are some remains which are not all turned to rock which can be dated by the Carbon 14 method, and there are some rocks (igneous or metamorphic) which one can also attempt to date by radioisotope techniques.

First the Carbon 14 dating[24] of bones and organic remains. This method was developed by Professor WF Libby[25] in the mid 1940s at the University of Chicago and is based on the knowledge that the Carbon 14 isotope is produced by neutrons combining with Nitrogen in the upper atmosphere. These neutrons are themselves produced as a result of the bombardment of the upper atmosphere by cosmic rays. The Carbon 14 forms carbon dioxide in the atmosphere and it is assumed that the ratio of Carbon 14 to Carbon 12 in the atmosphere is always the same and that living creatures have in their bodies the same quantity of Carbon 14 while living. The Carbon 14 enters plants through photosynthesis and also animals through the plants. In that Carbon 14 decays back to Nitrogen with a half-life of 5,730 years, in the living world it is assumed there is a constant ratio of the two isotopes of Carbon in the carbon dioxide of the atmosphere and in the living creature. When that creature dies, it is unable to take up further radiocarbon and that which is present diminishes due to radioactive decay. The half-life of this decay process has been determined at 5,730 years, so that measuring the amount of radiocarbon compared to Carbon 12 in a dead organism determines the age of dead organic material since death, on the assumption that the decay rate is unaltered. In fact there are six assumptions in all, as brought out by Monty White,[26]

i. That the amount of cosmic radiation, and hence the amount of neutron bombardment in the upper atmosphere, has been essentially constant over the last 50,000 years (the maximum supposed age that can be measured with this method).

ii. That the concentration of radiocarbon in the carbon dioxide of the atmosphere has remained constant.

iii. That the carbon dioxide content of the oceans and atmosphere has remained constant.

iv. That dead organic matter is not altered with respect to its carbon content by any biological or other activity.

v. That the rate of decay of radiocarbon is constant.

vi. That the rate of formation and the rate of disappearance of radiocarbon in the biosphere have been in equilibrium over the time period concerned (50,000 years).

Monty White[27] goes on to show that the first three assumptions are affected by variations in the sun's radiation and possible increases in the amount of carbon dioxide in the atmosphere, both of which are held to by evolutionists as reasons for the onset of the Ice Age(s)! It has also been shown that carbon dioxide levels have fluctuated because of the increased burning of fossils fuels[28] and that the amount of radiocarbon in the atmosphere has been steadily increasing since 1954.[29]

Furthermore, there is no certainty that the amount of cosmic radiation reaching the atmosphere was the same in the past, and thus the Carbon 14 production could have been much less. It has already been shown that the magnetic field was certainly stronger in the past and this would then deflect away more cosmic radiation than now. If there was more water in the atmosphere (which before the Flood is highly likely), this would also weaken the effect of cosmic radiation.

That dead organic material is altered with respect to its carbon content by biological activity has been certainly questioned. The following is a significant statement by radiocarbon scientists:

The most significant problem is that of biological alteration of materials in the soil. This effect grows more serious with greater age. To produce an error of 50% in the age of 10,000 year old specimen would require the replacement of more than 25% of the carbon atoms. For a 40,000 year old sample, the figure is only 5%, while an error of 5,000 years can be produced by about 1% of modern materials.[30]

The decay rate itself (assumption (v.)) may not necessarily be constant because it is known that radioisotopes have decay rates which can be affected by pressure[31] and the last assumption of equilibrium of Carbon 14 to Carbon 12 is questioned strongly by Slusher[32] who states that there is a 24% difference between the amount of Carbon 14 being produced to that decaying. This is certainly not a state of equilibrium.

The only way radiocarbon dating can be made to give any degree of accuracy is to calibrate it against known archaeological artefacts. Consequently its use is really somewhat restricted to the last 5,000 years for which we have firm records. Before this, the technique is so much dependent on assumptions that it becomes guess work. Even if scientists reject a global flood, there is very strong evidence from polar regions that there was a global semi-tropical climate with vast amounts of plant life all over the world. Thus the amount of carbon dioxide in the air would have been greatly changed and all the balances of Carbon 14 to Carbon 12 similarly affected.

Since Carbon 14 dating is often quoted as the answer to all dating problems, it is important we recognize the severe restrictions of this method.

We now turn to other radiometric dating methods which are used to date volcanic rock.

POTASSIUM-ARGON DATING METHOD

The advantage of these methods are that they can be applied to volcanic rock (but still not the 75% sedimentary rock). The details of the potassium-argon scheme are given in the excellent book of Monty White.[33] As with all these schemes, the parent isotope (potassium 40 in this case) is decaying to a daughter element (argon 40) and it is assumed that one can measure the amounts accurately in the rock today, that the logarithmic rate of decay is known and stays the same, that there is no contamination of the rate from another source of these two elements over the supposed long period of decay and that no daughter element entered at the time of crystallisation. Although it is certainly true that the amounts of argon and potassium can be accurately measured, it is exceedingly difficult to measure the logarithmic rate of decay of potassium 40. One of the main reasons is that potassium 40 decays into *two* elements, calcium 40 and argon 40. The proportion that decays into argon 40 compared to calcium 40 is called the branching ratio, and is only known by calibrating the dates that various values of branching ratios cause potassium-argon dating to yield, against the uranium-thorium scheme. That scheme itself is based on questionable assumptions. However, probably the major reasons why potassium-argon dating dates must not be relied on is because contamination and leakage is very easily performed. It is interesting to note that York and Farquhar (who would not accept a creation position) state:

Where the results of comparisons of this sort [i.e. of different dating methods] disagree, it is clear that some sort of transfer of material into or out of the rock or mineral has taken place. It has also become apparent from the number of published discordant ages that disturbances of this nature are far more common that was formerly realized.[34]

The difficulty of this method is that argon *very* easily diffuses from mineral to mineral so it can easily move down through the rock layers thus giving to those rocks, the appearance of age. Not only that, potassium can leak very readily from rock so that as much as 80% of potassium in a small sample of an iron meteorite was removed by running water over it for $4\frac{1}{4}$ hours.[35] Thus erosion can *easily* leach potassium out of rock again leading to the appearance of age. Andrews makes the important observation that:

we automatically factor-in ages of this magnitude by our choice of decay processes with half-lives of this order, so that if any result is obtained at all, it is almost bound to be within two orders of magnitude of the half-life … [the assumption is made] that no non-radiogenic argon is present at time zero. Yet the molten magma is known to contain significant quantities of argon and indeed this fact is frequently appealed to in explaining aberrant K-Ar dates! It would be just as logical to assume some 'universal' finite concentration of argon at time zero, with a consequent reduction of predicted age. If the present atmospheric concentration of argon were taken as this universal, non-radiogenic content, K-Ar dating would give ages close to zero for most rocks.[36]

Thus there is no reliability in this scheme.

THE ISOCHRON DATING METHOD

The matter of leeching of potassium *out* of rock and diffusion of argon *through* the rock is very relevant to the isochron method. This method[37] plots the abundance of the daughter element (argon in this case) against the abundance of the parent element (potassium) for set rock samples at the same location. It is found that the plot correlates closely to a straight line with positive slope. Each rock sample is represented as a distinct point on the graph. If the amount of parent element is not accurately known at the beginning, this method has the advantage that this knowledge is not essential for dating, since the larger (or smaller) amounts of parent element lead to correspondingly larger (or smaller) amounts of daughter element. However the method still has a very major assumption—that there was no slope for the curve to begin with. In practical terms this means this method still assumes no daughter element was there at the start, whatever the depth of the strata today. As is shown by Austin in his excellent summary of this more modern method,[38] there is no evidence from measurement of recent lava flows that daughter element uniformity at time zero is in fact a valid assumption. There is rather a change with depth at the start. This is so because (in the case of the K-Ar system [potassium and argon] for instance) argon *can* in fact be present throughout the lava when formed and can also diffuse through the rock, particularly near the surface. Consequently greater argon concentrations tend to be at greater depth from the initial year or two after formation! As a scientist regularly studying diffusion phenomena within porous media (for combustion studies[39]), I find this is a phenomenon very readily misunderstood and too easily relegated in importance. When considering long periods of time, as discussed earlier, the diffusion of gases can be a major factor.[40] It is quite incorrect for scientists to put confidence in dating methods by measuring gas levels on the basis of an original uniformity assumption.

OTHER RADIOMETRIC DATING SCHEMES

The next scheme that is often quoted is the uranium-lead dating method. This method is similar to the potassium-argon method although there are two isotopes of uranium which can be used (uranium 238 $\rightarrow$ lead 206 and uranium 235 $\rightarrow$ lead 207) and a similar thorium 232 $\rightarrow$ lead 208 method is also employed. To use any of these methods, as before, the logarithmic decay rate must be ascertained, it must be established that the decay rate is not changed by pressure, temperature changes and the original concentrations of uranium/lead, thorium/lead must be known. By examination of halo marks left by this sort of radioactivity, it has been shown that the decay rates of the uranium—thorium—lead decay sequences are in fact not constant. The reader is referred to Slusher[41] above for a detailed discussion of this finding. Even if one waives this embarrassing fact, the establishing of the all important parent/daughter ratio for the isotope at the beginning cannot be made and is *assumed* by the geochronologist. A guess is made from what the geologists think the original composition of the earth's crust would be when it was formed. Thus we find geologists admitting the following:

In practice very few uranium and thorium minerals have been found to exhibit this concordant pattern of ages and the much more common discordances ... have been facilely explained away as each investigator thought best.[42]

Similar difficulties exist with the rubidium-strontium scheme and other less well known radiometric dating methods. It would be far too hasty to state that the schemes are completely disproved. Rather the assumptions made by those who use them have not been carefully established. Thus when evolutionists make statements such as the following:—

Even allowing for some unreliable dates and for occasional lack of rigour in the practical application of principles, the pattern of ages which has emerged from radiometric studies from all over the world is impressive, both in its accord with the relative timing of geological events derived independently, and in the additional light it has shed on earth history.[43]

—it should be recognized that there are many hidden assumptions being made, which, when exposed, make these statements far less convincing. It is the detail which must always be carefully scrutinized, and it is at this level that these methods are at best questionable. The following quote by EH Andrews (Professor of Materials Science at Queen Mary College, London) is very salient to the question of so-called absolute calibration for these methods:

... Once one admits (as these experts do) that a significant proportion of dates are in error on account of 'contamination', material transfer, isotopic equalization ('resetting of the radiometric clock') and other hypothesized events, then the question arises as to how one differentiates an erroneous date from a true one. The answer to this question is surprising indeed, for it amounts to a calibration of the radiometric clock by the stratigraphical rates [i.e. supposed evolutionary slow rate of formation of the rock strata]. So, far from the radiometric time-scale providing an 'absolute' calibration of the geological column, we find the reverse is, in practice, the case.[44]

Professor Andrews then goes on to quote no fewer than six examples in the open literature of such circular reasoning where the radiometric dating is calibrated by the rocks. We illustrate with two of these quotes.[45,46] The reader is referred to the full article (footnote 44) for further detail.

The internal consistency demonstrated above is not a sufficient test of the accuracy of the [radiometric] age determinations; *they must also be consistent with any age constraints placed on intrusion by fossils in the country rocks.*

The Mississippian age for sample NS-45 cannot be correct because *it is grossly inconsistent with the stratigraphic position of the lavas.* No clues as to apparent preferential loss of potassium or gain of excess argon 40 from this sample are in evidence from thin section examination.

One of the most remarkable natural examples of sedimentary rock layers exposed to view is the Grand Canyon in Arizona, USA. The sediments sit above Precambrian rocks which contain Cardenas Basalt of volcanic origin. This dates (by radiometric techniques) at between 790 to 1,100 million years.[47] Above the sedimentary rock is a volcano which evidently is recent for the lava has flowed down the strata to the river bed. Yet these lava flows produced radiometric ages of from 1,300 million years using rubidium-strontium dating to 2,600 million years using other schemes.[48,49] Clearly the date was wrong, for it was coming out 'older' than the Precambrian basalt beneath! So the results of the top rocks were dismissed as 'fictitious isochrons', whereas those below are accepted. The reason? Simply because the data does not fit the preconceived view that the rocks were formed slowly over great ages.

When one realizes that these radiometric dating schemes are the backbone of the famous investigations by palaeontologists such as the Leakeys in the Olduvai Gorge in Tanzania, East Africa (see earlier discussion of Lubenow's[50] review of these findings), one becomes aware of the doubtfulness of the reasoning which places one questionable assumption upon another. This is particularly evident when one bears in mind that the rocks in the immediate vicinity of the skulls found in the Olduvai Gorge cannot be dated directly because they are in sedimentary rock. Rather the lava intrusions *into* these sedimentary rocks are dated by radiometric methods. The further, little known, but intriguing finding is that radiocarbon dating of the skulls such as Zinjanthropus and Australopithecus gives dates of the order of 30,000 years as against the claimed 2 to 4½ million years[51,52]—this can hardly be dismissed as experimental error!

Thus we must not be taken in by the rather grand statements by proponents of old-earth beliefs that radiometric dating has *proved* the age of the earth to be 4,500 million years old. The evidence is of a method which in no way is absolute but depends heavily on previously made assumptions about the stratigraphic record.

When these dating methods are applied to rock known to be young, the evidence is conclusive that the assumptions are faulty. Take for example the dating of the volcanic lava flows *known* to have originated from the Kaupeleha Volcano in Hawaii which erupted in 1800–1801. These were dated with a variety of methods.[53] According to theory, they were far too young to have produced much radiogenic argon or helium, and yet they contained enough to produce twelve dates ranging from 140 million years to 2,960 million years!'[54] This hardly inspires confidence.

A recent article[55] by Professor Colin Humphreys, a material scientist from Cambridge, shows far too great a confidence in these dating schemes and too quick a conclusion that a young earth position is untenable. We agree with Andrews, who has stated:

… radiometric dating is so frequently unreliable that practising geologists insist on using the stratigraphical record (based on sedimentation rates and index fossils) to control and calibrate the radiometric 'clock' rather than the reverse. It is thus totally misleading to claim, as many do, that isotopic ages provided an absolute time scale, against which the standard geological column and its fossils can be checked.[56]

The inexactness of this science would never be permissible in much tougher scientific arenas where safety and lives depended on it. If one used such guess-work to design aircraft, we would be no further than the men who jumped off towers flapping wings like birds. It was careful, exact scientific, testable techniques which led to the great inventions of pioneers such as the Wright Brothers. Apart from other philosophical beliefs, we need to bring the penetrating eye of good scientific method to radiometric methods and test *every* assumption before making bold, unfounded conclusions. A very good summary article on the question of rock dating is given by Peet.[57]

Indications of catastrophe in the rock layers

A classic text book on geology states:

It is the triumph of geology as a science to have demonstrated that we do not need to refer to vast, unknown and terrible causes for the relief features of the earth, but that the known agencies at work today are competent to produce them, provided they have time enough.[58]

However, this must now be questioned as many old-earth geologists are beginning to realize. As already noted in Appendix B (see section entitled, 'Large depths of volcanic lava'), the depth of volcanic flow is staggering in places on the Earth's surface. Whitcomb and Morris[59] discuss this matter at length and show that uniformitarian geologists acknowledge (but do not satisfactorily explain) this. Thus Fenneman states:

The physiographic history of this province begins with the ancient surface before the lavas were erupted. This is known to have been locally rough, even mountainous, partly by the fact that some of the old peaks rose above the lava flood, *which was at least several thousand feet deep.*[60]

It is therefore important as we conclude this appendix on the fossils and the rocks, to mention in the next three sections the remarkable rock layers which are known to have been formed catastrophically and recently. The great similarity to modern-day rocks bears great testimony to the creation/Flood model of rock formation.

Young igneous rocks

From November 1963 to June 1967, a volcanic eruption off Iceland created the island now called Surtsey. It only took months for bare volcanic rock to be changed into an island with beaches, sand and vegetation so that it had every appearance of age. The official Icelandic geologist Thorarinsson records the following intriguing description:

When [geologists] in the spring and summer of 1964 wandered about the island ... they found it hard to believe that this was an island whose age was still measured in months, not years ... What elsewhere may take thousands of years may be accomplished [in Iceland] in one century ... [in] Surtsey ... the same development may take a few weeks or even a few days.

On Surtsey only a few months sufficed for a landscape to be created which was so varied and mature that it was almost beyond belief ... wide sandy beaches ... precipitous crags ... gravel banks and lagoons, impressive cliffs greyish white from the brine ... hollows, glens and screes ...boulders worn by the surf, some of which were almost round on an abrasion platform cut into the cliffs.[61]

These eye-witness accounts of the very speedy change of a newly formed volcanic island to that which is very little different from previously existing and supposedly ancient terrain, give great weight to the belief that catastrophic forces were major factors in rock formation and that there are major unproven assumptions in modern dating techniques.

Mudflows

On 18 May 1980 probably the most well documented volcanic eruption took place at Mount St Helens in Washington State in the USA. The top of the mountain was completely removed and a hot blast cloud ripped away 150 square miles of forest. The movement of the mountain caused a wave nearly 900 feet high to move across Spirit Lake with the effect that of the order of 1 million tree trunks found their way into the lake.[62] Many others were pushed further down into lower regions by mud flows and were actually observed upright, roots down, moving at great speed in the mud flows.

It has to be appreciated that the force of the blast at Mount St Helens was small compared to known volcanic blasts such as that in 1883 at Krakatau in between the Sumatra and Java islands of Indonesia. This latter was heard 2,900 miles away with rocks thrown 34 miles high into the atmosphere and dust falling 3,313 miles away, ten days after the explosion.[63] A tsunami (tidal wave) 100 feet high was created which travelled right across the Indian Ocean at 450 m.p.h.[64] Volcanic mist circled the earth and turned the sun blue and green, creating effects that moved Tennyson to pen, 'For day by day through many a blood-red eve ... The wrathful sunset glared ...'[65]

Thus the forces of catastrophism in recent memory are known to be enormous. It is therefore quite conceivable that major volcanic activity was involved in the earth movements in the western United States with subsequent gigantic mud slides gouging out the Grand Canyon. This is consistent with the Scripture recording (Psalm 104:8) that at the time of the flood, '… the mountains ascend, the valleys descend …'. There is even today strong activity on the sea floor, as stated by Hamilton[66] (and quoted in Whitcomb and Morris[67]):

The present status of knowledge of the sea floor in the Pacific Ocean area is such that a surprising amount of evidence of large-scale faulting, mountain building, volcanic activity, and large-scale crystal movements is known; this is a marked departure from earlier assumptions, which, because of lack of information, held that this vast area had been relatively calm during geologic time.

Not until the eruption of Mount St Helens in 1980 had it been quite appreciated what the immediate aftermath of volcanic eruptions can cause. A number of studies have been made of this remarkable event. In particular, Austin[68] has rightly compared the events at Mount St Helens with the possible catastrophic cause of the Grand Canyon. The reason is that sediments 600 feet thick which were known to be formed from these mud flows are effectively a miniature $\frac{1}{40}$th version of the Grand Canyon. As Austin has stated:

The small creeks which flow through the head waters of the Toatle River today might seem, by present appearances to have carved these canyons very slowly over a long timed period, except for the fact that the erosion was observed to have occurred rapidly![69]

The similarities between the Toatle River Canyon and the Grand Canyon are not just superficial. There has long been a very great difficulty with the old earth interpretation of the Grand Canyon as it relates to the warping of the sedimentary layers as one moves away to eastern Arizona. This is called the Kaibab Upwarp and refers to the Kaibab limestone which sits as the top sediment. The distance from Grand Canyon village to the end of the Kaibab Upwarp is 250 miles. The top of the Canyon is 7,000 feet above sea level at the south rim and the same upper sediment drops to 2,000 feet in Eastern Arizona. The classical old earth explanation is that the plateau of the Grand Canyon was pushed up into its present position about 79 million years ago concurrently with the Rocky Mountains, and that the Canyon was carved through the uplifted plateau. The bottom layer (Tapeats Sandstone) is dated at 550 million years old by uniformitarian geologists and the top Kaibab limestone is dated at 250 million years. So the whole area was reckoned to be 180 million years old before the upwarp took place. Under those conditions to raise rock 5,000 feet *with no breakage* is some feat of engineering, particularly as one end is kept at the same height (2,000 feet above sea level) and what is more, all the layers are smoothly running in curves above each other. It is impossible to bend hardened rock without breakage due to its brittle consistency. This difficulty has never been satisfactorily solved, but as very clearly shown by Morris,[70] the problem has an immediate answer as soon as you consider the sandstone and indeed all the layers of upwarp being deformed while still in a soft plastic condition.

Fossilized tree trunks

Coal miners have been familiar for centuries with fossilized tree trunks in coal seams. Termed 'kettles' these circular shapes sometimes occur in the roof of a mine and are in fact the bottoms of upright tree trunks. If the lower parts, including the roots, are mined away, then there are dangers of it falling and crushing the miners underneath. The fascinating and instructive lesson is that these tree trunks are often very long, extending up through more than one layer of strata. They are then termed Polystrate fossils and these particular types are themselves proof that *all* the strata were laid at a similar period separated at the very most by a year or so, and probably not separated by more than a few days.

The uniformitarian answer is to say that the origin of coal was due to a peat swamp submerged by water, which then accumulated mud and sediment on the sea floor. Gradually this mud changed to rock (shale or limestone) with the peat underneath altering to coal through the action of heat and pressure from the rock layers above. All this is supposed to have happened imperceptibly slowly, so that we have the incredible situation of tree trunks extending 30 feet or more from the bottom of the ocean, staying upright for millions of years without rotting away? And what of polystrate tree trunks running through more than one strata? As Morris aptly puts it:

Did it ride the strata down and up and then down again for millions of years? From studying these trees, we can conclude that the length of time for accumulation of the peat (which later turned into coal) and the overlying sediments was less time than it takes for wood to decay. Obviously, wood decays in only a few decades at most, whether in an active ocean environment, standing in air, or buried in sediments.[71]

The argument above is really unassailable. To mix metaphors, the old-earth geologist is 'burying his head in the mud', if he tries to argue that the strata containing polystrate fossils were not laid at the *same time*.

Fossilized tree trunks (in coal or other sediments) are numerous and have been recorded in detail.[72] In fact the difficulties of understanding single layer tree trunk fossils have exactly the same problems of interpretation on a uniformitarian time scale as those which go through more than one layer. You still have to argue that 30 feet of wood remained unaffected by erosion while standing in air for at least a million years. That is not science, it is holding on to a religious presupposition against all rational explanation. For immediately one accepts catastrophic formation, the evidence, at least in this area of study, makes sense. Mudflows *carried* the tree trunks from their original locations. Indeed such is the only possible explanation of the 25–50 successive layers of sediment with vast numbers of tree trunks vertically embedded in them at Specimen Ridge in Yellowstone National Park[73,74] since uniformitarian explanations require successive forests one on top of the other with millions of years for sediment to bury trees in growth location. However, the erosion of the hillside where the ridge with its strata is dramatically visible, would require as much, if not more, time than that required to deposit the sediments. Again, catastrophic mudflow 'rafting' of tree trunks gives the answer which very readily fits the facts. It is significant that, as Morris has pointed out at Yellowstone:

The roots, while many times oriented in a downward direction, didn't have fully developed root systems. Often, in living trees, the roots are larger than the rest of the tree. The roots of these petrified trees appear to have been broken off near the base of the tree. Only 'root balls' are present, not the fully developed root system.[75]

This explains why marine animal remains are found in some 'root balls'.[76]

This is entirely as one would expect as uprooted trees are dragged by water/mud flows in a catastrophic fashion. The remarkable confirmation at the eruption of Mount St Helens in 1980 was astonishing. It was found that many tree trunks floated vertically in Spirit Lake[77,78] and as stated earlier, even in the mud flows, they often travelled away from their original growth position *vertically*. Such evidence lends great weight to the notion that the petrified tree trunks of Specimen Ridge in Yellowstone, those in Arizona's Petrified Forest National Park and those at Saint Etienne, France[79] and other strata throughout the world, were deposited by moving mud flows.

The evidence then changes our view of coal formation. Austin[80] has already investigated the peat formation at Spirit Lake and shown that it resembles certain coal beds of the eastern United States which are dominated by tree bark—and this within a few years after catastrophic origins. Further studies have been made by Nevins[81] on the catastrophic evidence for coal formation and an intriguing experiment has been reported by Hill[82] who produced a substance akin to anthracite in a few minutes by using a rapid heating process with much of the heat being generated by the cellulosic material being altered. Thus, the traditional view of applied pressure on organic material for millions of years producing slow coalification, is being replaced by the view that rapid heating (and possibly some self-heating) caused coalification in a short period of time.[83]

We conclude with a summary statement by Professor Andrews of Queen Mary College, Department of Materials in London. His comment pertains to his discussion of the Surtsey eruption of Iceland, but has much wider implications concerning rock formation: He wrote:

It is clear from this evidence alone that, *given sufficiently large forces*, the rates of geomorphological development may be speeded up by orders of magnitude. The validity of the uniformitarian time scale is thus based wholly upon the assumption that the forces acting historically within the earth's crust were on average, those observed in today's generally quiescent conditions. If conditions such as those that shaped Surtsey prevailed to any significant extent during geological history, the age estimates may need drastic downward revision. The evidence of massive volcanism, tectonic processes,

Appendix C

metamorphism and wholesale fossilization points to a turbulent rather than a quiescent environment over a significant portion of the earth's history.[84]

The author agrees with the statement by Don Batten that:

although evolutionists seek to keep to the original Darwinian premise that the present is key to the past, [i.e. supposedly current slow changes occurred in the past], we should reverse our thinking—the past [creation/catastrophic flood] is the key to the present.[85]

Appendix C notes

1 **SJ Gould,** *Natural History,* 86(5), May 1977, p. 13.

2 **G Chapman,** *Guide to Transitional Fossils*, Pamphlet 300, Creation Science Movement.

3 **T Beardsley,** 'Fossil Bird shakes Evolution Hypothesis', *Nature,* 322, 1986, 677.

4 **R Milton,** *The Facts of Life—shattering the myth of Darwinism* (London: 4th Estate, 1992), p. 105.

5 **DM Raup,** *Conflicts between Darwin and Palaeontology,* Field Museum of Natural History Bulletin, 50, 1980, p. 25.

6 **R Goldschmidt,** 'Evolution, as viewed by one Geneticist', *American Scientist,* 40, January 1952, p.98. See also **JC Whitcomb** and **HM Morris,** *The Genesis Flood* (London: Evangelical Press, 1969), pp.128–130.

7 **N Eldrige** and **SJ Gould,** 'Punctuated equilibrium: an alternative to phyletic gradualism', in **TJM Schopf** (ed.), *Models in Paleobiology* (San Francisco: Freeman, 1973), pp. 82–115.

8 **JW Oller,** *A Theory in Crisis*, ICR Impact Article, No. 180, June 1988.

9 **V Wright,** in **D Burke** (ed.), *Creation and Evolution* (Leicester: IVP, 1986), chapter 3, pp. 111–113.

10 **ML Lubenow,** *Bones of Contention* (Grand Rapids, Michigan: Baker Book House, 1994).

11 **M Charney** (Professor of Anthropology at Colorado State University, Fort Collins, Colorado), fly leaf of **ML Lubenow,** *Bones of Contention* (Grand Rapids: BakerBook House, 1994).

12 Thus for example see **ML Lubenow,** *Bones of Contention*, chapter 5 and chapter 16, p. 180—see in particular the discussion about Kanapoi Elbow fossil, KP271. This was dated by **HM McHenry** 'Fossils and the Mosaic Nature of Human Evolution', *Science* 190 (31 October, 1975) p. 428 and shown to be morphologically no different to modern Homo Sapiens by WW Howells. See also **BA Sismon** and **JS Cybulski** (eds.), *Homo Erectus in human descent: ideas and problems* (Toronto: University of Toronto Press, 1981), pp. 79–80.

13 **AK Betirensmeyer,** and **LF Laporte,** 'Footprints of a Pleistocene hominid in Northern Kenya', *Nature,* 289 (15 Janurary 1981), 167–169.

14 **BA Wood,** 'Evidence on the locomotor pattern of Homo from early Pleistocene of Kenya', *Nature,* 251 (13 September 1974), 135–136.

15 **CS Feibel, FH Brown,** and **I McDougall,** 'Stratigraphic context of Fossil Hominids from the Omo Group Deposits: Northern Turkana Basin, Kenya and Ethiopia', *American Journal of Physical Anthropology,* 78 (April 1989), pp. 611, 613.

16 **RS Corrucini,** 'The Forgotten Skhul crania and the "neopresapiens" theory' (Abstract), *American Journal of Physical Anthropology,* 81(2) (February 1990), p. 209.

17 **ML Lubenow,** op. cit., chapter 16, p.180.

18 **Lord Zuckerman,** *Beyond the Ivory Tower* (New York: Taplinger Publishing Co., 1970), p. 64.

19 **A Naismith,** *1200 Notes, quotes and anecdotes* (Pickering, 1963), p. 63.

20 **M Lambert,** *Fossils* (London: Ward Lock, 1978), pp. 16–20.

21 **C Schuchert and Dunbar,** *Outlines of Historical Geology* (4th ed.; New York: Wiley, 1941), p. 53.

22 **OH Schindewolf,** 'Comments on some stratigraphic terms', *American Journal of Science,* 255, p. 394, June 1957. The cyclical arguments used by geologists are discussed by **JC Whitcomb,** and **HM Morris,** in *The Genesis Flood* (London: Evangelical Press, 1969), p. 132.

23 **JD Morris,** *The Young Earth* (Colorado Springs: Master Books, 1994), p. 14.

24 **AJ Monty White,** *What about Origins?* (Newton Abbot: Dunestone Printers, 1978), p. 127.

25 **WF Libby,** *Nobel Lectures—Chemistry 1942–1962* (Amsterdam: Elsevier, 1964), pp. 587–612.

26 **AJ Monty-White,** op. cit., pp. 132–133.

27 **AJ Monty-White,** op. cit., pp. 133–136.

28 **HR Brannon,** et al., 'Radiocarbon evidence on the dilution of atmospheric and oceanic carbon' in *Transactions,* American Geophysical Union, 38, 1957, p. 650.

29 **Ingrid U Olsson** (ed.), *Radiocarbon variations and absolute chronology: proceedings* (New York: Wiley-Interscience, 1970).

30 **F Johnson, JR Arnold** and **RF Flint,** 'Radio Carbon Dating' in *Science,* 125 (8th February 1957), p. 240. See also **CB Hunt,** Radiocarbon dating in the light of stratigraphy and weathering processes, *Scientific Monthly,* 81 (Nov. 1955), p. 240.

31 **WK Hensley,** and **WA Bassett,** 'Pressure dependence of the radioactive decay constant of Beryllium-7' in *Science,* 181 (4104), 1973, pp. 1164–1165. See also **Monty White,** op. cit., pp. 135–136.

32 **HS Slusher,** *Critiques of radiometric dating* (San Diego: ICR, 1973), p. 39.

33 **Monty-White,** op. cit., pp. 142–147.

34 D York, and **RM Farquhar,** *The earth's age and geochronology* (Pergamon: Oxford, 1972).

35 HS Slusher, op. cit., p. 30.

36 EH Andrews, 'The age of the earth' in **D Burke** (ed.), *Creation and Evolution* (Leicester: IVP, 1986), p. 62.

37 S Austin, *Grand Canyon—monument to Catastrophe* (San Diego: Institute for Creation Research, 1994), chapter 6, pp. 111–131.

38 S Austin, op. cit., p. 127–128.

39 AC McIntosh, JE Truscott, J Brindley, JF Griffiths, and **N Hafiz,** 'Spatial effects in the thermal runaway of combustible fluids in insulation materials', *Journal of the Chemical Society, Faraday Transactions,* 92 (16) 2965–2969, 1996.

40 Slusher, op. cit.

41 Slusher, op. cit.

42 CF Davidson, 'Some aspects of radiogeology', *Liverpool Manchester Geological Journal,* 2, 1960, 314.

43 AG Fraser, *The age of the earth,* in **D Burke** (ed.), *Creation and Evolution* (Leicester: IVP, 1986), p. 31.

44 EH Andrews, 'The age of the earth', in **D Burke** (ed.), *Creation and Evolution* (Leicester: IVP, 1986), pp. 59–60 (explanation added in square brackets).

45 I S Williams, et al., *Journal Geological Society of Australia,* 22 (4), 1975, 502 [Italics added].

46 CM Carmichael, and **Palmer,** *Journal of Geophysical Research,* 73, 1968, 2813 [Italics added].

47 DP Elston, and **EH McKee,** 'Age and Correlation of the Late Proterozoic Precambrian Grand Canyon Disturbance, Northern Arizona', *Geological Soc. America Bulletin* 93, 1982, pp. 681–699.

48 JDMorris, *The Young Earth* (Colorado Springs: Master Books, 1994), pp. 58–60.

49 C Alibert, et al., 'Isotope and trace element geochemistry of Colorado Plateau Volcanics', *Geochimica et Cosmochimica Acta,* 50, 2735–2750, 1986.

50 ML Lubenow, op. cit., See particularly the Appendix 'The Dating Game' which concentrates on the dating of the KBS Tuff and the famous KNM-ER1470 skull.

51 AJ Monty-White, op. cit., p. 147.

52 RL Whitelaw, 'Time, Life and History in the light of 15,000 radiocarbon dates', *Creation Research Quarterly,* 7(1), 56–71, 83 (June 1970).

53 JG Funkhouse and **JJ Naughton,** 'Radiogenic Helium and Argon in Ultra mafic Inclusions from Hawaii', *Journal of Geophysical Research,* 73(14), 4601–4607 (July 1968).

54 JD Morris, *The Young Earth* (Colorado Springs: Master Books, 1994).

55 C Humphreys, *Can Science and Christianity both be true?,* in **RJ Berry** (ed.) *Real Science, Real Faith* (Eastbourne: Monarch, 1995) chapter 9, pp. 121–123.

56 EH Andrews, op. cit., p. 61.

57 JHJ Peet, 'The Bible and Chronology—a Geochronological point of view', *Origins* (the Journal of the Bible Creation Society) 22 March 1997, pp. 2–26.

58 LV Pirsson and **C Schuchert** *Textbook of Geology*, vol. 1 (New York: Wiley, 1920), p.5.

59 JC Whitcomb and **HM Morris,** *The Genesis Flood* (London: Evangelical Press, 1969), pp. 136–139.

60 NM Fenneman, *Physiography of the Western United States* (New York: McGraw-Hill, 1931), p. 229 [italics added].

61 S Thorarinsson, *Surtsey: the new island in the North Atlantic* (New York: Viking, 1967), pp. 39–40.

62 JD Morris, op. cit. p. 116.

63 N McWhirter (ed.), *Guinness Book of Records* (London, Guinness, 1983), p. 61.

64 JC Whitcomb and **HM Morris,** op. cit. p. 264.

65 D Plage, and **M Plage,** 'In the shadow of Krakatau', *National Geographic,* 167(6), June 1985, pp. 750–771, particularly pp. 754–756.

66 EL Hamilton, 'The last geographic frontier: the sea floor', *Scientific Monthly,* 85, December 1957, p. 299.

67 JC Whitcomb and **HM Morris,** op. cit. p. 127.

68 SA Austin, *Mount St Helens and Catastrophism,* Impact Article 175, 1986, Institute for Creation Research.

69 Ibid

70 JD Morris, op. cit. pp. 106–112.

71 JD Morris, op. cit., p. 101.

72 David TW Edgeworth, *The Geology of the Hunter river coal measures, New South Wales,* Memoirs of the Geological Survey of New South Wales, Geology No. 4, Part I—General Geology, and the development of the Greta Coal Measures, Deptartment of Mines and Agriculture, Australia, 1907. See in particular pp. 6–28.

73 JD Morris, *The Yellowstone Petrified Forests,* Impact article, 268, Institute of Creation Research, 1995.

74 JD Morris, *The Young Earth* (Colorado Springs: Master Books, 1994), pp. 114–117.

75 JD Morris, op. cit., p. 114.

76 SH Mamay and **EL Yochalson,** *Occurrence and significance of marine animal remains in American Coal Balls*, Shorter contributions to *General Geology*, Geological Survey Professional paper 354–I, US Dept. of the Interior, 1962.

77 HG Coffin, *Erect floating stumps in Spirit Lake, Washington,* Geology 11, 298–299, May 1983.

78 K Ham, 'I got excited at Mount St Helens', *Creation Magazine,* CSF 15(3), June 1993, pp. 14–19.

79 S Baker, *Bone of Contention* (2nd ed; Welwyn: Evangelical Press, 1986), p. 12.

80 SA Austin, *How fast can coal form?, Creation Magazine,* 2(1), CSF, December 1989, p. 51.

81 SE Nevins, *The Origins of Coal,* ICR Impact Article No. 41, Institute for Creation Research, November 1976.

82 GR Hill, *Chemical Technology,* May 1972, pp. 296–297. See also the discussion in **David CC Watson,** *The Great Brain Robbery* (Worthing: Henry Walter, 1975), p. 64.

83 R Hayatsu, et al *Organic Geochemistry* 6, 463–471, 1984. This article reports that wood, water and acidic clay heated for 28 days at 150° C produced high grade black coal.

84 EH Andrews, 'The age of the Earth', in **D Burke** (ed.), *Creation and Evolution* (Leicester: IVP 1986), pp. 55–56.

85 D Batten, Creation Science Foundation, Creation Seminar given at Liverpool, UK, 26 October 1995.

On giants' shoulders:
Studies in Christian apologetics

EDGAR POWELL

280PP, PAPERBACK

ISBN 978 0 902548 93 0

If you want facts with which to answer evolutionists, this book will help. It takes conviction and courage to stand up for the gospel and this book readily responds, with thought-provoking answers, to the propaganda from evolutionists.

Edgar Powell, BSc, MSc, PGCE, is a curriculum director in computing in a further education college. He teaches computing, information technology and geology, having over thirty years' teaching experience. He has contributed articles to *Creation Research Quarterly, Evangelicals Now, Evangelical Times, Grace Magazine* and *Monthly Record*. He and his wife have two daughters.

'A splendid overview of contemporary apologetic challenges.'
—*CHRISTIANITY TODAY*

'... an outstanding achievement ... food for thought on every page.'
—*PROFESSOR WILLIAM EDGAR, WESTMINSTER THEOLOGICAL SEMINARY, PHILADELPHIA*

On giants' shoulders

Studies in Christian apologetics

Edgar Powell

Foreword by Sir Fred Catherwood

Day One

Hallmarks of design:
Evidence of design in the natural world

STUART BURGESS

256PP, ILLUSTRATED PAPERBACK

ISBN 978 1 903087 31 2

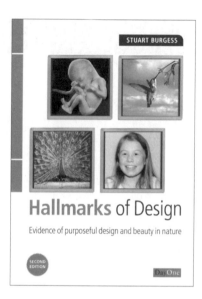

The Design Argument contends that design in nature reveals a Designer. *Hallmarks of Design* presents this in the light of the latest discoveries about the complexity and beauty of the natural world. Features of the book include:

- Six clear hallmarks of design;
- Over thirty diagrams;
- Description of how the earth is designed for mankind;
- Description of the Creator's attributes

Dr Stuart Burgess is Head of Department of Mechanical Engineering at the University of Bristol. His research areas include the study of design in nature. He previously worked in industry, designing rocket and satellite systems for the European Space Agency. He is winner of the Worshipful Company of Turners Gold Medal for the design of the solar array deployment system on the £1·4 billion ENVISAT earth observation satellite.

'Compelling presentation of the evidence of design in the natural world.'
—*BANNER OF TRUTH MAGAZINE*

He made the stars also:
What the Bible says about the stars

STUART BURGESS

192PP, ILLUSTRATED PAPERBACK

ISBN 978 1 903087 13 8

This book teaches clearly and biblically the purpose of the stars and the question of extra-terrestrial life. Dr Burgess explains how the earth has a unique purpose in supporting life and how the stars have a singular purpose in shining light on it. He explains why the universe contains such natural beauty and how the stars reveal God's character.

Dr Stuart Burgess is Head of Department of Mechanical Engineering at the University of Bristol. His research areas include the study of design in nature. He previously worked in industry, designing rocket and satellite systems for the European Space Agency. He is winner of the Worshipful Company of Turners Gold Medal for the design of the solar array deployment system on the £1·4 billion ENVISAT earth observation satellite.

'Dr Burgess has a very clear style and his book brims with interesting material. It will be greatly appreciated.'
—DR PETER MASTERS, METROPOLITAN TABERNACLE

The origin of man:
The image of God or the image of an ape?

STUART BURGESS

192PP, ILLUSTRATED PAPERBACK

ISBN 978 1 903087 73 2

Have humans descended from apes or were they specially created? Do humans have unique characteristics and abilities that set them apart from all the animals? The answers to these crucial questions determine whether man is just an animal or a special spiritual being. There is overwhelming evidence that man has a Creator. This book contains many diagrams and includes:

- Explanation of similarities between humans and apes;
- Unique characteristics and abilities of humans;
- Unique beauty of humans;
- Archaeological and fossil evidence;
- The importance and relevance of the origins debate.

Dr Stuart Burgess is Head of Department of Mechanical Engineering at the University of Bristol. His research areas include the study of design in nature. He previously worked in industry, designing rocket and satellite systems for the European Space Agency. He is winner of the Worshipful Company of Turners Gold Medal for the design of the solar array deployment system on the £1·4 billion ENVISAT earth observation satellite.

Life's story—The one that hasn't been told

MARK HAVILLE

64PP, PAPERBACK, POCKET BOOK SIZE,
ILLUSTRATED IN COLOUR THROUGHOUT

ISBN 978 903087 71 8

THE ONE THAT HASN'T BEEN TOLD

Written for anyone who is interested in the creation/evolution debate, but doesn't know where to start, this highly illustrated guide is the perfect introduction to the subject. Exploring the arguments, author Mark Haville thoughtfully analyses the flaws in the theory of natural selection. Beautifully illustrated in full colour throughout.

Mark Haville is a biblical creationist with a wide-ranging ministry.

The evolution creation debate has raged for more than 150 years
Now the debate is over!

DayOne

'The photography is breathtaking, the science is crystal clear and the application is thoroughly biblical. *Life's Story* is surely contender for 'Best in its class'.'
—*DR JOHN BLANCHARD, REVIEWING THE DVD ON WHICH THE BOOK IS BASED*

PHILIP SNOW

256PP PAPERBACK, ILLUSTRATED THROUGHOUT

ISBN 978 1 84625 002 6

Birds are amongst the world's most beautiful and beloved parts of creation, so it is not surprising that they have been so widely studied. This book closely examines their wonderful aerial lifestyle and unique, warm-blooded design—often so different from the cold-blooded dinosaurs that they are claimed to have accidentally 'evolved' from! This fascinating and beautifully produced book brings to light important facts from the world of science and is illustrated throughout by the author.

Philip Snow is a wildlife and landscape painter, illustrator and writer. His work appears in many publications and galleries, and he has illustrated, or contributed work to, over sixty books, and many magazines, prints, cards, calendars, reserve guides and decorated maps etc.

'Birds have played an important part in human history and have always been respected and loved for hreir beauty and amazing flying skills. Philip Snow has produced a unique book which expertly describes and illustrates the design, life and beauty of birds.'
—*STUART BURGESS, PROFESSOR OF DESIGN AND NATURE, UNIVERSITY OF BRISTOL*

An interview with C H Spurgeon
—C H Spurgeon on creation and evolution

DAVID HARDING

128PP PAPERBACK

ISBN 978 1 84625 021 7

C H Spurgeon, who is known to be theologically robust about the verbal inspiration, infallibility, perspicuity and preservation of the text of the Bible, made many forthright statements about Darwinism and his sermons and writings are liberally sprinkled with references to the subject. In this 'virtual' interview, David Harding takes us through his general thoughts on the matter, on science and the Bible, and then his more specific attitudes to science. There is advice to young people and then comments for preachers. What of those who disagree? He had a few words for them too! The appendix explores Spurgeon's attitude to his own fallibility and is relevant in view of his opinions and judgements about when the world was made.

David Harding is pastor of the Milnrow Evangelical Church, Lancashire, England, where he has ministered for the last thirteen years. His background was in local government work and he has also been an elder at Garforth Evangelical Church, and an evangelist and elder at Flitwick Baptist Church. He and his wife, Colette, have two adult sons, Matthew and Joel.

'A masterpiece of writing'

—*ANDY C. MCINTOSH DSC, FIMA, C.MATH, FEI, C.ENG, FINSTP, MIGEM, FRAES, PROFESSOR OF THERMODYNAMICS AND COMBUSTION THEORY, UNIVERSITY OF LEEDS*

'... A lucid, forceful, definitive, biblical answer to the theory of evolution in Spurgeon's own words. ... invaluable for both its historic significance and its timeless insight. I'm delighted to see this book in print.'

—*PHIL JOHNSON, GRACE TO YOU, USA*